PATRONISING BASTARDS

PATRONISING
BASTARDS

How the Elites Betrayed Britain

Quentin Letts

Constable • London

CONSTABLE

First published in Great Britain in 2017 by Constable

3 5 7 9 10 8 6 4

A CIP catalogue record for this book
is available from the British Library.

ISBN: 978-1-47212-735-8

Typeset in Sabon by SX Composing DTP, Rayleigh, Essex
Printed and bound in Great Britain by Clays Ltd, St Ives plc

Papers used by Constable are from well-managed forests
and other responsible sources.

Constable
An imprint of
Little, Brown Book Group
Carmelite House
50 Victoria Embankment
London EC4Y 0DZ

An Hachette UK Company
www.hachette.co.uk

www.littlebrown.co.uk

In memory of my sister Penny Rawlinson, 1957–2017,
and my brother-in-law Stuart Carrington, 1962–2016

NOTE TO READERS (AND LIBEL LAWYERS)

This is a work of peppery polemic. It should not be mistaken for Holy Scripture, or even the verdict of a modern Anglican bishop. It represents the subjective views of a scurvy parliamentary sketchwriter, critic and Marches blunderbuss, no more, no less. It sets about the Establishment as a savage to his privet hedge.

Contents

Contents

Revolution!

British voters hit breaking point

————————————•————————————

Two stunning election results. Two kicks in the kidneys for Britain's elite. The EU referendum 2016 and the general election of 2017 did not happen by accident. They were born of a weary truculence.

Before both votes the electorate was told firmly what to do. A vote for Remain would be safe and strong. A vote for Theresa May would be strong and stable. You know your duty, little ones, said the elite. Sod that, said the people. In the greatest citadel-storming since the French Revolution they chose to leave the obtrusive European Union. A year later, when asked by presumptive Mrs May to increase her majority, they did the opposite.

The spirit propelling these unexpected votes was not specific to Britain. Donald Trump's election showed similar things afoot in America. Elect that streak of grief Hillary? Hell, no. Nor can Right/Left conclusions be drawn. Brexit was broadly a Right-wing success and Jeremy Corbyn rose from the graveyard Left. Something bigger was in play. It went beyond manifestos. Nor will political scientists' put-down of 'populism' (by which they mean vulgarity) quite do. This was a yeoman impatience with our smug, self-perpetuating, invisible Brahmin caste.

For decades, Britons have been bossed about by a clerisy of administrators and managers and pose-striking know-alls. The old aristocracy having faded, in came a more furtive elite, driven by the desire to own minds, not acres. They were not interested in buying parkland and vistas. They wanted to control opinion and dictate our attitudes.

It was done on the sly. Of course it was. We are ruled by baby-boomers and the baby-boomer generation – as greedy for power as any of its predecessors – is embarrassed by outright leadership. Material chattels like stately homes can be taxed, so they submerged their swagger. They posed as liberals and dressed as and spoke like mechanicals – tattoos, mockney accents, crumpled clothes (you see more ties in economy class than at the front of a plane). They crouched behind 'enlightened' attitudes while imposing their views on a populace they claimed to esteem but more truthfully disdained. Politicians and civil servants and lawyers used a language few could understand. They became adept at smudged evasion, disguise, facade, until we reached the point where they all seemed the same – David Cameron and Ed Miliband were just variants of your basic Ford Cortina, one with a touch more carpet, the other with go-faster stripes. Miliband and his brother were so interchangeable, the public often got them confused. I am not arguing against elitism, an essential concept in any aspirational society. I am arguing against our elite, as exemplified by so many of its members.

Government was farmed out to agencies and quangos and privatised supply companies whose directors had the same tastes and handed one another sinecures. Verve vanished from parliamentary politics because the System sought anonymity, preferably in the back of a darkened BMW behind the smoked glass of cliché and small-print blether. Election promises were discarded like snakeskins. You promised us a referendum on the Lisbon Treaty, said the voters. Ah, but all that has changed, said David Cameron. You promised us a cash prize, said the scratch-card winner. Ah, but you didn't call the 50p-a-minute hotline in time, said the swindler. Read the small print, suckers.

Opinion gurus told bland 'leaders' what to think. National pride was diminished to the point that Labour MP Emily Thornberry could visit a working-class town and sneer to her followers about its flag-waving and white vans. *Look at what the common oiks are like,* said this millionaire lawyer. *Fancy actually liking one's national flag!* Cheap labour was imported, suppressing workers' wages, because that was what globalised bosscats at the international forums said was necessary. Could we criticise immigration? Only if we wanted to be called racists and fruitcakes. The elite's media munchkins had placed it on the top shelf, somewhere safe where it could not be touched.

Against our will, children were exposed to sex education by schools more interested in dogma than declension. Sex crimes rocketed. Sociologists said murderers must be released into the community. Re-offending rates rose. Smokers were made to feel like criminals. Criminals were encouraged to sue their victims. From every side came instruction as to what we must think: about diet, gender, sexuality, race, even the weather, with the TV forecasters telling us to put on sun cream and giving silly names to every incoming squall.

The most irritating moment in the day used to be when the old grump at the newsagent's called us 'love' or 'young man' (even when we were over fifty). Now the entire System was at it, badgering us, belittling us, patting us on the head, putting us in our place. Think this. Don't think that. Inappropriate! Hate crime! From *Blue Peter* presenters to the Chief Medical Officer, from that ninny Nick Clegg to railway Tannoys saying 'do not become a victim of crime' or 'see it, say it, sort it', they treat us like toddlers.

Even the most docile beach donkey, if repeatedly kicked, will eventually refuse to cooperate. It will bare its long, yellow teeth and walk in the other direction, pulling its tethers out of the sand. So it has proved with the British voters. Get off our backs, they said. Stop goading us.

Stop being such patronising bastards.

Independence Dawns
The morning we broke free

———————————•———————————

Where were you at dawn on Friday 24 June, 2016? I was in a poky hotel bedroom in London's Blooms-bury, shivering in my smalls. The previous evening had brought bad family news and I retired to bed at 10 p.m. to sleep fitfully. As daylight broke, I shivered not from cold but clammy nerves as the hotel's small television relayed the referendum results from around the country.

Our nation had voted on 'the greatest question to face this generation', millions turning out for the first time. One polling station, roughly in the middle of the country, was the Riverside Club in the Spital district of Chester-field, Derbyshire. On the Thursday morning a gaunt figure had entered, moving with difficulty. After collecting his papers, he leaned heavily on the stubby pencil while cast-ing his vote. Privacy did not much worry him. Why be secretive? Job done, he carefully dropped his ballot into the box, thanked the officials, winced a little and made slowly for the door. Aerospace engineer Stuart Carrington, fifty-four, had just voted for the last time.

A keen supporter of Leave – and normally a Labour

man, his dad having been a miner – Stuart had been determined to get to the Riverside Club and he had bloody well managed it.

Stuart was my brother-in-law. Well, as good as. He and my wife's sister Nicky were not formally married but they had been together years. Stuart's health had become a worry in recent months. Out of character, he took time off from the factory where he did laser coordinates. Stuart's machine, capable of the most intricate measurements, checked parts for aircraft jet engines. Stuart was proud of his work, just as he was proud of Nicky, her two sons and their flat. But he knew all that was coming to an end. The doctors initially told him he had a low-threat cancer but they changed their prognosis. That week we were told he was dying.

Into the early hours of Friday I woke repeatedly, thinking of stoical, taciturn Stuart. Those northern men don't always say much but by God they make their mark. Stuart was not a showy person. He did not consider himself important, not in the way we normally use that term. Not back then. Maybe things are a little different now. Maybe the balance of power has shifted a little.

As the hours passed, I peeped at the news a few times. No doubt the technocracy was going to win. It always did, didn't it? At the start of the evening, UKIP's Nigel Farage, normally Mr Perky, all but conceded Leave would lose. In my short bursts of sleep I had a nightmare about George Osborne as a sergeant major, bawling orders at those of us in the ranks.

By 1.30 a.m. the pattern of results suggested a result tighter than predicted. The experts had said defeat for Remain was unthinkable. But what is an expert? My

Abandon ship, Captain Ashdown!

Before the first results came in, former Lib Dem leader Lord Ashdown said: 'I will forgive no one who does not respect the sovereign voice of the British people once it has spoken, whether it is a majority of 1 per cent or 20 per cent. When the British people have spoken you do what they command. Either you believe in democracy or you don't.' Command! Such a Paddy Ashdown word. He himself was in the armed forces once, y'know – Special Boat Squadron Paddy paddling ashore by moonlight with a length of cheese wire to slit enemy throats before you can say 'lost deposit'. Well done, Paddy! The one snag? When he said all that about accepting the democratic vote, he thought Remain was going to win. Once Remain lost, he rapidly tried to contest the result. If it is possible for a commando to torpedo his own inflatable, dumbo Paddy did it.

brother-in-law Stuart was an expert. The job he did demanded training and concentration, ignoring outside interference, maintaining a steady hand and discarding the tiniest flaws. How often could we say that about the sort of experts – Treasury officials, opinion pollsters and almost the entire diplomatic corps – who idly presumed Remain would win?

More results came in. Remain was losing! Our dominating elite of parliamentarians, lobbyists, bankers, artists, political theorists, clergy, academics and sterile aesthetes was about to take a custard pie smack in the face. So many well-connected people had scoffed at Brexit. They had belittled anyone who suggested it could occur. But there it was, happening before our eyes on dawn television.

At 4.40 a.m. the BBC's presenter, David Dimbleby, stared at the camera lens and said:

> At twenty minutes to five we can now say that the decision taken in 1975 by this country to join the Common Market has been reversed by this referendum to leave the EU. We are absolutely clear now that there is no way that the Remain side can win. It looks as though the gap is going to be something like 52 to 48, so a four-point lead for leaving the EU, and that's the result of this referendum which has been preceded by weeks and months of argument and dispute and all the rest of it. The British people have spoken and the answer is 'we're out!'.

The cold print of the referendum ballot papers had merely asked voters if they wanted to stay in the EU. This result was the crystallisation of something bigger. It was the eruption of a long-building resentment at being bossed around by an opaque snootocracy, by prosperous fixers and people-in-the-know. The same thing happened in Worms five hundred years ago when Martin Luther ignited the Reformation against a money-grabbing, indulgence-selling, over-powerful Holy Roman Empire.

What had sparked the rebellion this time? Do we trace it back to 1980s Thatcherism, which started to dismantle big government and placed it in the hands of profiteering privatisers? Thatcherism showed that change could be made, albeit to a discordant mercantilism. Should we attribute it to the John Major years, when public trust in politics was loosened by destructive New Labour propagandist Alastair Campbell pushing the 'sleaze' agenda? In 1997, Princess Diana's death showed the public that they could bend remote authority to their will. Then came the Blair era, thick with hypocrisy, a government that flew under the colours of Islingtonian social democracy yet furtively pursued more privatisation (with added stealth taxes), outsourced our foreign affairs to the White House and saw a cabal of intimates bossing our civil service. Postwar liberal Blair affected glottal-stoppy mateyness. *Think of me as an ordinary kinda guy*, said the Prime Minister who ignored the ordinary people's feelings on immigration.

On my hotel bed that Independence dawn, after hearing David Dimbleby's words, I felt a giddying rush of patriotic pride. The applecart had been overturned. This was not just a public rejection of the EU. Thanks to Stuart Carrington and 17,410,741 other Leave voters, this was an act of thrilling dissent. Our arrogant elite, after years of self-enriching condescension, had been whupped.

Gather! Gather!

Celebs do politics

———•———

Film stars who win an Oscar go into clichés of disbelief: fanning of face, 'omigods!' and moans of 'Gather! Gather!' The rigmarole was much the same when the EU result came through. Celebrity luvvies hyperventilated.

Actress Amanda Abbington posted a dawn Twitter message: 'Why on earth we were given this choice to vote is beyond me. We are totally on our own now. Totally. Watch the collapse begin. Dark days.' Five minutes later, having had time to chew further on the matter, she added: 'Where can I move me and my children too? Where's nice? Italy? Canada?' They might have better grammar there, certainly.

Kit Harington, an actor from *Game of Thrones*, said it was a 'f***ing terrible result'. Harry Potter star Daniel Radcliffe detected a 'jingoistic "we don't want to take orders from bloody Frenchies"' attitude in Leave voters. The celebrity Twittersphere read like the Book of Lamentations. Niall Horan of pop group One Direction (his politics were certainly that) predicted Leave voters would repent their decision. 'It's a sad day,' he cried.

Tamal Ray, a 'celebrity pastry chef', put out a half-baked: 'I cannot believe this. What is going to happen to us now? Jesus . . . ' James Corden, who left Britain to present a TV show in California, transmitted from across the water: 'I'm so sorry to the youth of Britain. I feel you've been let down today. x.' From Philip Pullman, author, came this: 'We had a headache, so we shot our foot off.' J. K. Rowling: 'I don't think I've ever wanted magic more.' TV presenter and sometime footballer Gary Lineker asked, 'what have we gone and done?' Alexa Chung, model, resorted to 'scooping flesh out. Setting some aside in a jar marked "immigrant". Unsure where to scatter myself.'

Sometime triple-jumper Jonathan Edwards (and lead presenter for a European TV sports channel) let us know 'I feel I'm living in a foreign country now'. Danny Cipriani, rugby player, was appalled the people had been given a vote. 'It's ridiculous a decision this big can be left in our hands. I'm gutted.' Welsh rugby player Jamie Roberts, a doctor who studied at the University of Cambridge, called it an 'uneducated vote' and suggested politics should be made a compulsory subject in schools (taught objectively or not, Jamie?). Long-jumper Greg Rutherford called the result 'unbelievable' and said 'naughty world! Stop it! Down!'

The mood at Glastonbury pop festival was funereal. Coldplay's Chris Martin saw 'the collapse of a country'. Damon Albarn wore a black armband. Marianne Faithfull, famous because decades earlier she once did something filthy with a Mars Bar and Mick Jagger, said: 'We are back to where it used to be, the right-wing racist Little England. Those dreadful people, they've always been there.'

*

Emma Thompson, mother, director, writer, actress, intellectual, citizen, is her own greatest performance. Ems is luvviedom's head girl. In her various roles she gives it her all, widening her eyes, crumpling that pruney chin, gripping tight to the handlebars of what she laughingly calls her career. Hollywood loves her and pays her accordingly. She is thick into the brass.

But most of all, Emma cares. She cares so much that tears may soon spring to her spaniel eyes and her slightly bulbous nose may start to run; or maybe the moment calls for defiance mode with a jutted jaw and a lashing-out of bad language, substituting her habitual 'crumbs' and 'gollys' for 'f*** this' and 'f*** that'.

She cares about the planet and the poor. She aches for Labour (been a member 'all my life' – which means she backed Foot, then Blair, then Corbyn) and thinks Tories are evil, or something like that. Not evil in a biblical way, of course. She is a 'libertarian anarchist' when it comes to religion. As a tub-thumping atheist she has talked about how some of the Bible offends her and how she 'refutes' it. Fancy word, refute. It means 'prove to be wrong'. Millennia of religious teaching are thus overturned with one flick of an overpaid actress's ash-blonde hair.

Emma fights for feminism. When not beating her breast about Palestine or refugees or Aids sufferers or Heathrow airport's expansion, she campaigns for the Galapagos turtle, even though it looks a bit like Norman Tebbit. Ems is like that, you see. Forgiving. Big-hearted. So long as you're not talking about religion. Anyway, if she met rotten old Tory Tebbit she would probably want to win him over, because actors are like that. They yearn to be loved. So, she would try to josh nasty Norm along and do one of her little self-deprecating routines, which are always so amusing in a middle-class way. She's good with people, is Emma. She camouflages her blazing intolerance with English irony. What a star!

Why should we pay her political views any attention? After all, feminism (which seems to be her core belief) is based on egalitarian principles and if egalitarianism's logic of one person being no better than the next is to be pursued, why should a la-di-dah celebrity from a posh part of north London, brought up by an actress mum and a dad who did voiceovers for the 1960s children's TV show *The Magic Roundabout*, be any more worth listening to than a UKIP-supporting council-house knuckle-dragger from Boston, Lincs, or a Trump voter in Tallahassee or even a turbanned ayatollah in Tehran? Emma, however, does not see it that way. She argues that 'anyone with any sort of voice has a duty to plug into what they think needs to be said'. Crumbs. 'Anyone with any sort of voice'? That sounds like elitish self-justification – a manifesto for celebrity proselytising – does it not?

Who could resent Emma Thompson her public altruism? She is so valiantly earnest, shoulder-shrugging in an aw-shucks Cambridge Footlights way (she was at the University of Cambridge with the likes of Tony Slattery, Hugh Laurie, Stephen Fry and porcelain-petite heartbreaker Sandi Toksvig). Those Footlights people perfect the art of being patrician without ever quite seeming it. The British ruling class is artful at that sort of disguise. It has been perfected over centuries of self-survival, filing down the rough edges of autocracy and throwing in a few jokes so that hoi polloi don't notice they are jolly well being told what to do by the old boss types.

Life has certainly gone Thompson's way. She is wonderfully rich, allegedly worth £30 million, though that
looks like an accountant's under-estimate. A cynic would
say she made the money partly by being a brand – lovely,
Leftwing Ems, acclaimed by the Beeb and *Guardian* as a
national double-yolker. That sort of thing is terrific for the
bottom line. Em-pathy, you could call it. If only Vanessa
Redgrave had been a bit more crafty like Emma Thompson, a bit more SDP and a bit less Workers' Revolutionary
Party (ooh-er, Ems would say), then Vanessa, too, could
have made billions more bazookers. Fie such cynicism!
We fully accept that Ems is a sincere old biscuit and,
come the Corbyn revolution, will happily forego her holi-
days on private yachts and will settle for a wet week in
a beach-hut in Skeggy. Emma's socialism is of the elastic
variety. She is a great friend of Prince Charles, has a lovely
house in Hampstead and a second in Scotland. Oh, all
right, that probably means her carbon footprint is ginor-
mous – a very Emma word – and jetting round the world
from filmset to filmset must positively gobble down the
eco-equivalent of acres of Brazilian rainforest, but just
look at all the tax she pays. And she is using her voice,
remember. She is 'doing her duty'. Yes, she sent her pre-
cious daughter Gaia (named after the Greek goddess or
James Lovelock's theory of environmental synergy?) to a
private school, which might look like stinking hypocrisy
given her support for the anti-grammars Labour Party,
but at least that opened up another state-school place for
a poor person. Or a refugee. Like the Rwandan child-sol-
dier she and her handsome second husband Greg Wise
adopted. Husband number one was Kenneth Branagh,
since knighted. In their married days, Branagh was asked

if they planned to have children. Maybe, replied Branagh, but they had to save the planet first.

Duty, duty, duty. Emma T was, naturally, appalled by Brexit. She said she felt more European than English and she regarded Nigel Farage as a 'white nationalist'. Where that left the many non-white Leave voters and non-white UKIP supporters, it was hard to say. Before the EU referendum Thompson declared that it would be 'madness' to leave the EU and if we did so then Britain would revert to being the 'cake-filled, misery-laden grey old island' it had been in days of yore. In line with her view that 'we should be taking down borders, not putting them up', she said Britain should take in more refugees. 'We've got plenty of room for them,' she declared. How would she countenance a temporary refugee camp on Hampstead Heath? Maybe not so well. When Tesco proposed opening one of its Express mini-supermarkets in nearby Belsize Park, Emma (along with some fellow celebs) campaigned against it, arguing that the shop would blight that 'villagey' area. Village? Belsize bloody Park?

Socialist Miss Thompson is not a woman of the people. At one of those ritzy film-premiere nights she was stopped on the red carpet and asked if she would be taking selfies of herself with some of the evening's other stars. 'I wouldn't take a selfie with anybody,' she said with a shudder. 'I mean, God almighty, how to take narcissism to its unspeakable extreme. Get a life everyone.' By which she perhaps meant 'get a life just like mine'.

Despite her absurdities I still have a soft spot for Emma Thompson. It must be lingering affection for her late father's voice narrating *The Magic Roundabout* with Zebedee and Dougal and Mr McHenry & Co. But she is a

Lib Dems' new Youth Ambassador

Best celebrity endorsement of all time? It was hard to beat the time that pop musician Brian Eno came out as a supporter of the Lib Dems and was duly signed up as Nick Clegg's official youth adviser. Eno was sixty-one at the time.

hand-wringing Lefty pioneer followed by other actors and celebs, not all of them so likeable.

Lily Allen, a pop singer, has made plain her dimness by adopting drearily right-on postures on Brexit, refugees and other matters. Actor Michael Sheen was cross after his home area, south Wales, supported Brexit: 'Wales votes to trust a new and more right-wing Tory leadership to invest as much money into its poorer areas as EU has been doing.' A year later south Wales did no such thing and stayed loyal to Labour. Maybe its voters supported

Leave in 2016 because they saw how EU energy rules had wrecked its steel plants.

Do stars' managers calculate that a little Leftwing foghorning might help their celebs, attracting younger audiences? Is that the thinking? And where they already have the profile to make their own decisions, do they not realise how it comes across? *Sherlock* star Martin Freeman (an intelligent man) fronted a Labour party election broadcast in which he bragged that his values were 'community, compassion, decency'? Good grief, he'll be playing St Augustine next.

There is a word for Freeman and Thompson and their ilk – and, no, I am not about to contribute a tenner to the swear box, although Keira Knightley might. Knightley is a foul-mouthed little madam (and a poor stage actress) who was vehemently anti-Brexit. 'Stop others f***ing with your future,' she bleated in a message to yoof. The word talent managers use is 'influentials', celebrities who can influence the views of their fans.

Advertising agencies will cite statistics showing how sales of a certain brand of scent rise when someone like Helen Mirren stars in advertisements. Similarly, political strategists insist that voters are influenced when a Martin Freeman or David Tennant presents a party-political broadcast for Labour. Former *Doctor Who* star Tennant likes to parade his Labour support ('all my life,' he says) and desire for Scottish independence. He says Britain is in for a 'dark time' outside the EU and he went on American television to describe Donald Trump as a 'tangerine ballbag', a 'wiggy slice' and a 'witless f***ing c***splat'. Before the 2010 general election, Tennant backed Gordon Brown and said, 'I would rather have a prime minister who is the cleverest person in the room than a prime minister who looks good in a suit – I think David Cameron is a terrifying prospect.' How good to hear a much-packaged TV star decry image. But are voters really swayed by celebrity? I find it hard to believe.

Voters did not warm to Jeremy Corbyn because he was supported by the likes of Lily Allen and Arthur Smith and Steve Coogan. They were attracted to the simplicity of his message and the fact that he seemed to be outside the net-worky, money-driven System that enriches such luvvies. The status quo suits these stars just fine. In 2015 David Tennant, Julie Walters and Claudia Winkleman put their names to a campaign saying how marvellous the BBC was and how the public should 'celebrate and protect it'. The words 'so that they and their licence payers can continue to bung me pots of money' were not used but could have been.

Snooze Headlines

Lifeless politicians heighten
craving for excitement

———————•———————

How dare politicians be boring? Their trade should be the very stuff of life: freedom, gold, power. But so many of them make this dreary. Why do they go into politics if they have nothing electrifying to say?

Theresa May is so boring they should use her to dig for shale gas. She would not have prospered in the pre-TV age, when politicians had to quell vast crowds with their election addresses. Instead she made it to PM without ever hurling herself into a national campaign; when she did try her hand at it in the 2017 general election campaign, she was a dud.

Have you ever sat through a Philip Hammond speech? Your eyelids seem to become laden by fishing weights. To watch an audience during a lecture by Alistair Darling or Des Browne or Andrew Lansley or Patricia Hewitt is to see a scorpion slowly starved of oxygen in a bell jar. Onlookers reach the point where they would prefer to sting themselves rather than suffocate to death by dullness.

Even the decent prophet of Euroscepticism, Sir Bill Cash, is an Olympian snoozeroo. How could he make so riveting a cause so gluey?

Geoffrey Howe, Francis Maude, Stephen Byers, Geoff Hoon, Andrew Smith, Paul Murphy, Chris Grayling, Jeremy Wright: why did such morose, dog-eyed dullards ever go into politics? They must have known they were terrible at showmanship. We all now know that in private John Major was a hip-jiggling, afternoon copulator, as randy as Russell Brand, but in public Major had the speaking manner of a nasal nerd. In America, Hillary Clinton was hardly better.

It takes a warped audacity to go forth and stultify. At its root is the casual belief that the audience is peripheral to the process. The people are just bystanders whereas politics is for the cognoscenti. Don't communicate too openly with them, for goodness' sake. We don't want them to develop an unhealthy interest in ideas. And then these bozos are surprised when a ripsnorter like Nigel Farage or acid Alex Salmond or even Pied Piper Jeremy Corbyn comes along and grabs attention by being different.

Be Afraid, Children

Bank Governor Carney joins 'Project Fear'

———————————————•———————————————

For months before the June 2016 referendum, the System did its best to engineer things in favour of the EU. Cabinet Brexiteers were silenced. Eurosceptic ministers' civil servants were told to hide sensitive EU material from them. Some £9 million of our tax money was used for pro-Remain propaganda leaflets, which were posted through the nation's letter boxes. Quite a few were posted back, the words 'return to sender' accompanied by blunt suggestions as to what David Cameron could do with them.

The government machine was used remorselessly to help Remain. We were muck-spreadered with warnings of hideous consequences from Brexit. The Governor of the Bank of England, Mark Carney, was mobilised. For a bank governor to enter a political campaign was unusual but Carney ('Dr Carney', please) was unfazed. His friend George Osborne was Chancellor and, so far as the two of them could see, Remain was bound to win, and Clever George would become prime minister before the next general election.

© Supacharapong Buanark

Brexit supporters were long dismissed as weirdos. Michael Howard called UKIP's activists 'cranks and gadflies'. David Cameron called them 'fruitcakes and loonies and closet racists, mostly'. The delightfully disobedient Kippers, to whom 'fruitcake' became a badge of honour, cost Cameron a clean win in the 2010 general election. During the 2016 referendum campaign he reined in the insults, promised a referendum and duly won a majority. Oh no, that wasn't meant to happen! Now he had to hold the referendum. Had Cameron not been quite so rude about the Kippers in the first place, he might never have had to buy their support by offering a referendum, his EU friends could have continued on their anti-democratic way and he would still be prime minister.

Canadian Carney, a Centrist with a *soigné* manner, was bound to the status quo by instinct and career. Aged only fifty-two (he seemed older), Carney proved greatly helpful to Osborne and predicted Brexit would cause sterling to collapse, growth to stall and unemployment to rise. Scottish First Minister Nicola Sturgeon, herself a Remainer, told Downing Street such gloom-mongering would get Remain nowhere. Pah, what did Sturgeon know? She was merely a provincial. She didn't go to Chequers for weekend barbecues with Dave. She was never spotted at Matthew Freud's summer parties. Sturgeon was ignored and Carney & Co. put turbochargers on 'Project Fear'.

A much-feted American president (feted mainly for being black) made a visit to London and was persuaded to announce that Brexit would send Britain to 'the back of the queue' in terms of any US trade deals. When Barack Obama used that British formulation –an American might more naturally say 'line' instead of 'queue' – at a press conference on 22 April 2016, the Downing Street spin doctors were delighted. Mr Cameron's core adviser Craig Oliver practically purred with pleasure. Obama was basically issuing menaces to British electors not to get above their station – and these British officials were pleased! They had become so fixated by petty strategies that they could not see how unpatriotic this might look to many voters; and on the eve of St George's Day, to boot. But patriotism, to our elite, is like athlete's foot – an unfortunate embarrassment best not mentioned in polite company.

From comedians to bishops (hard to say which of those two groups is funnier), fund managers to charity-sector tsars, Brexit was as pongy as a bad sardine. They did not just oppose it. They *recoiled* from it. The reaction was not simply intellectual or even political. It was rooted in taste, aesthetics, manners. Let your future son-in-law have a wall eye, tombstone teeth, the clothes sense of Ken Dodd and a string of shoplifting offences to his name, but pray God Almighty he be not a Brexiteer. We no longer have widowed duchesses who clutch their dewlaps in horror when they hear the word 'serviette' but Brexit had the same effect on managerial and technocratic types. My wife, a sweet and liberal-minded soul, casually mentioned to a princeling of the Church of England that she intended to vote Leave. He gasped 'How *could* you?' He might have been less aghast had she admitted to witchcraft.

Fashionable 'opinion leaders' and pliable industrialists were pressed to the Remain cause to build the idea that superior people – *good* people – were of one accord. They crouched down beside the voters, looked them very gravely in the eye and told the boys and girls that Mummy and Daddy would be really, really sad if Remain did not win the referendum. The voters came to the conclusion that those prominent Remain supporters were only in it for themselves, chasing either business contracts or honours. Yet the barrage had been long and intense. It had been unrelenting. Opinion pollsters said Remain would win and in the last week of the campaign the Cameroons started to strut. Two days before the referendum, *Guardian* columnist Polly Toynbee, la-di-dah Leftist with the most perfect villa in Italy, opined that the result was in the bag. The headline over her article read, 'On Friday I'll get my country back. Britain will vote Remain'.

'Ignorant Masses'

How the caterwauling continued

———————————•———————————

That Friday morning after the referendum, I was soon out of my hotel, heading to Westminster in a taxi whose driver was cock-a-hoop at the Leave vote. Eight days earlier, Labour MP Jo Cox had been shot and stabbed to death in Yorkshire, a murder that had forced a temporary cessation of campaigning. My cab driver's scepticism showed that the respect quite properly afforded to Mrs Cox had not translated into wider admiration for Parliament.

At the gates to the Palace of Westminster I bumped into pro-Leave Tory MP Kwasi Kwarteng, a great bear of a man. 'This is bigger than any general election result,' boomed Kwasi. He was right. General elections are elections for Parliament. The referendum was an election against Parliament, in spite of Parliament. Abraham Lincoln once spoke of 'government of the people, by the people, for the people'. We had drifted towards 'government of the people, by the Parliament, for the Parliament and its fleas'.

The Establishment reacted with petulant disbelief. Tony Blair called it 'a foolish excursion into populism'. Lib Dem leader Tim Farron, forty-six, was concerned about 'young people'. 'They were voting for their future but it has been taken from them,' he said. Farron, normally a sunny fellow, was 'angry that today we wake to a deeply divided country'. Would he have said the same if the scores had gone the other way?

An American commentator, James Traub, was soon writing an article for the Foreign Policy website entitled 'It's Time for the Elites to Rise Up Against the Ignorant Masses'. Traub inveighed against 'voters' paranoia' and 'nativist parties' – 'nativist' had become the must-have insult for technocrats, a swipe at indigenous people. Traub deplored 'fist-shakers' in the electorate who had sided against the 'pragmatists' of the old order.

> It is necessary to say that people are deluded and that the task of leadership is to un-delude them. Is that 'elitist'? Maybe it is; maybe we have become so inclined to celebrate the authenticity of all personal conviction that it is now elitist to believe in reason, expertise and the lessons of history.

The Remain camp united atheists and the modern Church of England, with former Archbishop of Canterbury Rowan Williams and arch-atheist Richard Dawkins deploring the result. Dawkins raged that the voters had been 'ill-informed' and 'ignorant'. Personally, I blame evolution. Williams said,

> political literacy has to be rebuilt and the voices of properly independent civil society (frequently silenced by warnings from regulators and the like in this debate) – from churches

to local citizens' groups, from NGOs to universities (if they can ever free themselves from their present servitude to functionalist ideology) – have to be liberated.

Not a man for short sentences, is Rowan.

Another secularist, A. C. Grayling, wrote to MPs demanding that they reject the will of the people who, said Grayling, had voted on the basis of 'demagoguery and sentiment'. Too many voters were merely 'System One' thinkers, he argued, i.e. they acted chiefly on impulse and could be 'captured by slogans', unlike 'System Two' thinkers who made more considered, logical judgements. Shades here, of Plato, who regarded democracy as rule by the rabble and proposed the creation of elite 'Guardians' or 'Philosopher Kings' who could be selected in youth and trained to rule. Plato's thinking is most clearly seen today in the French *grandes écoles* that train the cadre of Brussels Eurocrats who propose and draft EU treaties.

British Europhiles read with approval an article by a Georgetown University philosopher, Jason Brennan, who floated 'the rule of knowledge', or epistocracy, in which only the cleverer people would have a vote. That would solve the problem of what Hillary Clinton called 'The Deplorables', i.e. supporters of Trump. Tony Blair soon made a speech calling on people to 'rise up against' . . . er, themselves, basically. He argued that voters had not known what they were doing. 'The people voted without knowledge of the terms of Brexit. As these terms become clear, it is their right to change their mind. Our mission is to persuade them to do so,' he said.

Tory Europhile Lord Heseltine was so horrified by Brexit that he made a speech in the House of Lords (where he had hardly stepped foot since 1997). He said: 'My opponents will argue that the people have spoken, the mandate secured and the future cast. My experience stands against that argument.' One old man's experience against the majority vote of the British public on a 72 per cent turnout! This was the same Heseltine who, after quitting Mrs Thatcher's cabinet, remarked: 'It was the most appalling waste of my life.'

Time and again it was argued by anti-Brexiteers that Leave voters did not understand the vastness of their decision, that they had swallowed lies, that they had 'not voted to make themselves poorer' and that 'they did not vote to leave the Single Market'. The elite was indignant and fearful – and that only made many Leave voters all the more certain they had made the right decision.

George Osborne's 'Project Fear', which tried to scare us into voting Remain but came to resemble a ghost-train ride at a funfair, was not even original. Pro-Europeans tried the same thing before the 1975 referendum. In a mesmerising speech at the Oxford Union that year, Labour Eurosceptic Peter Shore said: 'The message that comes out is fear, fear, fear. Fear because you won't have any food. Fear of unemployment. Fear that we've somehow been so reduced as a country that we can no longer, as it were, totter about in the world independent as a nation. And a constant attrition of our morale. A constant attempt to tell us that what we have and what we had as not only our own achievement but what generations of Englishmen has helped us to achieve, is not worth a damn.'

Edward Heath, who had been recently ousted as Prime Minister, also made a strong speech at that Oxford debate.[1] Unlike Messrs Cameron, Osborne and Clegg in the 2016 referendum, Heath admitted the argument was not really one about prices or tariffs or jobs. It was to do with the nation state. The Eurosceptics were 'content to remain with the past development and institutions and organisations of the nation state' whereas those on the pro-Brussels side 'want to move forward into a new organisation which is going to have greater success in meeting the needs of its peoples than the nation state has done in the past'. Heath's side won the national referendum – and there was no quibbling, then, about a stupid electorate having been out of its depth. Robin Day, presenter of the BBC's Oxford Union coverage, asked his colleague Ludovic Kennedy for his view of the applause Mr Heath won at the end of his speech. Kennedy said he thought it was 'very deserved' for it had been 'a marvellous speech'. Ah, the old BBC balance!

---

[1] Victor van Amerongen, president of the Oxford Union that night, recalls Heath won the Union debate's vote easily and that he, Victor, was persuaded joining the EEC was wise. By 2016, Victor was an enthusiastic campaigner for Leave.

Beauty Banished

State Art and its 'experts'

———————•———————

O ur elite received its Brexit boot up the backside because electors did not believe the institutional 'experts' who instructed them to vote Remain. Who was responsible for this loss of trust? Dodgy bankers ('Sir' Fred Goodwin and his ilk) and promise-breaking politicians (Nick Clegg with his tuition-fees betrayal) did not help. But one of the main culprits was a man who was neither politician nor banker, economist or diplomat. He was art-gallery director Sir Nicholas Serota.

Serota, seventy-one, is a sterile figure, sinuous, sober. For the past three decades this automaton ran the Tate galleries, accumulating extraordinary clout as he asserted the might of State Art, by which he meant weird conceptualism. You'd think three decades was more than enough for any one person but Serota was recently appointed to another big job, running the Arts Council. It is unusual – improper, I would say – for a single person to exert such grip over public patronage for so long. It is even less usual for that person, on departure, to bag another position commanding even larger sums of taxpayers' money with which to debauch national taste.

Why was Serota allowed to stay at the Tate so long? Were politicians scared of him? Were they daunted by modern art? They would not be the only ones. The character of art – or Art, as it became when staged by state commissar Serota – has changed. Beauty has gone. In its place is an aggressive self-assertion, even though the 'selves' in question are pathetically dependent on the taxpayer.

Nicholas Serota was born to the comforts of Hampstead's intelligentsia, his father an engineer, mother a Labour busy-boots who made it to the House of Lords under Harold Wilson (she had never dirtied her hands by being an MP). Her son, likewise, rose to prominence without mastering his métier's raw craft. Young Nicholas was little cop at mixing flesh tones on an easel. He would struggle to draw the outline of a horse's body or prepare the cast for a figurative bust. But he was ace at office politics and administrative strategy. If it was squaring a committee, stroking donors, putting ministers' minds at rest, creating a cabal of intimates with whom to brutalise the bourgeois aesthetic: at these, Serota was *maestro di color che sanno*.

At Cambridge he read economics before switching to art history; he was never some emotion-ravaged creative, wielding chisel or paintbrush and teaming hand, finger, eye and brain. Making something authentic, expressive and soulful was not his desire. Did a tendril of inadequacy weed its way into his breast because he lacked artistic genius? Probably not. That would be too emotional a response. But at times it has been as though he was on a campaign to destroy skill and redefine art as something anyone could do, though few could comprehend and none define.

Celebrating work that people don't understand: that is what the 'Serota tendency' (copyright the late Brian Sewell) does. It makes us feel small and the gallery experts can then look big when they deliver their explanations in pseudish phrases.

Serota's first job was at the Arts Council in 1970. After three years he was placed in charge of Oxford's Museum of Modern Art, one of the Arts Council's client galleries. By that, one means the small number of galleries that received state cash and fell into line with an unwritten expectation that the galleries would pursue the new, the vulgar, the obscure. The traditional, figurative, beautiful, sentimental, Christian, pastoral? These, most firmly, were not wanted. Beauty, to these modernisers, is to be regarded with suspicion. Like so much religion, it belongs to the heart and the heart cannot always be conquered by reason and intellect, which are their modernisers' weapons.

The Arts Council was created in the 1940s out of the wartime Council for the Encouragement of Music and the Arts. The original dream, a good socialist one, was to enrich the working-class by exhibiting high art, thus lifting lives, particularly in drabber industrial areas. We may not all be born equal but we can all benefit from artistic nourishment. Since then it appears that that ideal has been hijacked by a group of people who could be described as bureaucrats and shysters who have attempted to redefine and obscure 'Art'. Serota seems to be their head boy.

A 1965 policy document by Jennie Lee, Arts Minister, said in its opening paragraph 'no one would wish State patronage to dictate taste' in the arts. Lee was soon ignored. By the 1970s, the Arts Council was effectively running several galleries such as the Institute of Contemporary Art, the Hayward Gallery, the Serpentine Gallery, the Whitechapel, Camden Arts Centre, Oxford Museum of Modern Art and more. At the same time the Arts Council funded arts magazines, whose critics slavishly praised the whizzy new

The BBC recently said it would revive Kenneth Clark's *Civilisation* programme, which in the 1960s educated viewers about Western art history. Great! But then stubble-chinned James Purnell, BBC 'head of strategy and digital', said this series would be called *Civilisations*' (the plural being multicultural) and would take the 'opposite' of Clark's pukka approach. 'It won't be the Auntie that dispensed culture from on high,' mewed Purnell. 'It will be much more of a thoughtful friend, prodding us to keep our resolutions, helping us to ask and find answers.' He envisaged 'expertise without elitism'. Elitism has done Purnell well enough. After public school and Oxford this pampered smarmer landed a holiday job in Tony Blair's office, went full-time as a Downing Street fixer, became a Labour MP and was quickly made a minister, becoming Culture Secretary. Having quit politics not long after Blair (without his protector Tony it lost its savour for him), Purnell sashayed into a top job at the Beeb – a rankly improper transfer, given his former responsibilities as minister for broadcasting. When you watch a documentary on telly, do you want to be 'prodded' and 'helped to ask questions'? Who is really the nasty elitist here? A smartly suited patrician who tried to share his knowledge? Or a lispy careerist who thinks the little people are too thick to understand art without having it dumbed down by 'a thoughtful friend'?

products being pumped out by the Arts Council's galleries. The public were unenthused by contemporary art but their preferences were ignored. In previous centuries, art patrons were able to insist on their taste being satisfied but this time the patron (i.e. the taxpayer) was told to stop complaining. This was not art for art's sake, or even art for artists' sake. It was art for the benefit of a small number of art experts on state salaries.

State Art pushed the new, the minimalist, the puerile and plain nasty. It may have begun with a pile of bricks but it soon became pickled sharks, an unmade bed, mounds of cigarette ends, heroin needles. Politicians could have intervened, saying 'This is disgusting and a waste of hard-earned money,' but they lacked the guts to do so for two reasons. First, they subscribed to the 'arm's-length' principle, which (*pace* Jennie Lee) holds that it is improper for any elected politician to set artistic tastes; second, Westminster feared looking out of touch with groovy youth. Inverted snobbery is nowhere so fierce as in the arts.

At his Oxford museum, the young Serota gave exposure to Joseph Beuys, a German 'Fluxus, happening and performance artist and pedagogue'; that is, a prize bullshitter. His work included *The End of the Twentieth Century*, a collection of lumps of basalt shaped like cigars or turds (and bought by Serota's Tate in 1991 for an undisclosed sum). These rocks lie on the floor at various angles. You can look at them for ages and still not have a clue what they mean. Thank goodness for the curator notes, which tell us:

> Although Beuys made some initial sketches that illustrate possible ways of arranging the stones, there are no fixed rules for installing *The End of the Twentieth Century*.

This poses a challenge for curators, who must decide how to display the installation and whether to base their decision on previous displays of other versions that the artist helped to install.

Translation: 'We try to put them in the same place as last time but can't always remember exactly where the bits go'. Fret not. The arrangement does not affect the artistry. We know because we have been told so by the all-powerful galleriste.

Should art not derive its eloquence from precise line and balance and shape? Without such precision, what is to distinguish it from bric-a-brac (or, in the case of this basalt, rubble)? Beuys, who died in 1986, tried to explain what he was saying with *The End of the Twentieth Century*. 'This is the old world, on which I press the stamp of the new world,' he burbled. 'Take a look at the plugs. They look like plants coming from the stone age.' No, they don't. They look like cigars or turds. 'I took great pains to drill them out of the basalt in a funnel shape and then set them back into the hollows using felt and clay,' continued Beuys, 'so they cannot do each other harm, and can keep warm. It is something agile, eruptive, lively in this solidified mass.' Beuy oh Beuy.

Leaving Oxford scratching its head, Serota in 1976 moved to another of State Art's client galleries, the Whitechapel in London. He was then, as he is now, an intense figure with all the warmth of a Swiss banker. One imagines his calculating mind whirring and clicking like some metallic computer device. What would create controversy? Again, he turned to Germany and to a glum buddy of Beuys, Anselm Kiefer, who uses 'encoded sigils' in his work; and if you don't know what they are, you are not good enough to complain about the way your tax money is being spent on these important German artists. The art may have been dire but Serota, who is nothing if not an empire expander, extended the building. He proved himself adept at parting rich supporters from their banknotes, extracting grants from officialdom and persuading tame artists to donate work for a fundraising auction. Directors, being jealous of their editorial judgement, would once have hesitated to owe favours to artists.

When the Tate was looking for a new director in 1988, Serota's neophile zeal and budgetary competence won him the job in a weak field. The chairman of the Tate when he was appointed was architect Richard Rogers. Simply in terms of the property portfolio, Serota's twenty-nine years at the Tate were a success. Tate Modern was opened in the former Bankside power station and the building is big and striking. People stand in awe inside. It beckons them like a cathedral. But are they moved by the gallery's contents? Very seldom.

In terms of art and ethics, the Serota years at the Tate were a decadent failure. His narrow, insistent interest in the new has dominated to the exclusion of most else. There was a bad episode when the Charity Commissioners found 'serious shortcomings' in the conduct of the Tate's management after £700,000 was spent on work by a politically appointed Tate trustee, Chris Ofili (best known for using elephant dung on his canvases). This was not the only instance of Tate patronage being dished out to a trustee. Ofili's ex-girlfriend, artist Tomma Abts, also had her work bigged up by Serota's Tate.

Most glaring of all was the annual Turner Prize, Serota's big idea to 'widen interest' in contemporary art and reward 'a British artist for an outstanding exhibition or presentation'. Every year, with diminishing returns, the Tate (collaborating recently with the BBC) brought us a parade of artistic incompetence, obscenity and trash. They strained for controversy. The more we reactionaries in the tabloid press said the Turner Prize was rubbish, the happier they claimed to be. Yet they were damaging our body politic. The Turner Prize merely cemented, in the public's mind, an impression that State Art lived in a privileged world of its own, where a male potter became famous chiefly for dressing as a woman and where Damien Hirst became a multi-millionaire even though some of his ideas were second-hand and the work was done by helpers. Lay people looked at the sort of rubbish that won this coveted prize and thought 'we know more than the experts'.

The nominees for the 2016 Turner Prize were:

Josephine Pryde – her *lapses in Thinking By the person i Am* (the odd capital lettering is intentional) was formed mainly of a toy railway track with a locomotive dragging two sit-on carriages covered in graffiti.

Anthea Hamilton – an old boot had lichen and fungus glued to it; a woman's suit was patterned like brickwork; a metal chastity belt was suspended from the ceiling; an enormous model of a human bottom was shown being parted by two hands, as though about to let rip a silent-but-deadly.

Helen Marten – various pieces of plastic, some of it looking like surgical ware, were joined together to make robotic shapes.

Michael Dean – a work entitled *(United Kingdom poverty line of sixteen thousand seven hundred pounds sterling translated at an exchange rate of 1.27 on Christmas day 2014 into two million one hundred and twenty thousand nine hundred euro cents.)* was, as the Turner Prize brochure explained, a pile of 2,120,900 Euro cents. This was 'an emotive quantity made physically apparent ... implicating all who stepped on the coins in a shrewd questioning of value within the art world and, more widely, of how wholly democratic access to the arts really is'.

The £25,000 prize, paid boringly by cheque rather than in a pile of tuppenny bits, went to Marten.

The oddest thing about State Art is not that it is so bad. It is that it is tolerated by professional critics and politicians. With a few honourable exceptions (after Brian Sewell's death the best being David Lee, editor of *Jackdaw* magazine), art critics fawn at the feet of Serota and his gang. How can these suck-ups call themselves journalists? Broadcasters are absurdly respectful, too, that windy head-wobbler Simon Schama droning on about Damien Hirst's pickled mutton having an 'ancient, perfervid religiosity' owing to evocations of biblical sheep sacrifice. Radio 4 is normally assiduous about not giving free plugs to commercial concerns, but when arts correspondent Will Gompertz talks about contemporary art, where is the scepticism? He should be given greater editorial freedom to indulge his journalistic independence. Would the listeners not thank him for occasionally laughing his teeth off and admitting that it is all a load of cock?

The politicians continue to go along with this con because they want an easy life and they know that a whingeing art establishment will be given a sympathetic hearing by the BBC. Ed Vaizey, a long-serving Tory arts minister, admitted within days after he left office that the arts world lived in a bubble and was immune from the taxpayers who subsidised it. State-supported artists and actors were ridiculously hostile to those who did not share their 'massive, relentlessly leftwing groupthink,' said Vaizey. What a pity he never had the courage to say so when he was a minister. He excused himself, saying that had he been so outspoken when he was minister, he would have been 'murdered'. His use of 'leftwing' is open to question, mind you. The subsidised arts world is not Left-wing in terms of having solidarity with the working people of this country. They take funding for granted and they scorn common taste.

Art critic Robert Dixon has concluded that State Art 'is no longer art but a cultic practice, involving holy relics, temple architecture, civic theatre, public ceremony and mythic belief in something invisible, an idea of Art'. Attacks on it are 'absorbed as proof of "challenge" of "provocation" or "innovation", and called the virtue of Art'. That may be how the Serotas see it. At the other end of the sewage outlet, the people of Britain were simply reinforced in their suspicion that the Establishment was taking the mickey. State Art, though useless in many ways, had at least symbolised the deeper truth of corroded values in our elite.

Boaty McVolteface

How to torpedo an election result

———————————•———————————

Elites can soon acquire a taste for ignoring public votes. The EU has repeatedly forced member states to have a second go at elections until they reach the right decision (i.e. capitulation to Brussels). Likewise, in March 2016 the Natural Environment Research Council quango decided to do some outreach and invite the public to choose the name of a new £200-million polar research ship being built on Merseyside. You could almost call it a referendum. Merry disaster ensued when the public chose the name 'Boaty McBoatface'.

Westminster seadog and Labour peer the Rt Hon. Admiral the Lord West of Spithead GCB DSC declared that the public had 'gone mad'. But had it? In some ways the jovial name rather suited a vessel that had a big, red, rounded prow and pleasingly chunky proportions, like something out of *Thomas the Tank Engine*. Was it really so bad for a polar research ship to have an amusing name? The penguins were hardly going to take offence.

The world of science was ap palled. Yes, two words – appalled, with as long a mid-pause as you like. Royal

Research Ship *Boaty McBoatface* would bring polar research into disrepute. Foreign dignitaries would be perplexed. And could we imagine – could we? – the naming ceremony when some lord lieutenant or minor royal had to say, 'End ay name this ship . . . *Boaty McBoatface*'?

What a wonderful moment that could have been.

Jo Johnson MP, science minister, scuttled the wheeze. He announced that the moniker was 'not appropriate'. The authorities had been 'looking for a name that would fit the mission and be in keeping with the tradition of the royal research vessel and scientific endeavour. It is going to be doing science on some of the most important issues facing humanity – global warming, climate change, rising sea levels. So you want a name that fits the gravity and importance of the subject . . .' Blah blah blah, drone drone, boring snoring. Mr Johnson's brother Boris would not have hesitated to seize on the name 'Boaty McBoatface' as a wonderfully British jape. If global warming is half so bad as the snoots say it is, a little humanisation of the problem would be no bad thing. But airs and graces had been offended. People At The Top decided a joke had gone too far and it was time for the grown-ups to intervene.

Having ruled that the name poll was merely advisory – does this pattern of events not sound familiar? – the authorities announced that the ship would be named the RSS *Sir David Attenborough*, in honour of the Establishment's preferred television presenter. They love old Attenbore. He is so reliable, so house-trained. In fact, his name had come only fifth in the ship-naming poll, nautical miles behind not only 'Boaty McBoatface' but also 'Poppy-Mai' (a little girl who had died of cancer), 'Henry

Worsley' (a polar explorer who died in 2016) and 'It's Bloody Cold Here'.

Gummy old Attenborough was soon heard deploring the very principle of referendums. After the drubbing he had received in the naming poll, are you surprised? The dreary poot also came out as a Brexit Remoaner, saying the EU referendum had left Britain in a 'mess' and citing an old remark of Ken Clarke that if the people were given a referendum choice between having a National Gallery and a funfair, they would opt for the latter. Well, er, yes, of course they would – that explains the honourable role, through the centuries, of arts patrons.

Attenborough went on to defend 'experts' and added that Members of Parliament were chosen because the people saw that MPs were wiser than us. It is no wonder that lofty Sir David spent much of his life as a senior executive at the BBC.

Two footnotes. First: in November 2016, Labour MP and firm Remainer Paul Flynn (whose constituents voted by 56 per cent for Leave) suggested that Parliament should ignore the EU referendum result the same way the 'Boaty McBoatface' poll had been cast aside. The public had been influenced by racist arguments and were not as 'mature' as MPs. Second: after a public outcry at the dumping of 'Boaty McBoatface' the authorities had a small change of heart and allowed the name to be bestowed on one of two inflatable vessels attached to RSS *Sir David Attenborough*. You've had your fun now, people. Hurry along.

Crazy Clothes, Crazy Gal

Kids Company: a cautionary tale
for our times

————•————

Episodes of *The Two Ronnies*[1] would end with plump Ronnie Barker donning outrageous drag outfits for a song-and-dance routine. But nothing Ronnie Barker ever wore came close to matching the outlandish garb of his lookalike Camila Batmanghelidjh, founder of the Kids Company charity.

What the heck was she wearing? A djellaba? Timothy Leary's bedsheets? Had there been an explosion in a fruit-salad canning factory? Or was this a cynical 'look at me, I'm multicultural' gambit, made in the knowledge that bizarre clothes placed her beyond the bounds of criticism? She knew that the British Establishment was so terrified of being thought 'judgemental', it would have to tolerate any amount of social-worker hokum if its source was wearing a cod-tribal costume.

---

1 For readers younger than the bottle of Angostura bitters in my drinks cupboard, *The Two Ronnies* was a 1970s BBC TV comedy sketch show starring Ronnie Barker and Ronnie Corbett.

Two comedians   Multiculturalism in action

From the tottering turban to the Turkish slippers or yellow Croc beach shoes customised with jazzy inlays, Camila Batmanghelidjh's look was designed to shout multi-ethnic challenge. It also spoke volumes about the muddle of her ideas and the chaos of her charity's multimillion-pound accounts. With those clothes, Batmanghelidjh was asserting her difference and that difference was her trump card. The dresses, wrappings, swaddlings, bandage-weave top-knots or whatever they were, presented a quilted multiplicity of patterns and hues, as myriad as the filigree layers of pastry in a croissant. She wore everything from tartans to Maasai tribeswomen's prints, sickly greens, garish yellows and the sort of swirly circles drawn by first-year primary-school kiddies when testing new felt-tip pens. All this would be completed by old-man Steptoe tipless gloves.

Camila Batmanghelidjh: crayzzee name, crayzzee laydee. Was she real or were she and her moniker a hand in Scrabble?

This bizarre figure was taken seriously by our governing intellects. They managed to suspend their critical faculties and gave her millions of pounds. When they saw her striding round the corridors of Westminster and Whitehall, they overcame the natural instinct to think 'Jaysus, what the hell is THAT?' Conditioned by years of political teaching that no oddball must be judged and that every viewpoint is valid, they gave the woman pot-fuls of public dosh. Oh, and will you come along to our party-political conference, O swami Camila? Will you help us to show the media village what a tolerant party we have become? I'm a liberal pasha. Let me be part of your charity!

Batmanghelidjh became a regular guest speaker at the autumn political party conferences. 'Before we hear from the Shadow Minister, please give a special welcome, con-ference, to a woman who works on the front line of our cities with drug-dependent kids.' The politicians adored her. She was so 'real', they felt. Party members were never quite as ecstatic. They used to peer at this rotund genie, unsure if she was nuts, a fraud or a liability.

Kids Company, founded in 1996, aimed to help problematic youngsters avoid trouble. Batmanghelidjh was raised as the daughter of wealth in the Shah's Iran and claimed to have a gift for talking rough children off the path of misfortune. The way she told it, she tamed violent and drug-addicted youths by showing them love and 'emotional leadership'. It was after speaking to Batmanghelidjh that David Cameron made his 'hug a hoodie' speech.

Soon she was lionised by politicians and celebs alike. Ministers gave Kids Company millions of pounds. Both David and Samantha Cameron became supporters, as did Sting's wife Trudie Styler, about whom it is hard to think without imagining her and Sting hard at it like a couple of tantric-sex yogis, conjoined in the lotus position. Boris Johnson bigged up Camila – she made him look neat. Ditto Sir Richard Branson, Cherie Blair and pop band Coldplay, which helped to raise £10 million for Batmanghelidjh projects. She was photographed alongside the Prince of Wales, or vice versa. Look, there she was at the BAFTAs, upstaging film stars. And there she was surrounded by gorgeous Claudia Schiffer, Stella McCartney, Natalia Vodianova (whoever she might have been) and Gwyneth Paltrow at an event called Fashion's Night Out.

Soon she was being called 'The Angel of Peckham'. Polly Toynbee was a convert, saying: 'She is a brilliant exponent of the cause of the child everyone is scared of. She is a great writer, a great talker. She has terrific descriptive powers of what it is to be a young black kid who is utterly adrift and never had anyone to talk to.' Batmanghelidjh vouchsafed an audience to *PR Week* magazine – not the most sceptical of titles – about her scientific theories on youth criminality. The magazine was a bit baffled by her spiel but concluded that she had 'quite complex ideas' and said she was involved in 'pioneering research' into the way stunted emotions could cause 'physical changes in the brain'.

As bees to a giant honeysuckle, so the technocracy to Camila Batmanghelidjh. She was named Businesswoman of the Year in the Dods and Scottish Widows 'Women in Public Life' awards. Ernst & Young, supposedly shrewd accountants, made her their Person of the Year in 2006, to top their Social Entrepreneur of the Year award in 2005. Various universities gave her honorary degrees and doctorates – the likes of Nottingham Trent University, the Open University, Goldsmiths, Brunel, the South Bank University – with vice-chancellors falling over themselves to be seen encouraging the Great Batmanjelly, beacon of modish social theory. Radio 4's *Woman's Hour*, whose monochrome Miss Prims seldom wear anything more colourful than raven, included her in a poll of powerful women. A CBE came her way. Even the Right-wing Centre for Social Justice scampered after her, giving her a 'lifetime achievement award' in 2009 when she was only forty-six.

Slowly the facts of Batmanghelidjh's charity work started to unravel. She claimed to be helping 12,000 youngsters. The true number was found to be a great deal lower. She claimed to be a psychiatrist; oh dear, she was not. At best she was a psychotherapist, a less regulated field. This turbanned Madame Arcati had dismissed one of her early critics, freelance journalist Miles Goslett, as 'a fantasist' but in due course it turned out she was the one who had trouble discerning reality from fluff.

Batmanghelidjh proved adept at wringing money out of Whitehall. Blackmail would be too strong a word but she engaged in public brinkmanship, daring politicians to allow her much-publicised charity to go bust. BBC executive Alan Yentob, who chaired Kids Company, put his name to a hysterical letter that told ministers that unless Kids Company was given another £3 million urgently, parts of Britain could 'descend into savagery'. Strong language. And of course the letter had its desired effect, for Yentob was part of the power network. He knew people. He went to the big arts launches. And in an attempt to suppress bad news about Kids Company he threw his weight around at the BBC. He was putting his own convenience and his personal political agenda over the corporation's journalistic reputation.

Politicians finally started to regret creating this high-profile media monster, this woman who kept screaming for more cash and who had gone through £37 million of public money. Much of that was handed out to young ruffians in cash, in weekly wads as big as £200; these were called 'poverty intervention payments' and were nominally given to pay for things such as bus passes, food and 'emergencies'. Could they include drug debts? When Tory MP Bernard Jenkin put that to Yentob, the BBC's creative director reacted with theatrical shock, saying it was 'a terrible allegation'. Terrible, indeed, to think that public money was being used to pay off drug dealers. But might it not have been true? Was that not the reality of the 'savagery' of the streets? Should a creative ace such as Yentob not be able to imagine such things?

His fellow trustees at Kids Company were: former WHSmith chief executive Richard Handover; Sunetra Atkinson, former wife of Rowan Atkinson; Erica Bolton, an arts-world PR person who makes all the right political noises and whose clients include the BBC, Arts Council, Anish Kapoor, Tate, Serpentine Galleries and British Council; lawyer Jane Tyler, an expert in EU law; Francesca Robinson, posh headhunter; and Andrew Webster, human-resources wallah.

David Cameron kept telling his ministers to support Batmanghelidjh. She had become an embodiment of his fast-sinking Big Society idea. Eventually the debts became too much and Kids Company collapsed. Yentob adopted an expression of hollow-eyed victimhood. The trustees put out a statement saying that there was no suggestion they had acted 'dishonestly or in bad faith' but they possibly slightly spoilt the effect of that defensive declaration by getting a law firm to make it on their behalf.

The House of Commons's Public Administration Select

Committee concluded that the trustees had relied on 'wishful thinking and false optimism'. The MPs added that Charity Commission guidance to charity trustees gives a warning that trustees 'would not allow their judgement to be swayed by personal prejudices or dominant personalities'. 'This is what happened in Kids Company,' said the MPs. 'This resulted in trustees suspending their usual critical faculties.'

Batmanghelidjh had presided over a crony culture in which some staff had their children's school fees paid. The children of Richard Handover were employed by Kids Company on generous salaries. Handover by name and nature! Some of the young 'clients' of Kids Company were being paid many thousands of pounds a year to keep them off the street. It would have been cheaper to send them to Eton. But that would never have been countenanced because it would have gone against the political orthodoxy of the egalitarian society grandees who regarded Kids Company as a treadmill on which to exercise their social consciences.

What was it that attracted the Establishment to Camila Batmanghelidjh, this galleon in full sail? Her intellectualism? She was more a figure of blunt assertion. Her humility? She came across as an imperious figure. At a select committee I watched her roll her eyes to the ceiling and moue her lips in belittling gestures as MPs probed her charity's ruinous mismanagement.

Ministers could have put a stop to it. They could have said 'something's not quite right – let's stop giving her public money'. For too long they did no such thing. Equally, their civil servants could have said 'that woman is spending the public's money without achieving the results she claims'. But Camila Batmanghelidjh was exotic. She had become a symbol of rainbow politics.

What, too, of the professional consultants who were hired to oversee her activities? One was PricewaterhouseCoopers, one of the biggest auditing firms in the Western world. The report by MPs was withering. Professional advisers, said the select committee, 'tend to limit the scope of the terms of their investigation in order to limit their own exposure to risk'. What a damnation – brilliantly crystallised – of the way these prancing snoots operate. The MPs continued: 'In this case, they were able to avoid making any examination of the wider issues that threatened the charity's existence. In the partial assurances they offered, the resulting reports may actually have obscured more than they revealed to those who read them.'

We are forever being told we must hire expert advisers, jump through the hoops of professional scrutiny, submit to 'compliance' by la-di-dah shysters with lots of letters after their names – but here was the high court of Parliament saying such contracting out of common sense and salty scepticism can merely achieve obfuscation and confusion.

The Kids Company scandal was 'an extraordinary catalogue of failure', to quote the Commons inquiry. Yentob, that player of liberal-London contacts who over the years asserted himself as the BBC's great arts critic, was exposed as a politicised sucker. What is art if it is not about truth? Yet here was our most high-profile critic gulled. Yentob had, in Batmanghelidjh, possibly thought he had found a living, breathing Roy Liechtenstein canvas. She was a piece of performance art all by herself. Her turban alone should have had an Arts Council grant. But in the end it was not art. It was artifice.

Yentob and his friends fell for that. With their 'personal prejudices' (to cite the Commons select committee) they were keen for it all to be true, for this wild, intoxicating figure, acme of Leftish wish-fulfilment, to be proved correct in her altruistic meddling. Camila Batmanghelidjh appeared to put flesh and bones on all those theories, cherished by the moneyed Left for decades, about discipline being inferior, when raising youngsters, to tolerance and cash handouts. If the Batmanghelidjh social experiment was wrong, then their whole world would collapse, would it not?

Lording It

Patronising bastardy's Mother Ship

Parliament is topsy-turvy. Today's House of Commons is like yesteryear's Lords and today's House of Lords is in many respects the old Commons.

The twenty-first-century Commons contains so few working-class members, it is barely 'common' at all. It protects the interests of the clerical/political caste. The number of former manual workers in the House fell from ninety-eight in 1979 to just nineteen in the 2015 Parliament. Today's Commons has roughly as many lawyers as it did forty years ago (more solicitors than barristers now). In the Blair years there was an influx of teachers but several were expelled by the voters. The percentage of MPs who are doctors has barely altered; journalists and former civil servants have dropped a bit and there are half as many farmers. The number of former businesspeople (this includes accountants and personnel officers) has swollen from 22.3 per cent to 30.7 per cent, but the biggest rise between 1979 and 2017 was in the 'white collar' and 'political organiser' sectors. 'White collar' means union officials, PR people and charity executives.

The modern peerage

They rose from 1.5 per cent in 1979 to 11.1 per cent. Political organiser (up from 3.4 per cent to 17.1 per cent) means party apparatchiks/spin doctors.

The Commons thus became the House of Accountants, the House of Third Sector lobbyists, trade-union researchers and former ministerial special advisers. Politics has been professionalised, making the Commons less representative. Our national debate is not being moulded by politicians who have mixed it with factory workers or experienced cold mornings in a warehouse or been joshed by lads on a construction site. Our laws are being made by soft-palmed Herberts and Hatties adept at bureaucratic one-upmanship and making themselves look good in meetings.

Recent leaders have not had a wide experience of life. Tony Blair was a junior barrister for not very long before becoming an MP. Gordon Brown was a lecturer in ... politics. David Cameron worked briefly as a television company's PR man but otherwise his working life was in politics. Ed Miliband was a political schnoodler (a noodle who schmoozes) from day one of his extended adolescence. Nick Clegg wrote speeches in Brussels. Jeremy Corbyn's adult life was spent as a trade-union organiser before he became a Labour backbencher but at least he remained on those backbenches for a long time. Corbyn's former challenger for the Labour leadership, Owen Smith, was a ministerial special adviser and briefly a lobbyist for the manufacturers of Viagra – and yet he flopped. Theresa May was briefly in central banking, Tim Farron worked in higher education for a while, Harriet Harman was legal officer for the National Council of Civil Liberties and Nicola Sturgeon spent four years as a baby solicitor. The Greens' Caroline Lucas was a press officer for Oxfam, London Mayor Sadiq Khan was a human-rights solicitor, John Bercow was a special adviser. On it goes: a litany of limitation.

In Edwardian days, the House of Lords was similarly ossified, drawn from a sliver of society. The peerage had long been to the same educational establishments, married their children to one another and spoken a language distinct to the ruling class (in the thirteenth century it was Norman French, later it became bureaucratese). Thus does today's Commons resemble the Lords of the past. Meanwhile, today's Lords has become a recycling bin for failed and former MPs.

The red benches of the House of Lords were once reserved for barons who would bop Marches marauders with their spiked maces. The survival of the hereditary House into the twentieth century was an anti-democratic outrage but over the years many peers acquired an artful charm. They learned not to push their luck too hard when it came to opposing the Crown. They perfected a genial eccentricity, which made them harder to hate. Some hereditary peers attended the House so infrequently that they were known as 'backwoodsmen', like far-flung Wild West frontiersmen coming into Medicine Bow for their annual bath. The state opening of Parliament became a colourful pageant when hereditaries would turn up with their consorts, some of them jowly trouts, some slender corkers, all done up in ancestral bling. Even amid that costumery these aristocratic couples radiated horsey diffidence, understanding they were just playing a role and that by the late afternoon they would be back home in motheaten pullovers, mucking out the stables and throwing mice to the Jack Russell.

In 1999 Tony Blair botched his reform of the Lords. Despite fine words about reconnecting Westminster to the voters, the Blairites seized power over the Lords. More than that, they seized power *beyond* the Lords because they increased the numbers of life peers being created. Yum yum – the power of patronage, reaching out across the agencies and councils and quangos of the land. Bureaucratic Britain is full of fixers who would do almost anything to be made a member of the Lords. What a prize: to become a member of the legislature for the rest of one's days and never have to meet a single, unwashed voter. Third World dictatorships have 'presidents for life'. We have parliamentarians for life.

The red benches are thus now filled by a legislative gloop no more democratically accountable than the old hereditaries but more arrogant, for they have not acquired that patina of eccentricity. The old peerage at least had a connection with the land (which they owned/farmed) and their localities (they were often lord lieutenants or high sheriffs or magistrates or church wardens or trustees of county charities). The new peerage is rooted in the professions. It grabs its privileges greedily and has a far greater sense of its magnificence than the toffs did.

Look, there's Neil Kinnock, election-losing former Labour leader and Brussels commissioner. Who's that next to him? Hooray, it's his beady-eyed wife Glenys, the prototype Cherie Blair who became an MEP. Both Kinnocks being life peers, they can trouser £600 a day of our money in allowances. Tidy. Between them they are said to have six public-sector pensions worth some £250,000 a year. One estimate reckoned that over the years the two of them had ker-chinged £10 million from Europe. The Kinnocks' son, Stephen, is in the Commons and his wife is a former Danish prime minister who now leads a big charity in London, its work subsidised by the government. The Kinnocks' daughter Rachel is in politics, too, having worked as an adviser to Ed Miliband. When the dukes and earls were members of the Lords they at least, by dint of taxation, sat there as net contributors to the state. The Kinnocks are net graspers, sucking harder than anything James Dyson has yet invented.

Brussels was a staging post for many peers – Lords Richard, Mandelson, Balfe, Tugendhat, Liddle, Kirkhope, Tomlinson and all stations to Milford Haven, plus the Ladies Ashton, McIntosh, Crawley (good name!) and more. The European Commission's Justus Lipsius building did for our new peerage what Swiss finishing schools once did for Chelsea debutantes. Several peers are on delicious Brussels pensions, whose small-print has been interpreted by credible sources as a demand that recipients should not attack the European Union. How did such a constraint on free expression ever get past the lawyers? Simple. The lawyers are in charge and they are mainly pro-European because Europe creates more complex laws, which only they, the scriveners, can authenticate.

Across today's Lords, questions about character, suitability and political judgement arise. You think, *Jeepers, how did* that one *get through the swimming-pool filters?*

Look at Lord Davies of Stamford, as oily and sneery a piece of work as exists this side of the late Terry-Thomas's film work. Tory MP Quentin Davies defected to the Labour Party in 2007 soon after Gordon Brown became prime minister. Brown made Davies a defence minister. Was that part of his price for crossing the floor? Three years later Davies (who would never have won Stamford as a Labour candidate) was given a peerage in Brown's resignation honours. Was that because he had been such a fine defence minister? Or was it – I ask this merely out of curiosity, not for a moment believing our system could be so whiffy – part of the original deal under which he left the Tory party to join Labour?

Defectors have often made it into the Lords. Peter Temple-Morris, a low-impact Tory MP for Leominster, slithered towards Tony Blair's Labour not long after the 1997 election. He was made a peer in 2001. Alan Howarth made the same journey, becoming Lord Howarth of Newport. Hugh Dykes, John Lee and Emma Nicholson migrated from the Tory benches to the Lib Dems in the Commons. None was exactly a first-eleven player yet all received peerages. A place in the Lords was a tool in the hands of prime ministers and they were using it blatantly to promote second-raters.

Among our Upper House's eggheads squats Lord Sugarlump, runty little property developer, shouty presenter of TV's *The Apprentice* and sometime computer salesman. Should we cry or laugh at his presence in the panoply? Lady Mone, underwear model and lingerie tycoon, sits there in all her finery. Nearby is West Ham FC's Lady Brady, who once worked for a pornographer (though not, indeed, as a dolly bird). David Cameron's resignation honours jemmied a busload of his loyalists into this quagmire.

This whole process of ennoblement is dressed up still with ceremonial, with the ermine robes once worn by the old peerage. The introduction formalities still involve a royal herald and the reading of a long, cod-medieval citation – the only way of making it bearable is to imagine it being said by Michael Palin with a stutter. Squalid new peers acquire coats of arms and elaborate titles – all the appurtenances and privileges of the old nobility but with none of the inherited sense of duty to the nation. We have ended up with the worst of both worlds.

Standards of behaviour in debates plummeted. Heckling increased, as did party political polemic. Attendance rates increased, but not always in a good way. Some, like the Tories' former convict Lord Hanningfield, 'clocked on' briefly to claim his daily smackers before buggering off again, £300 the richer.

Peers shout over one another, younger ones thrusting themselves to the fore, men perfectly happy to barge women aside. Chivalry has shrivelled. In the Commons that might be excusable because the parliamentarian speaks for his or her constituents. The Lords is supposedly just an assembly of experts ready to serve as and when the country wishes to hear from them. Its new occupants mistake 'duty to speak' for a 'right to shout'.

Seldom have they screamed and stamped their feet as they did in the Brexit debates in early 2017, when faced with a Bill that would let Theresa May trigger Article 50 and confirm to Brussels that we intended to leave the EU. For days the unelected House seethed. The place was packed, peers arriving from far and wide, buffalo gathering at a water hole for some rare lunar event.

Here was a chance for the Lords to block the Prime Minister from carrying out the orders of the British people. Had the referendum been a general election, Leave might have won by more than 100 seats. And yet Lady Smith, Labour leader in the Lords, cried: 'We will not be threatened into not fulfilling our normal constitutional role.' The issues were 'complicated – they are complex and require wisdom, experience, thoughtful strategy and serious negotiation'. The electorate should not get above itself. The wise and thoughtful Lords was in command.

'The process of Brexit cannot be run solely by those who have no doubt,' averred this Lady Smith, a one-time anti-hunting zealot. Lord Newby, a former spin doctor and now Lords leader of the Lib Dems (they have one hundred peers) was indignantly pro-EU. 'Many of us have always been proud internationalists,' said Newby. How he ever managed to get his tongue round the oath he made when he became a peer, when he promised to serve the British Crown, one can but wonder. Former Labour MP Lady Jowell said that in twenty years of weekly surgeries and doorstep meetings, 'never once' did a voter raise with her the issue of Europe. 'Never.' Perhaps voters thought it would be pointless complaining about the EU to a political class that so adored Brussels. Lachrymose Lord Lester (Lib Dem) compared the Brexit plans to George Orwell and Humpty Dumpty and said Britain would become 'an offshore island, semi-detached from Europe'. By George, I think he's got it. The Bishop of Southwark called the referendum result 'quixotic'. Young Lord Oates (Lib Dem), a former spin doctor to Nick Clegg, tremulously said politicians seeking to enact the will of the majority of voters were behaving with 'the arrogance of a medieval monarch'.

Lord Alli (Lab) knew better than the elected ministers supervising the Brexit negotiations. Why? Because he was a businessman. 'For those of us, and there are many in this House, who have run, built or managed big multibillion-pound commercial operations, we know that putting the trainees to run our most important deal is a mistake. That is what looks like will happen. In this House there are eight former EU Commissioners, two of whom have already spoken. There are current and past CEOs of some of Britain's biggest companies. There are chairmen, past and present, of many of our most successful businesses. This House is a resource and a place to find advice, help and skills that are not available in the other place.' We were back to the superiority of experts.

Lady Armstrong (Lab) claimed that the Leave vote showed Britain was insufficiently multicultural. She added: 'Bullying has to be confronted. Certainly we women know that.' Thus were Leave satirists slandered as wife-beaters. And Lady Wheatcroft (Con) complained about the 'irrational hostility' she had faced when she said Brexit should be resisted. Was it really so irrational of people to become angry at a hoity-toity peer taking it upon herself to resist the majority decision after a plebiscite involving thirty-four million voters? Wheatcroft, with her nasal, Sybil-Fawlty voice, said there was no reason the referendum should not be repeated. After all, general elections were re-run every four or five years. 'A Parliament is not for life,' she said. No. But a ruddy life peerage is.

What weeping and wailing, what threshing of limbs we had from this House of Inertia. Former MEP Lord Balfe (Con) condemned the 'foolishness' of the electorate. Lady Henig (Lab) said, 'this is the problem with direct democracy: the public do not necessarily come up with the optimum answer'. Lady Lister (Lab) had been 'bereaved' by the vote. A hearse, a hearse, my kingdom for a hearse. Crossness, exasperation, disgust: that was their reaction to the electorate's independence of mind. How very dare the voters not do as the elite wished?

Lady Altmann wailed that 'politics is being put above economics'. Quite apart from the possibility that the economics of Brexit could be a great success, let us just look at that statement. Is it so wrong for politics to be more important than short-term economic benefit? 'Where is the risk assessment?' asked Altmann. 'Think again!' intoned Lord Liddle, sometime briefcase-carrier of Lord Mandelson. Liddle – whose wife Caroline Thomson was once number three at the BBC and was daughter of a European commissioner – sounded close to emotional breakdown as he deplored the 'jingoists and imperialists . . . in the working-class electorate'. Reflecting on his own fine career, Lord Kerr reminded the House: 'I speak from experience.' Something similar came from Kerr's friend and fellow former diplomat Lord Hannay. After venting theories about how we should yield ground to the EU on citizens' residency rights, Hannay murmured: 'I say that as someone with a little experience of EU negotiation. I negotiated our accession to the treaty, in a very modest way, as well as the budget rebate, the establishment of the single market and the opt-out on the euro. Of course, I cannot be sure that I am right, but I do think that there is a reasonable chance that I am right.'

My favourite part of that quotation is the phrase 'in a very modest way'. Hannay is a man who, even when looking in his shaving mirror, surely adopts an expression of pained superiority.

In a telling exchange, Lib Dem Lord Tyler snapped at Lord True (Con). True had elegantly taken the mickey out of the Remainers and suggested that 358 anti-Brexiteers in the Lords effectively had a power of veto over Brexit, and thereby an improper level of power compared to the Commons. Tyler, scorn dripping off his upper branches, said: 'I have now served in Parliament for over twenty-five years – roughly half that time in each House. I do not think the noble Lord [i.e. True] has had experience of the House of Commons.' What did Tyler mean by that? Did he mean, 'I was an MP once so I am superior to you?' It sounded like that. But the thing about being an MP is that the distinction ceases the moment you stop being an MP because your importance flowed only from the people you represented. A politician should not think he is important thanks to his own person, rather than his constituency.

Lib Dem Lord Thomas of Gresford hollered, 'We are the enemy to Brexiteers, to Trump's vision of America and to populist politics everywhere – we are progressives! We stand instinctively for cooperation.' He compared himself and his fellow 'progressives' to the cavalry officers who took part in the charge of the Light Brigade. He even started quoting from Rudyard Kipling's 'The Last of the Light Brigade':

> O thirty million English that babble of England's
>   might,
> Behold there are twenty heroes who lack their
>   food tonight;
> Our children's children are lisping 'to honour the
>   charge they made –',
> And we leave to the streets and the workhouse
>   the charge of the Light Brigade!

Kipling (who taught my grandmother how to skate, by the way) would surely have been a romantic Leaver. The astonishing thing about Brexit was that it was a battle indeed fought by a tiny band of dissenters who took on the pounding guns of the Established order – and won.

Life peerages were introduced in 1958 as a way of refreshing and intellectualising the hereditary Upper House. The original idea was to bring august figures into the legislature. Life peers would wear their political preferences lightly and attend when they felt they had something to say. These would lend their knowledge to the nation. Membership of the Lords would be an honour, not a living.

Today's life peers include:

Lady Adams – sometime Labour MP Irene Adams, who inherited her Commons seat from her late husband. She was booted upstairs to the Lords when her constituency was merged and Scottish Labour bosses wanted someone else to be MP.

Lord Alderdice – multiple election loser with Ulster's Alliance Party, now sits as a Lib Dem.

Lord Allan – a youthful Lib Dem MP for Sheffield Hallam, then one of the Lib Dems' few safe seats, until making way for Nick Clegg. A seat in the Lords followed.

Lord Archer – juicy Jeffrey, always on the make. Writhed like a rattlesnake to get himself a peerage. Did time in prison for perjury. An adornment to any black comedy.

Lady Bakewell – ex-TV presenter, ex-mistress of playwright Harold Pinter. The House of Lords likes to embrace experts and here is one on betrayal.

Lady Bakewell of Hardington Mandeville – former secretary of Paddy Ashdown. One shudders to think of what she must have seen in her time.

Lord Barker – resigned his Commons seat to spend more time with his business interests.

Lord Bassam – sometime squatter known as 'Lord Swampy'. Failed to become a Labour MP.

Lord Beith – long-standing Lib Dem MP who retired in 2015 just in time to avoid defeat by the Tories. His wife Diana Maddock was made a peer after contriving to lose Christchurch to the Tories in 1997.

Lady Benjamin – Floella Benjamin, ex-presenter of TV's *Play School*. Moving to the Lib Dem benches in the Lords was not so much of a leap.

Lady Bertin – ex-press officer to David Cameron, just thirty-eight when made a peer.

Lady Bonham-Carter – ex Lib Dem press officer, now popsy of Lib Dem peer Lord Razzall.

Lady Brady – Karren with two Rs once worked for garish porn-to-footie tycoon David Sullivan and later collaborated with cerebral Alan Sugar on *The Apprentice*. Was it working with those two refined gents that made her a keen feminist?

Lord Brennan – personal-injury barrister with Cherie Blair's Matrix Chambers.

Lady Brinton – Lib Dem twice rejected by the voters of Watford.

Lady Burt – Lib Dem who lost Solihull seat in the 2015 election and within weeks was back at Westminster as a peer. In-out-in like a fiddler's elbow.

Lord Caine – special adviser to several Conservative ministers. *Not* Michael Caine.

Lord Carter of Barnes – communications wonk who lasted roughly as long as a snowball in a hot room as Gordon Brown's chief of staff. Then did nine months as a minister. One of life's stayers!

Lord Cashman – *EastEnders* actor turned Labour MEP.

Lady Cavendish of Little Venice – Downing Street strategist who was bunged a peerage in David Cameron's resignation list; quit Tory whip after three months because she said she was off to do a big job not yet identified.

Lord Chadlington – PR man, brother of John Gummer (Lord Deben).

Lady Chakrabarti – Liberty pin-up turned thirsty Corbyn

apologist. Looks a bit hunted these days, following accusations she has sold out.

Lord Chidgey – Lib Dem plodder who vacated his seat in 2005 just in time for Chris Huhne to inherit it; a peerage to that man surrendering his parking slot.

Lord Cooper – 'Calamity Cooper', David Cameron's polling guru; made Mystic Meg look like an Old Testament prophet.

Lord Cotter – formidably dull little man who was Lib Dem MP for Weston-super-Mare before being kicked out by the voters in 2005. One of life's grey socks.

Lady Doocey – was Vince Cable's Lib Dem election agent.

Lady Falkender – Lady Forkbender was Harold Wilson's lavender-tinged amanuensis.

Lady Fall – David Cameron's bag-carrier.

Lord Fearn – ah Ronnie, ex Lib Dem MP; more usefully, a panto dame.

Lady Featherstone – hereditary millionaire dumped by the voters of Hornsey and Wood Green in May 2015; six months later was back as a Lib Dem peer.

Lord Foulkes – Labour blowhard and W. C. Fields look-alike who, when an MP, nose-dived into a gutter after a whisky tasting. Recently filmed by BBC dozing in the Lords chamber.

Lady Garden – a title that makes some laugh. Failed MP; made a life peer a month after the death of her husband, Lord Garden.

Lord Grabiner – Grasper Grabiner, a barrister and

business schmoozer, was once Robert Maxwell's lawyer. Close to Sir Philip Green, too. Classy guy!

Lady Greenfield – telly scientist once married to militant secularist Peter Atkins.

Lady Grender – ex speech writer for Paddy Ashdown, now a TV pundit.

Lord Hall – ex-head of the Royal Opera House who was paid some £400,000 a year; now director general of the BBC.

Lord Harries of Pentregarth – former Bishop of Oxford. When Lords Spiritual retire as bishops they normally leave the Lords but *Thought for the Day* bore Harries is such a Left-wing pin-up he was made a life peer.

Lady Healy – special adviser to Harriet Harman and then, poor thing, John Prescott; was also a Labour press officer.

Lord Hoffmann – senior judge who came a spectacular cropper in 1999 when he ruled on a case involving Chile's former dictator Augusto Pinochet but did not declare his family links to Amnesty International. Hoffmann replied: 'The fact is, I am not biased. I am a lawyer.' Magnificent!

Lord Horam – was a Labour MP, an SDP MP and a Tory MP. Bingo!

Lady Howe of Idlicote – widow of Geoffrey Howe and sometimes said to have exhorted him to topple Margaret Thatcher.

Lady Hughes of Stretford – B-list Blairite former MP and demonstrably useless immigration minister.

Lady Kennedy of Cradley – former 'strategic adviser' to Ed Miliband. That went well.

Lord Kerslake – mumbling, bumbling Bob, former head of the Civil Service, his mere name is enough to raise ironic laughter around Whitehall.

Lord Layard – economist and 'happiness expert' who argues that money does not make you happy. He and his wife, Lady Meacher, both have comfortable parliamentary incomes.

Lord Leitch – outwardly unexciting insurance bod who became the improbable 'fourth man' in the political sex saga surrounding sometime *Spectator* magazine floozie Kimberly Quinn. Vamp devours mouse.

Lord Levene – arms-trade schmoozer who was also – how agreeable – a government adviser on procuring weapons.

Lord Levy – played tennis with Tony Blair and never – NEVER – offered peerages to Labour donors.

Lord Martin – dire Commons Speaker who left that position at the height of the expenses scandal.

Lady Mone – businesswoman and queen of the cleavage; has moved out of bras, so to speak, and into fake-tanning.

Lady Morgan of Huyton – former Downing Street fixer for Tony Blair.

Lady Nye – Gordon Brown's former diary secretary.

Lord Ouseley – sometime local government clerk who has made a lucrative career out of racial equality; Parliament's only Herman.

Lord Palumbo – property owner and art buff who was friendly with Margaret Thatcher. Seldom seen or heard in Lords.

Lord Palumbo of Southwark – son of the above; was a director of the Ministry of Sound nightclub and used to let his friend Nick Clegg (who put him up for the peerage) hold Lib Dem events there; little more active in the Lords than his father.

Lord Pannick – complete and utter lawyer.

Lady Parminter – animal rights nag and sometime researcher to Lib Dem MP Simon Hughes.

Lord (Chris) Patten – as puffed up as the most perfect Indian poori, this former BBC chairman (not to mention Tory party chairman, Hong Kong governor and EU Commissioner) is condescension made flesh. His eyebrows rise like sloths, out comes a froggy croak – everyone else is wrong, I'm right.

Lady Pidding – sometime bank clerk; a Tory best known for her *terrifying* orange lipstick.

Lady Rawlings – once a Tory MEP but better known as a leading society beauty of the 1950s and for having an interest in antiques. Get her in the Lords, pronto!

Lord Rennard – Lib Dem election planner who was the target of sex-pest allegations, which he denied.

Lord Rose – was good at selling smalls when boss of Marks & Spencer; less efficient as head of the Remain campaign in the EU referendum, which he ballsed up bigtime.

Lord Ryder – Establishment man who was John Major's Chief Whip at the time of the Maastricht Treaty; later showed his colours when a BBC governor and took it upon himself to apologise for the way the Beeb had behaved in the David Kelly affair.

Lord Strasburger – no fan of the press, this property dealer has given more than £700,000 to the Lib Dems. They made him a peer. Would a thank-you letter not have sufficed?

Lord Sugar – ratty little sort, has made much of his money in property and from telly. Not one of life's instant orators or political thinkers.

Lord Taylor of Warwick – sentenced to a year in prison in 2011 after an expenses fiddle.

Lord Truscott – goatee-chinned, keen on Russia; suspended from House for six months in 2009 after a lobbying scandal.

Lady Uddin – she had to repay £125,000 in wrongly-claimed expenses; yet she still sits in the House!

Lady Young of Hornsey – social worker turned artful quangocrat but not quite in the league of . . .

Lady Young of Old Scone – who picks up quango jobs as a magnet collects iron filings.

Cordon Bleuh

Culinary one-upmanship our speciality

———————————•———————————

Your starter for ten: What is umeboshi dressing? Is it,

a) a Japanese medical procedure that allows a sup-
    purating wound to breathe through strips of
    sterilised liniment?

b) a pickled-plum sauce for salads, revered as a
    health tonic?

c) saffron-dyed clothes typical of the nomadic
    Umebosh women of the south Sahara?

Now try these posers.

Tamarind: a lizard, a bulbous stringed instrument or a
leguminous tree whose fruit is used in Worcester sauce?

Tabbouleh: meditative copulation technique popular-
ised by Joan Collins and her Percy, a salty Levantine dip
or the transsexual heroine of H. Rider Haggard's novel
Tabbouleh, Princess of Madagascar?

Courgetti: 85 cc mopeds in Sardinia, fine noodles made by pushing baby marrow through a mincer, or Middlesbrough FC's goalkeeper in the 2008/9 season?

Daikon: radish grown in Japan, a fifth-century BC phallic toy (found at a 1960s dig in Mytilene, Lesbos), or a new brand of budget van made at a Thai-owned factory in Ebbw Vale?

Each is the food. Not that Mrs Beeton would have known. Nor would sixties TV chef (and bigamist) Fanny Cradock. Cooking advice used to be about taking everyday ingredients and making something palatable. Today it is about showing how sophisticated you are – what obscure commodities you can 'source' (like some geologist). You then turn those foreign objects into something that may well be repulsive. Is the intention to give friendly advice to amateur chefs or is it about swanking and making us feel small?

Umeboshi dressing is recommended by the Hemsley sisters, Jasmine and Melissa, thirty-something south-London beauties much promoted by Channel 4 as 'passionate foodies'. Neither looks a convincing trencherwoman. Some of their critics become indignant that the Hemsleys do not have qualifications in nutrition. That worries me less than the fact that they are so skinny. Have these girls never had a real pig-out?

For the Hemsleys' roasted carrot and fennel salad with umeboshi dressing you need quinoa, fennel, carrots, sesame seeds (black and white), asparagus, pink radishes, spring onions, coconut oil, fresh mint and coriander, umeboshi puree, sesame oil, fresh ginger, tamari, raw honey,

Fanny: more fun than Ella Mills

fresh chilli and, phew, water. Until writing that just now, I did not even know what tamari was. Since you ask, it is a Japanese soy sauce made without wheat and therefore acceptable to people with wheat allergies. Did anyone have wheat allergies in the 1960s? The entire salad not only sounds horrible – I dislike fennel – but also tricky to whip up on the spur of the moment. How many of us have quinoa and tamari and raw honey and umeboshi purée on our larder shelves?

The Hemsleys preach 'clean living' and promote a philosophy based on '15 pillars' that will help their disciples to achieve a state of 'wellness'. Here are some morsels from the sisters' pulpit:

The Hemsley + Hemsley business grew organically as people became interested in our approach to health, wellbeing and food. Our books act as a go-to guide for anyone looking to create meals that are simple, nutrient-dense and utterly delicious. In our books, we not only talk about bulk cooking, nose-to-tail eating and share tips on sourcing ingredients of good provenance but also emphasise the importance of good digestion, explaining everything from the virtues of thoroughly chewing to the importance of natural probiotic foods. Our ethos encompasses a holistic mindset. We believe that what you eat, how you care for your body and the way you feel are intrinsically linked. We champion a philosophy which is simple, mindful and intuitive, steering clear of 'quick-fix' answers which are abundant in the health and wellness (and even fashion) industries by teaching a long term lifestyle change.

'Thoroughly chew' on that lot as long as you want, it may still give you indigestion.

Customers possibly bought the cookery book to see if there was something more interesting to be done with a block of mousetrap and the leftovers from last night's roast chicken. Instead they find themselves being subjected to a homily about being 'kinder to your body', avoiding 'bad' ingredients, making chocolate brownies from black beans rather than wicked flour and whisking up a quick beetroot and cinnamon smoothie (don't forget the raw cacao nibs, the desiccated coconut – and a sick bag for the moment after tasting it). The message here is not so much about healthy living as expensive living, posing with a superior 'I know what spirulina powder is' expression on your vegan chops.

Posh crisps have taken over. Candy-stripe beetroot, lobster cocktail, goat's cheese with garlic and rosemary: these are some of the flavours sold by Tyrrells, which illustrates its packets with sepia-tinted snapshots of olden days. Would madam be interested in seeing other succulents on today's crisps menu? Firecracker lobster from Burts, horseradish and sour cream Salty Dog crisps 'that bite back', Salty Dog jalapeño and coriander crisps: these are selling a dream, a class statement, and more often than not a dig in the gums, ouch (posh crisps are sharp). All you craved was a packet of Golden Wonder ready salted. It is the same with party nibbles. Nothing beats a cheese straw, a bite-sized ham sandwich or a sausage on a stick. We are not allowed anything so sensible. Round come platters of citrus-cured sea bass on blinis with Ossetra caviar and crème fraîche, gravadlax (does *anyone* like dill?), warm bonbons of foie gras à la Basque, Roquefort pie with aromatic apricots. Here, Fido, scoff-scoff.

The Hemsleys have a deadly rival on the clean-living front: Ella Mills (née Woodward), a young honey from an immensely rich background blessed with good media contacts. Ah, Ella, so fey, so pure, so fond of avocado that she even uses it to make cheesecake. My wife and I tried it once. It nearly made me boke on my plate. Ella, whose mother is a Sainsbury and father was a New Labour cabinet minister, has made a tidy little business out of her innocence. Admire the retro typewriter script of her website and the use of golly-gosh adverbs. *Deliciously Ella* was her first book, sold with the catchline 'Love Your Life, Love Your Food, Love Your Self'. What happened to the chef as giver, as spoiling feeder of friends?

Clean-living cookery writers list ingredients that anyone on the minimum wage would struggle to afford. Ella looks and sounds a sweet-enough girl but her proselytising feels horribly cliquey. Does she look so gorgeous simply because she is a trust-fund millennial who makes her own almond milk (the better to go with her date and chia pudding, to be eaten en route to 'work, gym, school')? Or does she look diaphanously pretty because she has enviable genes and her parents were loaded?

A mirthless duo called Dr Patrizia Collard and Helen Stephenson produced *The Mindfulness Cookbook – Eat in the 'Now' and be your perfect weight for life*, which combines recipes with a form of Buddhism and the sort of religious superiority more commonly associated with flagellating adherents of Opus Dei. 'This book is based on the idea that behind every weight problem is a human being,' write Collard and Stephenson. They obviously haven't met our neighbours' Labrador. 'We all look for quick solutions to our inner dissatisfactions by seeking satisfying experiences through food. Unfortunately, this doesn't work. We can't feed the longings of our mind with food. You can start to find other ways – developing new neuro pathways – of dealing with unhappiness and pain.' Hunger is being cast as something the superior being (i.e. these authors) can control. Each recipe is accompanied by 'awareness points'. When preparing corn and bacon muffins, Collard and Stephenson say, 'take a moment to really appreciate the sizzling sounds of frying bacon and onions'. With their layered nutty bars, 'explore touch – use your hands to grease the tin, noticing the coolness of the metal'. With the mushroom stroganoff, they write, 'this recipe is incredibly simple to make – how will you spend the extra time?' By laughing your knackers off at their dotty 'aware-ness points', perhaps.

There is nothing new about melding philosophy with cookery. Chapter 1 of *Mrs Beeton's Book of Household Management* (1859) opens with a quotation from the Book of Proverbs ('she looketh well to the ways of her household and eateth not the bread of idleness' – a gluten-free statement, even). Mrs Beeton compares the mistress of the house to the commander of an army ('her spirit will be seen through the whole establishment'). Early rising, cleanliness, frugality and the avoidance of hastily formed friendships are just some of the lifestyle options, as she does not call them, recommended by Mrs Beeton. She was, quite possibly, an insufferable old boot.

Yet the tone of Mrs Beeton's book differs from that of the Hemsley sisters and Ella Mills and our Buddhist bores of mindfulness. Mrs Beeton is bracingly utilitarian, addressing the reader as a comrade in the trenches rather than handing down (as if from some scented, Zenned-out cloud) advice on how to be as beautiful and successful as lovely, lovely us. Mrs Beeton barks out her receipts for cheap onion soup or roast widgeon, or gives brisk instruc-tions on how to dress a plover or ptarmigan. She does not pass comment on good and bad enzymes or the cleansing of your kidneys or breaking down your cellulite. Looking at gorgeous Ella, or – ping smile! – Jasmine and Melissa Hemsley, you doubt they have ever been afflicted by fat-bottomed cellulite in their lives. They look such physical perfection, even their burps must be frangipani-scented.

This was not something that could be said of the Two Fat Ladies, Jennifer Paterson and Clarissa Dickson Wright (both dead, alas, but both snortingly sensible women of the world). It could not be said of the Galloping Gourmet, Graham Kerr, who starred in TV cookery shows in the 1970s and injected his programmes with chaotic mishaps. Although Fanny Cradock appeared a snob, could we not all see that she was, under those hawk-wing eyelashes and the smeared lipstick, a tottering desperado, possibly a couple of gins already down the hatch? Fanny and her monocle-popping husband Johnnie were fun to watch. The clean-living brigade are unutterably joyless.

London publishers recently went mad for *hygge*, which is Danish for domestic cosiness. *Hygge* was ordained a 'word of the year' by both the Oxford and Collins dictionaries. Only, perhaps, in London publishing circles. If you said '*hygge*' to an Aldi till operator in Sunderland you might receive a blank look. *The Art of Hygge* by Jonny Jackson and Elias Larsen was just one of numerous how-to-*hygge* books, illustrated by photographs of open fires, mugs of cinnamon-infused cocoa and home-knitted socks. Readers were taught how to go for winter beach walks, carve pumpkins, make lavender bags, stack firewood and have a candlelit bath. A *hyggelig* life could be achieved through 'crafting, baking, experiencing natural wonders, lingering over everyday rituals'. Another *hygge* expert, Marie Tourell Søderberg, quoted Nordic interior designer Christina B. Kjeldsen as saying *hygge* could not be achieved by following décor instructions. 'A home decorated "in the right way" with furniture and aesthetic style chosen exclusively from some kind of formula that is thought to be "correct" is seldom very hyggelig.' So why be an interior designer and why publish books about *hygge*?

The whole *hygge*-guide business was basically bølløx.

Can cooking be about self-denial? Keith Floyd, 1990s TV chef, never thought so. You could argue that heavy-drinking, fag-puffing, debt-ridden, wife-hopping Floyd (he was felled by a heart attack at the age of sixty-five) was no 'role model'. Sod role models. The nannies who bleat about role models are the sort of people who happily tolerate bad language and coarse behaviour on television programmes because, they say, we need to be aware of the world about us. Role models are invariably waxen, stunted stiffs. Show me today a toothpastey, gleamy role model with faultless Californian uplift, a liver pink and healthy as soft nougat, and I, in a decade, will show you a rough-as-pumice has-been with bloodshot eyes, receding hairline and all sorts of iffy inclinations. Keith Floyd may have been a toper but was there not something uplifting about him? He took cooking outside and bunged in flavours with abandon – none of that tight-bottomed Delia approach to measurements. Delia is a New Labour supporter, and wouldn't you know it?

Floyd glugged away in front of the camera. Sometimes he omitted important ingredients. For all these so-called faults, he spread fun and encouraged us to try the new. He did so without making himself sound superior.

In their miserable *Mindfulness Cookbook*, authors Collard and Stephenson urge their readers to 'try giving up' things they crave. A panel lists some of the sins we should attempt to do without for a while: 'sugar, snacks, your favourite caffeine, dairy food, white flour, alcohol, meat, pre-packed food, complaining, internet, mobile phone, car'. Imagine the cackles of laughter if anyone had ever put such a suggestion to Keith Floyd.

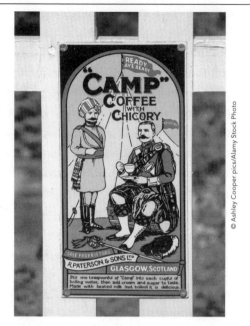

'We haven't had much call for Camp since
John Inman died, sahib'

Michelin still adorns its garages and restaurant guides with its
Michelin Man motif. What a pleasingly porky fellow – lots of
spare tyres, and that is the message they want to promote.
The Michelin Man's official name is Bibendum, Latin for 'drink
up'. Don't tell the police. In earlier decades Bibendum would
be depicted with a cigar, a napkin in his collar and even with a
sloshing wine glass in his hand. He is soberer these days –
they slimmed him down a bit in the late 1990s – but at least he
is still there as a public sybarite. Camp Coffee had a less
happy time with its corporate device. Labels on bottles of
Camp, the world's first instant coffee and made in Glasgow
from the nineteenth century by the Paterson Company, used
to show a smartly turbanned Indian bearer bringing a tray of

coffee to his sahib, a kilted Scottish soldier with a Village People moustache. 'Ready Aye Ready,' said a jaunty slogan. The finger-waggers descended. Mukami McCrum, director of the Central Scotland Racial Equality Council, adjudged the label 'racist' and 'offensive in the way it portrays other cultures as being subservient to the white man. They should be using a picture which gives out a message of equality. Young people going into supermarkets and seeing this on the shelves will be getting an outdated message.' Now that really was absurd. Since when has any 'young person' bought Camp Coffee?

Hoggs a-Troughin'

The hoggy Hailshams, snootocracy's
first family, bring in the bacon

All may not be well at the minor stately home Kettlethorpe Hall, Lincolnshire. Tinkle! Is that the smashing of priceless porcelain? Splash! Has another under-valet – some warted Baldrick – been booted into the hall's infamous moat by its owner, the 3rd Viscount Hailsham?

M'lud Hailsham, a crabbed, staccato, glowering presence, was formerly known as Tory MP Douglas Hogg. This trilby-hatted grump was the one who managed to mention moat-clearing in his parliamentary expenses claims. There was also talk of piano tuning and a Kettlethorpe housekeeper being stuck on the public tab. Although Hogg contested the details, he went down in the public's imagination as the grasping toff who had his moat – a ruddy moat! – dredged at public expense. It was the end of his Commons career.

He has since wormed his way back into Parliament, having been bunged a life peerage by David Cameron in 2015. An earlier attempt by Cameron – or maybe his chancellor, George Osborne – to palm Hogg a peerage

Spot the difference

was stopped by an advisory committee. Hogg/Hailsham was also rejected in a ballot of hereditary peers when a vacancy arose in their ranks in 2013. But sometimes a Prime Minister becomes insistent on enobling a friend whom others would say was unsuitable. Feet are stamped. I will, I will, I WILL! It happened when Mrs Thatcher elevated Jeffrey Archer (later prisoner number FF 8282) and it happened again now. Cameron felt emboldened by his election win of 2015 and did his old pal Douglas a favour. Truffle-hound Hogg was back in the legislature he possibly regarded as his blood-right.

He was soon using his unelected perch to oppose Brexit. Hailsham pooh-poohed referenda as being 'profoundly divisive'. He compared Theresa May's Britain to Idi Amin's Uganda. He called himself a Roundhead in favour of greater parliamentary power to rein in the power of ministers. Time and again the 3rd Viscount rose to make interventions during Brexit debates, shoulders hunched.

The more he was complimented by Left-wing Remainers, the more he licked his tortoisey lips with relish.

'Lord Moat' was brazenly insisting that the votes of more than seventeen million electors must come second to parliamentary prerogative – more specifically, the opinion of some eight hundred unelected peers. The will of the populace was wafted aside with one sweep of Hailsham's claws. His eyes glinted. Spittle gargled in his beak. The old buzzard was in his element. How tenaciously he applied his legal mind to the deficiencies of the Leave vote. Hailshams didn't get where they are today – no, sir! – by allowing popular sentiment to translate into law. Such matters as treaty, Act, statute: these are not for the pilfering lower orders. You should no sooner let the voters dictate such matters than you would grant your average butcher's boy admission to your current wife's boudoir. There is a time and a place for butcher's boys, by all means. Let Hailshams not be thought unreasonable. In the encasement of forcemeat, slicing of tongue, the pedalling of black-framed bicycles with large wicker baskets, such fellows are to be acclaimed. But within the purlieus of constitutional law they have little proper business.

The 3rd Viscount's father was, as these things tend to go, the 2nd Viscount. He was better known as Tory MP and peer Quintin Hogg and in 1976, while delivering a Dimbleby Lecture – always a high point on the Patronising Bastards' calendar – he used the expression 'elective dictatorship' to describe the powers of recent British governments. Hailsham was by that point in the House of Lords. He had originally gone there in 1950 when he inherited his title but he renounced his viscountcy in 1963 to become an MP. He hoped one day to lead his party and become prime minister. He did not win the Tory leadership because, it was felt, he was too – oh dear! – vulgar. Grandees frowned on his love of a photo opportunity, be it whacking a Labour poster with a truncheon or going swimming in goggles and flippers in the sea at Brighton during a party conference. Hailsham was one of the first modern exponents of the photo opportunity. And yet he scorned populism.

> Quintin Hogg's 'elective dictatorship' phrase described what he saw as the inability of the 1970s Parliament to stop ministers passing laws they wanted. But Brexit flowed from an extra-parliamentary plebiscite. It was the decision of the people *in defiance* of Parliament. It was the verdict of an electorate that saw that parliamentarians – some bent by financial interests – had a sunnier view of the European Union. If there was any 'dictating' being attempted here, it was being done by the Westminster claque.

The current viscount resides at Kettlethorpe with his wife Sarah, economist and businesswoman. Her father, Lord Boyd-Carpenter, was a Tory cabinet minister in the era of turn-ups and Humber Sceptres. It's not keeping up with the Joneses that matters. It's keeping in with the party leaders. We have not yet had – nor possibly ever will, if the Hailshams have their say – a prime minister called Jones.

Sarah Hogg has graced various boards in her time, including those of the BBC, P&O Cruises, Eton College and the 3i Group, which she chaired. A BBC governor? You don't get to be one of 'em without passing muster. Sure enough, when Greg Dyke was in trouble as BBC director general after Radio 4 accused the Blair government of 'sexing up' the case for the Iraq War, la Hogg was one of the governors who pushed for Dyke to be sacked. No doubt the Establishment was duly grateful. We can't have the BBC rocking the canoe, can we? It's there to cement the snootocracy's grip on power, not be difficult. Dyke later claimed that he had wanted the BBC to be more inquisitive about MPs' expenses but he had been opposed by various forces of inertia including the governors. Yes, you can see why Douglas Hogg's wife would have been horrified by the thought of the Beeb pursuing such inquiries. It would be another six years before, thanks to a leaked computer disc, the expenses scandal broke.

Sarah Hogg was formerly a rather grand scribe on the *Independent* and *Daily Telegraph*, as well as doing a stint at Channel 4. Her period in telly might have lasted longer had she not sounded so disapproving. On Fleet Street she was known less for her sparkling prose than for her social acquaintance with much of the Establishment. In the 1990s she was given a life peerage after serving as head of John Major's Downing Street policy unit.

But back to Kettlethorpe, a pretty spot blotched by recent misfortunes. Quite apart from the intolerable Brexit business there was an unfortunate to-do concerning the Hailshams' daughter Charlotte. In January 2017, she was appointed to the deputy governorship (markets and banking) of the Bank of England. She had previously been the Bank's chief operating officer, back when the chancellor was George Osborne. Why do I again mention Mr Osborne? Well, it so happens that his first big job in politics, as a young bachelor, was as special adviser to Douglas Hogg. He met and warmed to the elegant Charlotte, a shade older than him. Did favouritism play any role when, two decades later, Charlotte was made Threadneedle Street's chief operating officer? We must hope not. Once Charlotte Hogg landed the promotion to deputy governorship, she was spoken of as a future governor of the Bank. The incumbent governor, Mark Carney, himself seen as an Osborne stooge, was said to be 'a fan' of the Hon. Charlotte. The Bank deputy-governorship came with pay of £270,000 a year plus hefty perks.

Alas, alack, Charlotte suffered a horribly public downfall. Amid all the hyperbole about her brilliance, it was discovered that she had contravened a code of conduct that she herself had written for Bank employees. She had failed to declare a potential conflict of interest: her brother was a senior strategist at Barclays Bank. Why she omitted this connection it is hard to be sure. Did she just assume that, the Hoggs being so jolly well-known, everyone would know what her bro' did? The Commons Treasury Committee said her 'professional competence fell short of the very high standards required to fulfil the additional responsibilities of deputy governor for markets and banking'. Ker-twangggg! The sound this time was not of some imaginary vassal sailing through the air towards Kettlethorpe's algae-fied moat. It was of the dainty Hon. Charlotte hurtling over the Bank of England's battlements as she left in disgrace.

Would she have been so harshly treated if her stupid father had not made such a fuss about Brexit? Would she have survived if her booster, Mark Carney, had not irritated some members of the Treasury Committee by being so anti-Brexit? Those theories may have more to them than the absurd suggestion from George Osborne (him again) that Charlotte Hogg was a victim of sexism.

We can note that Charlotte Hogg is on paper a formidably clever woman. Just look at the curriculum vitae she submitted to MPs before her 'pre-appointment hearing'. I use inverted commas on that term because the hearing was arranged at a rush, *after* the Treasury had announced her appointment. Her c.v. showed that she was educated at pukka St Mary's, Ascot, at Hertford College, Oxford, and won a Kennedy scholarship to Harvard. In 1992, she became a junior Bank of England officer specialising in hedge funds and derivatives.

Executive stints with management consultants McKinsey & Co. in Washington, DC, with Morgan Stanley in New York and with Santander bank followed. From the start, she was in the fast lane, top of the class, gliding effortlessly into enviable jobs.

When she appeared before the Treasury Committee, she was asked what fresh insights she would bring to the top of the Bank of England. Would she be able to challenge 'groupthink' in the Bank's 'court' (as its senior managers are called)? The nine members of the Bank's monetary policy committee came from worryingly similar educational establishments, banks and backgrounds. Hogg tried to talk about 'diversity' at the Bank solely in terms of gender and race. She said she had a 'range of cognitive experiences'.

When both your parents and both your grandfathers have been members of the unelected legislature, when you have swished from top job to top job like an ice skater on one foot, when you have been to wonderful schools, sat in boardrooms and been brought up within footman-lobbing distance of a moat, it is probably not a good idea to claim such a thing.

BBC governors are 'safe pairs of hands', altar-servers of the System, non-political yet artfully politic. They know what needs to be done and do it with mirthless efficiency. Repress the irrepressible. Dial down dissent. Sarah Hogg's BBC board colleagues included Dame Pauline Neville-Jones, an ex-'Foreign Office diplomat'. I have met a number of the Dame's acquaintances who disliked her sharply. She chaired arms company QinetiQ (a former state asset, which had been privatised in smelly circumstances) before becoming security minister, briefly, in the Cameron government.

Other BBC board stooges around this time: serial Leftist quangocrat Lady Young of Old Scone, wet-as-celery theatre director Sir Richard Eyre, a race-equality wallah – they always like to have one of those – called Ranjit Sondhi and Lord Ryder, who had been government chief whip when John Major was ramming the Maastricht Treaty down the Tory party's goosy gullet. Recent BBC boards have been no sparkier. They have included: Suzanna Taverne, daughter of a Lib Dem peer who compared Brexit to the work of Hitler, Mussolini and Stalin; Mark Florman, a European merchant banker and associate of Bob Geldof; a former (Labour) ministerial special adviser, Lord Williams of Baglan; and Richard Ayre, a sometime civil service commissioner and Law Society insider prone to oozings about the sanctity of free speech, even while running the BBC Trust's Orwellian editorial standards committee.

Is it not time we had a *Panorama* investigation on the sort of complaisant boobies who decorate the Beeb's board?

Tsar Ascendant

Social mobility, a job-creation
scheme for the elite

———————•———————

Alan Milburn was that sparky, larky New Labourite once spoken of as a possible prime minister. You remember Milburn: good-looking, nice legs and a mouth as small and round as a cat's bottom. He spoke in a refined Geordie accent closer to Inspector Clouseau than *Auf Wiedersehen, Pet*. Quick to first names and with a joshing laugh, he was happy to mix with business types ('here's my card – don't be a stranger'). From a distance, there was perhaps the suspicion he might wear designer underpants and apply excessive applications of aftershave yet some women found him captivating. Gordon Brown couldn't abide the fellow.

Milburn was good on television and had a bluff manner around Parliament, usually content to have a beer with the lads – though it might have been Peroni rather than Newcastle Brown. His government career? Patchy. He began as a health minister, doing much to encourage the Private Finance Initiative, which enriched so many venture capitalists at public cost. Cabinet promotion followed but he lacked staying power. He quit in order to spend more time with his family. They often say that.

Some allege that Brown duffed in Milburn's political career to make sure he was no threat to his chances of leading Labour once Blair turned to vapour. At the start of the 2005 general election campaign, Gordon did an Achilles, sulking in his tent until Tony agreed to make Alan less important in the election-planning team. How sulphurous Cabinet hatreds can be. Not so much shoulder to shoulder as fist to nose. Others said Milburn did not possess the intellectual rigour, bloody-mindedness and physical stamina required in high office. With that boyish charm and that thatch of hair, he had been blessed with many natural gifts. He was one of life's fly-halves. It is, however, the way of the world that sunny-go-lucky souls such as Wor Alan do not always have the tenacity found in drabber specimens (e.g. G. Brown). Things sort themselves out in the end. Talent alone is not enough. The dour shall inherit the Earth.

What became of Milburn? For that matter, what became of several of those New Labour floaters? David Miliband took himself and his banana off to New York to work for International Rescue. Helping poor people in distant and dusty lands has proved a canny move for Miliband (Ma). He is paid the best part of half a million pounds a year and is the toast of *soignée* Manhattan's Democrat billionaires. As mentioned, his former cabinet colleague James Purnell wormed himself into an executive position at the BBC. How public-spirited Purnell was to devote himself to non-commercial broadcasting for a mere £295,000 per annum (plus generous extras). Ruth Kelly was gently escorted by men in white robes to a cloistered perch at a Roman Catholic university in Twickenham, working under former Blair policy adviser Francis Campbell. The much-maligned masons some-times have nothing on the way the modern Establishment looks after its own. Former House of Lords leader Lady Amos went on a global wander, first becoming High Commissioner to Australia (lucky Aussies); she briefly washed up at that desert island for wrecked politicos, the United Nations, before London's Left-leaning School for Oriental and African Studies came to the rescue and made her its director. Meanwhile, Geoff Hoon is selling helicop-ters. 'Chopper' Hoon, Defence Secretary at the time of the Iraq War, was much vilified in a lobbying scandal but at least he is now engaged in proper wealth creation.

As for Alan Milburn, he is sucking on the teat – really more of a Zeppelin – of 'social mobility'. Never in the field of politics have such juicy sinecures been found for so many social democrats in the service of our poverty-stricken masses – well, not if you discount overseas aid. Here is a grand example of how political correctness, far from helping the needy and frail, serves the interests of the citadel's elite. Soon after quitting as an MP in 2010, he became the coali-tion government's 'social mobility tsar'. He chaired the Panel on Fair Access to the Professions and the Social Mobility and Child Poverty Commission. In 2012, this turned into the chairmanship of the new Social Mobility Commission.

The Panel on Fair Access was a humdinger. Its members included such orthodox trundlers as publisher (and Labour peer) Gail Rebuck, whose late husband was Tony Blair's pollster, and TUC General Secretary Frances O'Grady. Also:

KPMG partner Neil Sherlock, a Lib Dem who advised Paddy Ashdown and Nick Clegg; soapy ex-Tory minister Gillian Shephard; luvvie Jude Kelly of the South Bank Centre; lawyer David Neuberger, who would lead the Supreme Court in 2017; the police's 'PC' Sara Thornton; architectural quangocrat Sunand Prasad; Girton bluestocking Madeleine Atkins, who sucks some quarter of a million pounds out of the public purse as head of the Higher Education Funding Council (a woman worth knowing – she gets to propose people for honours and is a gatekeeper of tickets for Buckingham Palace garden parties); and Trevor Phillips, the TV producer-turned-equalities campaigner who at that point had yet to complete his brave recantation of multiculturalism. The Panel of Fair Access was such a classic that in any game of Establishment bingo you would soon be shouting 'full house!'

Commissions are splendid things for a former minister because they come with Swanksville offices, business cards and spin doctors. According to twenty-first-century Whitehallspeak, Milburn was given the task of

being an advocate for the social mobility agenda: holding to account and challenging key institutions in areas such as higher education and the professions; building and sustaining effective working relationships with a range of stakeholders, including ministers, senior government officials, representatives from local communities and experts in the field; being a public spokesperson for the commission, and ensuring active engagement by all members in the business of the commission.

Does it never occur to the authors of such stodge that one reason working-class youngsters are deterred from aiming at the professions and public institutions is the sheer deadness of the jargon?

Milburn did not over-exert himself. He posed for a new photograph, which captured the handsome philosopher in a sharp suit and intellectual-looking spectacles. When the Commission issued its occasional reports into social mobility – which, miraculously, it found to be worsening, for what is the point of busy-body commissioners if they do not demonstrate the world is riddled with the problem they are paid to identify? – he would pop up on the television news to vouchsafe a few Cloueseauish soundbites. He may have been speaking complete tosh but you have to give him this: he did always look terrific in the latest whistle and toot.

Talking of fashion, one of those reports found that 'bright youngsters' were being turned away from bank jobs because they wore brown shoes and garish ties to interviews. Milburn complained that 'bright working-class kids are being systematically locked out of top jobs in investment banking because they may not understand arcane culture rules'.

While it was welcome to hear so modish a former Blairite renounce the questionable value of appearance over substance, was Milburn really arguing that working-class lads could not understand that garish ties and brown shoes might be thought prattish? If you can't pick up a simple unwritten dress code, what hope is there that you will be able to read the mood of a rich client? Or was Milburn just trotting through the hoops, spouting rubbish written for him by aides? Was he told 'this will make a good story – let's accuse employers of fashion snobbery'? It would have made a much stronger story if Milburn had told twenty-something lads, 'Don't dress like plonkers – wise up to the real world and buy yourself a £20 pair of black shoes if you are going for an interview with one of those big City firms.'

Since quitting the Commons, Milburn has made as much as half-a-million pounds a year from business interests. He was a director of AM Strategy (his personal consultancy) and had involvements at Bridgepoint Capital (a private healthcare provider to the NHS), Mars foods and two further health companies. How lovely for this socialist drum-beater to be so in with big business. Those years he spent semi-privatising the NHS did not go to waste. And how congenial for those businesses, not without their controversial nature, to be able to brandish on their corporate teamsheet the name of the Rt Hon. Commissioner for Social Mobility. Look at us. We've got Milburn on our books. He cares, and so do we!

Not fair. That is the claim made by opponents of selective and private education. Among these stovepipe-hatted theorists: playwright and grammar school-educated Alan Bennett, supposedly such a dear old thing with his cardigans and that ooh-Betty Leeds accent. Is he Bennett the droll and cherished chronicler of genteel, lower-middle-class northern ladies with handbags that fasten with a 'clack'? Or is he an acid class-warrior who wants to abolish private schools, even while making a fortune out of mocking his working-class parents?

Bennett was once a new-wave satirist. He was part of the *Beyond the Fringe* team that in the 1960s helped to rip down the old order, loosening respect for the Church, the Macmillan Tory party, judges and the military. What juicy targets they were, ripe for the plucking. Not that it was particularly brave work. Those purple-nosed boobies of the bench and those gowned beaks at minor public schools were already on the way out. A really brave satirist is the one who takes on the incoming regime.

In his play *Forty Years On* (1968), Bennett attacks the past: Empire, tradition, retiring authority. Among his targets are superannuated majors in south-coast guesthouses who still use their military rank despite having long ago left the Army. To have made that point in the 1940s would have been edgy. To have examined it in the early 1950s might have been interesting from a psychological aspect. But to swipe at them in the late 1960s? Were those ageing chaps really a threat? Or were they not just sad and lonely figures who in their egg-stained regimental ties and hankering for a daily routine were gamely trying to keep body and soul together?

John Betjeman covered the nostalgia beat with greater charity. Betjeman wrote of sun-burnish'd Aldershot beauties and elderly maids contentedly praying in church light scented by lilies. Bennett writes of timid working-class mams and aunties worried about their p's and q's, furtively gossiping about their neighbours. Both writers peddle memories. Both may be touched by a rueful melancholy. But Betjeman's verbal watercolours have a faint wash of solidarity whereas Bennett's words are written as though from higher ground. Where Betjeman sympathises, Bennett surreptitiously places himself above his subjects, even his own flesh and blood. In *Untold Stories* he describes his parents and their social hesitations.

He extracts laughs from their wonderment that he, their Alan, had started mixing with all those posh folk down south. Many writers of comic fiction exploit their families but with Bennett there is bitterness in the ink. At times, it feels distinctly as if he is laughing *at* his parents. Betjeman memorialises with benevolence and, for that reason, is less revered by the Left, which wants to attack the past in its quest for constant change.

Butcher's boy Bennett is no longer working-class because he went to a grammar school – an elitist establishment, based on selection. It was thanks to that education that he got to the University of Oxford, another sharply selective establishment, and met the likes of Peter Cook, Dudley Moore and Jonathan Miller. He became a supporter of the Left, much feted by the Arts Council and the public universities and the big prize-giving bodies. The same Left attacked grammar schools out of spite (if you doubt that, consider the words of their midwife, Anthony Crosland, who said, 'if it's the last thing I do, I'm going to destroy every f***ing grammar school in England') and brought in the bog-standard comprehensive schools, which dumbed down British education for decades. Although comprehensives at last may have been discredited – getting the Left to accept that has been like getting antibiotic tablets down a Doberman – the same educationalist Levellers are now in the process of imposing social-class requirements on our top universities.

Bennett, meanwhile, wants to smash the private sector – smash it until the last neo-classical, Portland-stone frieze of public-school culture lies in splinters, like the monasteries after Henry VIII. 'Private education is not fair,' wheedles Bennett, himself childless.

Those who provide it know it. Those who pay for it know it. Those who have to sacrifice in order to purchase it know it. And those who receive it know it, or should. My objection to private education is simply put. It is not fair. And to say that nothing is fair is not an answer. Governments, even this one, exist to make the nation's circumstances more fair, but no government, whatever its complexion, has dared to tackle private education.

Is that really what governments are for? To make life 'more fair'? Welcome to the Ministry of Defence, citizen, our Trident missiles with their bulbous warheads are here to make life more fair. Oh look, there's the Lord Chancellor. We can rely on him to run courts that deliver judgments based on a squashy idea of fairness rather than rigorous justice. Unemployment benefits: how are they fair on people working for the minimum wage?

What the hell is fair? Is it fair that some of us are good at maths and others cannot even count their regrets? Is it fair that Jonny Wilkinson was both brilliant at rugby and wonderfully good-looking? Is it fair that bragging Sir Philip Green is a billionaire? The answer to those questions is 'quite possibly' because their achievements may all, in their way, have involved personal graft and self-discipline. But is it fair your parents lost their first son in infancy, that your sister died of cancer and that your child has autism? Fairness has bugger all to do with it.

What a pointless, plastic, lazy, Lefty, arrogant word this 'fair' is, all the worse when uttered in a maudlin, moany accent. Does Bennett mean 'wrong'? There is no right or wrong in providence. What Alan Bennett probably means by unfair is 'unequal' or 'inegalitarian', but he is too canny to use those expressions because they would expose him as a droning socialist and that would be bad for his image. It might upset his lawn-mowing, *Daily Telegraph*-reading fans. For all his complaints about the materialism of post-Thatcher Britain (when Lady Thatcher died, Bennett gloated and said she should have been buried at dark of night) this is a man who now lives with a civil partner, one Rupert, who edits the entirely materialist *World of Interiors* magazine.

If you want to make something less unfair that will probably mean taking something away from another person, and how 'fair' would that be? A mother has saved hard to send a little girl to, say, a private dance school where she can do ballet to her heart's content: are they now to be told that this is illegal? A father wants to send his youngsters to the same school his family has attended for four generations but is now told that the government has nationalised the site and he must instead go to the educational establishment assigned by a local council office? Eton, perhaps the world's greatest school, is to be bulldozered in the name of egalitarian 'fairness', as demanded by a playwright who has made his fortune out of cosy Radio 4 nostalgia but now says he is concerned about the poor people?

Despite having sent my own children to fee-paying schools, I am not an unalloyed enthusiast for private education. Today's public schools are appallingly expensive and not as tough as they should be, scholastically and culturally. They have become so internationalist that they have nearly lost the British dimension that was possibly their great attraction. Yet to demand the abolition of these establishments simply in the name of social engineering: that is the stance of an acidic and liverish old bastard.

Harmful Harriet

The woodworm of statutory Equalities

———————————●———————————

Harriet Harman should have been in the Special Air Service. She may not have the biceps of your average SAS operative. Nor, one suspects, would she take easily to being called 'you 'orrible little woman' by one of those moustachioed sergeant-majors. Taking orders from a man is not a Harman forte. It may, furthermore, be hard to envisage the Rt Hon. Lady, QC, with her Greenham Common peace-camp views, abseiling through the windows of a foreign embassy to hurl stun-grenades at hostage-takers, or bashing down the door of a stinking hovel in the Khyber Pakhtunkhwa badlands – 'go, go, go!' – to spray hot lead at some sultan of terrorism. Harriet with her face smeared in camouflage cream, lighting up a Marlboro after despatching turbanned zealots, or 'members of our ethnic community' as she might prefer, to their gurgling deaths? Only in the more vivid, sheet-ripping dreams of Boris Johnson would this occur.

Yet Labour's venerated mother hen, Peckham's pop-eyelashed Eva Perón, would have been a good fit for our special forces and for the following reason: booby traps.

We will whistle through the biographical record: Harman, Harriet, born to privilege in 1950, schooled privately, a cousin of the Pakenhams. She made it to the University of York, easier in those days than now. Having qualified as a solicitor, she became an MP in 1982. In 1997 she became social security secretary, a vast brief that would have challenged anyone with twice Harman's brainpower. It overwhelmed her. She liked emoting about the poor in a posh accent dented by glottal stops – having once sounded like Julie Andrews, she was by now known as 'Arriet 'Arman – but the more theoretical, policy-laden side of the brief was left to her deputy, Frank Field. Harriet did not demonstrate much relish for the necessary business of imposing departmental spending limits.

Bookish Field was told by Blair to 'think the unthinkable'. Rashly, he did just that according to his churchgoing principles. Did his Merseyside constituency give him a different view from his London-orientated secretary of state? Yet Field was himself reared in Battersea, not far from Harman's constituency. He was the son of a factory hand (his father worked at the Morgan Crucible factory, a place sooted by carbon) whereas Harriet Harman was the daughter of a Harley Street doctor who wore sponge-bag trousers, a top hat and charged his patients in guineas. When it came to assessing the working-class poor, Field had an advantage in that he had sprung from them. Harman romanticised them.

Field felt welfare spending could prevent the poor from making the most of their lives. It held back their 'motivation, their actions and thereby their character'. Certain benefit payments were creating a feckless, infantilised underclass. Harman (and much of the Parliamentary

Labour Party) was horrified. The underclass served an important function: they gave New Labour people to patronise. And here was Frank Field talking about their 'motivation, their actions and thereby their character'? You can't talk about the 'character' of the poor, man! That's judgemental! In the ensuing hoo-hah, both Field and Harman left their jobs.

A period of entrenchment and reapplication followed and in 2001 Harman was back in the middling position of solicitor general. She rose an inch in the hierarchy when she became minister of state at Constitutional Affairs, working under the more congenial Charles Falconer. There she might have stayed had Tony Blair – never entirely convinced of Harman's abilities – not quit as prime minister in 2007. John Prescott stood down as Labour's deputy leader at the same time. Harman stood for the vacant deputyship and, thanks to a woman-and-minorities pitch, beat Alan Johnson. The deputy leadership of the Labour Party never translated into the deputy prime ministership – a male conspiracy, or did 10 Downing Street have other reasons? – but Harman did become leader of the Commons and minister for women and equality. The leader of the Commons is in charge of apportioning parliamentary time for debates. Labour's time in office was clearly running short. Harman used her twin positions to secure the necessary legislative time for a Bill that would hard-wire political correctness through every aspect not just of Whitehall but also British public life. This was her booby trap.

One of the skills required of an SAS soldier is sabotage. My wife and I used to live near a tough old man who had fought in the Second World War. After a few whiskies, John Wright would admit that his wartime service had included 'making things go bang' in the Far East. Exploding wall safes, trip wires, lavatory cisterns that went ka-boom when 'Tojo' (as John called all Japanese) pulled the loo chain: these were the sort of escapades our kindly old neighbour had got up to in his wartime days. The idea was that you left behind nasty surprises.

Harriet Harman did the political equivalent. She may not have left bundles of gelignite all round Whitehall. That sort of thing we tend to leave to the Irish Republican Army and its successors. Instead she left the Equality Act 2010. It only just squeaked through Parliament in time before Westminster broke up for the general election in May of that year, which Labour lost. The Bill received Royal Assent on 8 April, along with such vital measures as the Anti-Slavery Day Act, the Sunbeds (Regulation) Act, the Debt Relief (Developing Countries) Act and the Bournemouth Borough Council Act.

Chewing on the full ramifications of the Equality Act 2010 is not my purpose here. It might be necessary to fell the New Forest for the wood pulp to do so. Let us concentrate on just one aspect of the Act: Equality Impact Assessments. Equality whats? If you do not know what one of those is, you are not a member of the ruling class.

Equality Impact Assessments are considered necessary in order to ensure that the Public Sector Equality Duty is fulfilled. They have become the legislative equivalent of blobs of Semtex, stuck to every new doorway encountered by government ministers following in Harriet Harman's wake.

The Public Sector Equality Duty has three 'limbs', as the jargon puts it (limbs do not often come in threes but to make that point might contravene the spirit of the Equality Act, being possibly hurtful to tri-dexters and amputees). A public authority must do three things: eliminate discrimination, harassment and victimisation; advance equality of opportunity between minorities and the majority; foster good relations between those minorities and the mainstream. Forgive the verbiage but this is a boiled-down version of the original.

These legal stipulations came as a tremendous career-boost to finger-waggers because they meant public bodies had to be able to show they were actively being nice to minorities. It was no longer good enough to avoid being nasty to them. They had to demonstrate that they were patting minorities on the head. The easiest way of showing clearly that you are fulfilling that sort of behaviour is to spend money on it. It doesn't matter how wisely the money is spent. Just SPEND THE STUFF! Then you can say, 'Look, here is our budget and we have employed lots of people with approved certificates.' A certificate, no matter how pointlessly acquired, no matter the quality of the people awarding it (provided they themselves have a certificate!), is a tick in the box. It is evidence that you have bowed to the system and spent money in the temple.

If you are to 'eliminate discrimination' and so forth, you need to have people who can not only identify discrimination – sniff it out under the floorboards – but also measure it, box that data into reports and present those reports back to their employers, who can then wave them at lawyers to show that the Act's requirements have been satisfied. The one important thing is that everything must bear the watermark of officialdom.

Thus, ladies and gentlemen, is an entire sector created. A profession is born.

For the People Who Know Better, nothing is so handy – so deliciously clerical and legalistic – as an impact assessment. At general elections, voters may be told that by electing a certain politician and party, policy changes will be made and society will alter accordingly. This is the basis of most election campaigns: vote for our manifesto, vote to change things. Change. At that very word, many bureaucrats shudder.

Voters usually fall for these promises. Civil servants know better. They understand that Equality Impact Assessments have made them masters and mistresses of inertia. Politicians can propose what they want but if their reforms fail to pass an Equality Impact Assessment, well, that's the end of the reform. If politically motivated special advisers try to cut corners and hurry impact assessments through the system faster than the system wants to go, the impact assessments may be sent for judicial review and even the smallest infraction of officialdom's 'best practices' guidelines may be enough to see the policy halted on the orders of a judge. You have here the most tremendous device for gumming up the works. Secretaries of state rarely last more than three years at a department. By the time the impact assessment has been commissioned, conducted at glacial speed in the face of shrieking objections from the special interests and their professional lobbyists, checked, sat on, published, objected to vociferously by the special interests and their PR people, sent to the courts, processed by the courts amid continued agitation on the *Today* programme by the professional classes' hired hands, rejected by the courts, sent for appeal, again rejected by the courts, sat on, submitted to further dilution and spin, and finally discussed in cabinet after 'further work' in focus groups, the original policy – which was approved by the electorate – will be found to be 'not worth the candle'. It will then be quietly dropped, politicians saying that they have 'listened and shown we are not unreasonable'. Democracy 0, Status Quo about 20. Behold the paralysis of democracy and a feast for litigators and approved assessors (approved, that is, by Whitehall civil servants who do not want any change).

When the European Union (Notification of Withdrawal) Bill was before the House of Commons in early 2017, Remainer MPs yearned to block it any way they could. They naturally reached for impact assessments. Labour frontbencher Matthew Pennycook argued that before the government confirmed we would be leaving the EU – as demanded by 17.4 million voters – it should be forced to publish official assessments of the impact on 'women and those with protected characteristics'. By that he meant 'black, Asian and minority ethnic people, disabled people and lesbian, gay, bisexual and transgender communities'. Pennycook seemed to doubt that anyone from one of those minorities could have supported Brexit.

Hansard for 7 February 2017 (columns 338–346 if you wish to savour them in full) lists the impact assessments proposed by Pennycook and his friends. They range from impact assessments on everything from the European Union Intellectual Property Office to the Community Plant Variety Office, from the British Overseas Territories to every region of England, from farm incomes to chemical-safety regulations, skills training to charities law. The amendments demanded that Brexit be held up until the bureaucratic class had conducted a full risk audit of Brexit on all those areas of official life. Only then, and only if the government had shown all the legal due diligence required of that process, would the Pennycooks of this world deign to admit the democratic desire for Leave.

'Equalities' is now a whole field of careers and consultancies, piggy-backing on the greater bureaucratisation of life. More rules and forms? More work! The sector is composed of training courses, indoctrination procedures, away-days and conferences, advice leaflets, solicitors' symposia, compliance officers, ombudsmen (ombudspersons? – Ed.), race relations, gender neutrality awareness, diversity managers, inclusion examiners, exclusion litigation specialists, key equality partnerships, community outreach programmes, equality implementation strategies, intervention advisers, inclusive environment auditors and more. These and other juicy occupations have sprung from dingbat Harriet's booby trap. The pay is high.

The University of Salford was recently prepared to pay more than £46,000 a year for an 'inclusion and diversity manager'. I hesitate to make your eyes glaze at the speed at which super glue sets, but the job ad said the successful candidate would:

> Lead the implementation and continuous development of the university's newly approved Inclusion and Diversity Strategy and supporting action plan, with the aim of creating a genuinely inclusive environment for our students, staff and stakeholders. Reporting directly to the Human Resources Director, the role holder will work closely with a range of internal and external stakeholders to ensure the university continues to meet its statutory requirements. They will also facilitate achievement of specific outcomes, including for example work towards various charter marks including

Athena Swan. The role will involve benchmarking diversity practices and work collaboratively and creatively to engender an inclusive culture. The successful candidate will be experienced in the field of I&D, possess management and leadership ability and be able to operate effectively in a fast paced environment. An ability to interpret complex data, communicate effectively at all levels and lead on change through influencing and networking are all key requirements. The role also has line management responsibilities for the Inclusion and Diversity Officer.

Translation: spend what you have to; cosy up to the minority lobbies; just make sure some whinger doesn't sue the knickers off us as a result of that ruddy Equality Act 2010.

Harriet Harman might bridle at the term 'queen bee' – a touch gender specific – but it is suitable given that a queen bee gives life to thousands of worker bees, henceforth to be known as inclusion and diversity managers. As the SAS might say, mission accomplished.

Murray-go-round

Dame Jenni enters the transgender
minefield – and is blown to smithereens

When BBC Human Resources (i.e. Personnel) decided
Dame Jenni Murray had to be ticked off for
remarks about transgender people, there must have been
buttock clenching in the room. Which unfortunate would
be given the task? Did the quick-witted ones say, 'Bags-
I-bloody-not'? Disciplining staff may normally be an
agreeable task, a power kick when a manager can adopt
pitying airs. 'I'm afraid we need to have a talk, Jennifer.
You don't mind if we shut the door, do you? There's a box
of tissues on my desk if you'd like to blow your nose.' But
this case was different. To upbraid Dame Jenni, the mighty
Murray? And over a breach of political correctness?
Gulps. If anyone would be needing tissues it might be the
manager – to staunch the torrent of nose blood.

The dame is one of the great cow walruses of British
feminism. She is presenter of Radio 4's *Woman's Hour*, a
patron of the Family Planning Association, supporter of
the British Humanist Association. Such connections ring
triple cherries on the fruit machine of public life. They are

Another satisfied 'Woman's Hour' listener

badges of virtue, proclaiming a medalled grandee of the Establishment game. Most of all, Dame Jenni is president of the Fawcett Society, crack troops of finger-wagging. As Pope Theodoros II is to observant Copts, so la Murray to liberals; and yet she was to be disciplined for saying something untoward about transpeople? Egad. *Gut Gott.* Pass the gin bottle, Mabel.

In her time Jenni Murray has been a presenter of *Newsnight* and *Today* and an occasional bowler on ITV's *Loose Women*. She inherited *Woman's Hour* from Sue MacGregor thirty years ago and is so indomitable that there has never been any nonsense about replacing her with a younger model (the fate of many other BBC women in their mid-sixties). Jenni has endured breast cancer. She has written a guide to the menopause. She has had very public battles with her waistline – and even if the waistline usually won, that is not mentioned, thank you very much. Throughout, the dame has reigned unchallenged as a juddering tribune of approved attitudes. She has guided us through the rapids of parenting classes, home births, teenage eating disorders, period poverty, craftivism and more, and if her voice has occasionally sounded haughty, well, we deserve it. We need keeping in our places, particularly if we are male. Flay, flay your glistening backs, ye men of Albion.

For such a figure to be charged with political incorrectness was like accusing Buzz Aldrin of being a stay-at-home cissy, or alleging that Mahatma Gandhi was a greedy-guts who scoffed all the pies. What on earth had happened?

Our dame, in the course of one of her important perambulations of the feminist estate, declared that transsexuals who became female were not proper women. Having grown up as boys, they had not experienced the injustice of sexism throughout their years. No. They had been (dark chords, please) men.

This theory did not slip out of the moorings like the inadvertent loosening of wind from the hindquarters of a much-tupped ewe. It was not a case of said ruminant straying beyond its pasture and stepping a hoof in a minefield, one moment tugging at lush grass with its sweet little neck-bell tinkling, the next – kaboom! – being reduced to a pink, sheepish mist. In her offending article, which appeared in the *Sunday Times*, the dame said she knew she was 'entering in the most controversial and, at times, vicious, vulgar and threatening debate of our day. I'm diving headfirst into deep and dangerous waters.' In she went. Out it came.

To say something critical about transgender types? Was she mad? Murray kith and kin should have rushed to stop her. They should have implored her to withdraw the article, at very least to apologise once it appeared, for in this era of flash-flood disapproval a quick apology can stem controversy. Yet in she waded, recalling the 'anger' she felt when she listened to an Anglican priest called Carol, who had once been a bloke. Carol's primary concern, observed Murray, had been on issues of wardrobe and cosmetics. What should she wear? Should she apply make-up? 'I thought of all those women who had spent years and years challenging what being female had meant as they sat in the pews on a Sunday morning: 2,000 years of institutionalised patriarchy,' wrote Murray. 'It was news to Carol that life as a woman, especially a middle-aged woman, stepping into male territory in which she was unwelcome would be extremely tough.'

Having biffed Carol, the dame meted out treatment to someone called India, once a man but now keen to be thought 'a real woman'. India had intimated that hairy legs on a lass could look 'dirty'. This displeased the dame, who proceeded to give a precis of feminist thinking on body hair (legs and armpits, knees and toes, knees and toes) before saying India was 'ignoring the fact that she had spent all of her life before her transition enjoying the privileged position in our society generally accorded to a man'.

To say 'the balloon went up' would be an understatement. The balloon turbo-lurched for the heavens. The transitioning community threw up varnished fingernails in horror. Egalitarian theorists spluttered. And the 'executive director, campaigns and strategy' of gay-rights group Stonewall, one Rachel Cohen, descended from the upper slopes of Olympus to deliver admonishment. Sister Murray was rebuked for 'questioning the identity' of

Messrs Carol and India. 'I do not question your identity, Jenni, and in return I would not expect you to question mine or anyone else's,' said this Cohen. Savour those words for their clipped, Brahmin disdain. This was high-class scorn, as uppish as Cumbria's steeper fells, flavoured by the patient but stern disappointment of the Anger Management School.

As happens in modern Britain, the insulted party ran to the ref and demanded a penalty. What sneaks we have these days. India gathered her skirts and declared that she had been verbally goosed. Murray was 'transphobic' and was 'spouting bile'. India demanded that the BBC sack Murray there and then. Stick her on the sharp end of a pikestaff and wave her severed head from the battlements. Revenge this day! It was 'ridiculous' that such a 'dinosaur' as the dame was permitted to present a BBC radio programme.

The nation was agog, watching this shoot-out at the Right-On Corral. As with the Iran–Iraq War of the 1980s and with most football derbies in the north-west of England, it was possible to resist taking sides. In the red corner: an over-indignant transwoman revelling in victimhood. In the blue corner, peering over her habitual half-moon spectacles with all the jowliness of the late Robert Morley: J. Murray, OBE, DBE, hon' graduate of the University of Salford and lay Professor of Gender Grievances who had once announced that marriage was legalised prostitution.

The BBC could have told India to grow a pair, although on reflection that might not have been wise. And so the corporation part-grovelled, saying Dame Jenni would be pulled into a corporate lay-by and 'reminded that presenters should remain impartial on controversial topics covered by their BBC programmes'. Ha! She had been political much of her professional life and that had not stopped them placing her at the helm of news and current affairs programmes. Similarly, prissy Chris Packham, a presenter of wildlife shows on BBC TV, had been rude about people involved in country sports ('the nasty brigade') and had got off scot-free. The BBC could not give a fig about its presenters being political when the politics are, indeed, politic. Had Dame Jenni only taken a pot-shot at terrier men or the Masons or campanologists or some such unfashionable band of innocents, she'd have been fine. It would have been 'box on, Jenni' and 'don't mind if you do, darling'. But she had made the schoolgirl error of saying something about transsexuals. Gender preference has become the most heavily defended pillbox on the liberals' Maginot Line. Dame Jenni had to be punished.

What boring self-absorption grips the sexual-politics sector, demanding that we listen to people's proclamations about their wobbly bits and what an unhappy time they have had. Most of us are really not that interested. It's a free country. Live and let live. But please don't bore the smalls off us by banging on about your 'journeys'. You were born Eric but now want to be Edith? Fine. Carry on, Tootsie. But leave us to our sudoku, if you don't mind.

England's shires are a lot less fazed by transgender matters than some urban-based equality campaigners imagine. In our local town, Ross-on-Wye, there is a middle-aged chap who walks round in bovver boots, sideburns, tartan leggings and a pink dress, swinging a handbag over his shoulder. No one pays him the blindest bit of notice.

Drive them off the road. Close down debate. Muffle and mute. These are the tactics of the intolerant elite, sniffing out offence where none was ever intended. That little green figure at traffic lights telling pedestrians when to walk across a junction? Discriminatory! And so the Mayor of London, Sadiq Khan, goes to all the elaborate trouble of turning the figure into a gender-neutral diagram. Ditto the squabbles over public lavatories. Signs marked 'ladies' and 'gents'? Prejudice against transpeople! The Barbican arts centre in London duly altered the signs so that they read 'Gender Neutral Toilet – cubicles only' and 'Gender Neutral Toilet – with urinals'. Result: even longer queues for women during the interval. At the root of this is an assumption by officialdom (after being hounded by well-paid gender-rights lobbyists) that trans urgings may lurk in us all.

Equality campaigners argue that loose talk must be silenced because it might offend. Really, they want to starve the populace of views that differ from those of the ruling class. Thou shalt not think.

Universities should be open-minded places where philosophies can be tested against one another but when Germaine Greer was invited to speak at Cardiff University, the Women's Society there went on the warpath. It said veteran feminist Greer would not be welcome because she held unacceptable views on transgender matters. Granted, fruity Germaine did once say about transwomen, 'just because you lop off your d**k and then wear a dress, it doesn't make you a f***ing woman; I've asked my doctor to give me long ears and liver spots and I'm going to wear a brown coat but that won't turn me into a f***ing cocker spaniel'. By Germaine's standards, that was pretty tame.

Impure attitudes to transgender politics have also seen the likes of Julie Bindel (founder of the Justice for Women organisation) and Peter Tatchell (valiant campaigner for gay rights) boycotted by students. People who think Peter Tatchell is intolerant need their heads examining. Yet this madness has gripped the world of LGBTQ+ (the Q stands for questioning and the + means any other business). The National Union of Students has a 'no platform' policy of preventing controversial people from speaking at universities because they might imperil the 'safe space' of campuses in which everyone can be cocooned from upsetting views. It's a wonder lecturers are ever allowed to posit an antithesis these days.

What Rhymes with 'Schmooze'?

Abbey's Frost pocket illustrated the
worship of networking

————————•————————

Poets' Corner at Westminster Abbey salutes great writers. Geoffrey Chaucer was buried there in the 1340s. Later burials included Charles Dickens (interred at first light as he had requested no fandango), Alfred Tennyson and Rudyard Kipling. There are memorials to the likes of Christopher Marlowe, C. S. Lewis and Anthony Trollope, plus a few fabled actors such as Henry Irving and Peggy Ashcroft. These were creative talents of a high order and by marking their memory at the abbey we are saying something about the value of their art and perhaps a divinity in creation. When you consider Trollope's prolific output or Kipling's swirling verses it becomes harder to *not* believe in God.

But Poets' Corner also has a plaque commemorating David Frost. Frost? As in that nasal, drawling telly presenter who used to swank it around on Concorde, flying to and from America every week? The Frost who co-launched TV-am, had a show on Al Jazeera and gave a big drinks party in London every summer? What is he doing at Poets' Corner?

Patronising Bastards

'People are dying to get into the Abbey, I believe'

'Sir David Frost OBE Broadcaster,' says the memorial stone. A poet or artist may sometimes broadcast but a broadcaster, howsoever fluent, is hardly an artist. 'Frosty' was convivial and he spent a lot of money. He may even have invited deans of Westminster to his drinks parties and donated generously to the choristers' Christmas-present fund. He was an incorrigible talker, the familiar of thousands. But a poet?

Frost, in his youth, had a quickness of wit. He possessed business acumen, stamina and a facility at the various powers of bluster and exaggeration that television presenters need. But what he did was not art. It was not even particularly creative. It may suit media executives and small-screen showbiz to promote broadcasting

118

as a noble vocation but it is not. It is just glorified waffling. Spiel. Veneer. Frost was a good talker, not some miner of artistic truths. The abbey's Chapter may have felt it was combining whizzy populism when it admitted Frosty to our Elysium of poetic geniuses but all it really achieved was the diminishment of a shrine.

One of the characters in 'Peter Simple', the *Daily Telegraph* satirical column of a generation ago, was Lieutenant General Sir Frederick ('Tiger') Nidgett, sometime commanding officer of the Royal Army Tailoring Corps. Rasping Nidgett held that the answer to most problems was 'leadership, initiative, vision, initiative, leadership'. Yes, leadership!

People who bang on about leadership are themselves often frustrated megalomaniacs. Leadership gurus have become one of the curses of the age. Every bookshop seems to have a shelf of books about 'the art of leadership', packed with guff about commanding your 'team'. Themselves invariably self-employed, leadership gurus deliver PowerPoint presentations to middle-management cannon fodder. Their audiences stare at them dumbly, too knackered by corporatism to laugh at the pointlessness of it all. Do you wish to bestride the fresh-fruit logistics world like a colossus? Do you have it in you to become a Hannibal of the back office, an Alexander the Great of MegaBucks Ltd's cardboard-packaging division?

There is a woman called Julia Middleton whose mania for 'leadership' is sold on an even bigger scale. Her aim, no less, is to create leaders for the entire world. Middleton runs a charity, Common Purpose, which hopes to create 'the next generation of global leaders'. By that she does not envisage the next Trumps or Farages or Le Pens or Corbyns but something rather more Centrist, i.e. to her own liking.

Middleton aims to turn business executives into a cadre of liberal grandees, massaging society towards certain goals. All who come to her door will be schooled in the enlightened leadership of multiculturalism and suspicion of tabloid newspapers. Yes, she is rather agin the free press. It does not conform to her world view. Middleton's munchkins become part of a discreet network of Common Purpose 'graduates'. They do not have a school tie or roll their trouser legs but the idea is otherwise not dissimilar from the old-boy network or Masonic lodges.

Are you a leader? Do you have what Julia Middleton considers the right stuff? Or are you going to be one of the little people on a low wage for the rest of your life, one of the bleating goats? Are you patrician or pleb, squire or serf, doer or grunt? Common Purpose does not quite use those words but that is the upshot of the sales pitch it makes to the civil service, the police, big business, the Church of England and other such organisations. Over twenty-five years Middleton has worked her way into the minds of some of the highest counsels of our land and she now operates around the world. Global domination, comrades – let us seize the levers of cultural and political power!

She herself keeps a lowish profile. No Richard Coeur de Lion, she. That sort of leadership is not to her taste, being too male and swashbuckling. She prefers to push her agenda in a subtler way. The few photographs of her that exist suggest a stocky, short woman prone to the sort of high collars worn by Sloane Rangers in the 1980s.

Think beady-eyed county type with a muscular gait, a tendency to flick the lank hair off her brow, a brisk voice and rather too keen an eye for the custard creams. This potentially comical figure, alas, is never hauled on to the public airwaves for scrutiny by Eddie Mair's *PM* on Radio 4 or cocky little Krishnan and Kathy on Channel 4, even though she runs a public charity that is indoctrinating thousands of public employees at taxpayers' expense. You might have thought our broadcasters would strive to investigate Julia Middleton and Common Purpose but they have hardly ever touched her. Point of information: the BBC sends numerous top executives on Common Purpose leadership courses. At about £5,000 a pop, they are not cheap.

Leadership can be a troubling notion for liberals. They quail at the idea some people have natural authority while others are so flaky they could barely run a bath. Are we not all born equal? And yet these liberals can see that some folk – by which they naturally mean themselves – need to boss others around. The Julia Middleton answer to this conundrum is that leadership can be taught. That makes it okay. You can go on a course to become an office dictator. Yessir. 'Tiger' Middleton, in exchange for a fistful of spondoolicks, often from the public purse, will show youngsters how to become the Nelson Mandelas (or at least Peter Mandelsons) of tomorrow. That is the theory.

'Draw out your circles' is her first tip. These are the 'circles of authority' that chart your ambition to reach beyond your core group or circle. Middleton wants graduates to influence first their wider company, then the whole of society. 'Think about your personal brand' is another tip. 'Do your own 360-degree appraisal. Ask others what words they would use to describe your personal brand.' Next: 'Think about the setting on your radar screen.'

Comrade Middleton lays down these and other steps over 172 pages in a 2007 book, *Beyond Authority – Leadership in a Changing World*. She argues that networking between prominent people is a vital civic duty and that leaders must be prepared to shade the truth a little, using slyness and disguise to achieve their goals. She even recommends that they occasionally appoint 'useful idiots' and 'expert idiots' to help them see off the threat from Right-wing sceptics whom she calls 'black holes' (because they suck out the energy from life). *Beyond Authority – Leadership in a Changing World* is infused with a belief that certain types of networky people are entitled to run the world. It envisages careerists volunteering to help their communities not out of simple neighbourliness or decency but because it might give them and their companies an inside edge. 'Go to a meeting or an event that you, and others who know you, would consider it unlikely that you would normally be at,' it suggests, as this will help leadership pupils be seen as outward-looking and therefore better able to command obedience in committees. What a fake way to live. How cold and scheming. 'Seek out opportunities that will give you the experience of being in a minority, an outsider,' declares Middleton. One imagines a chi-chi merchant banker telling her husband, 'I'll be home late tonight because I am off to the diabetic amputees' mobility rights workshop to gain experience of being in a minority – it should help me outmanoeuvre my rivals for the chair of the bank's remuneration committee.'

Eric Hobsbawm (d. 2012) was a Marxist historian, perhaps the last defender of Stalinism this side of the Urals. His daughter Julia (b. 1964) takes a more modern view of power: she is Visiting Professor of Networking at Cass Business School, London. Cass students are told that 'although it is not compulsory to attend networking events, they are encouraged to make the most of these opportunities which can contribute towards their career development'. Bag a first in schmoozing. In the Darwinian world of networking, is there any space for friendship? Would the Julias (Hobsbawm and Middleton) ever make the acquaintance of someone who was no use to them?

Middleton says that if you are going to make it into the 'outer circles' (by which she means the inner circles of her global elite) you have to believe in diversity. Diversity is meeting people from 'every sector, background, race, creed, sexuality and set of beliefs, every political place and conviction, able-bodied and disabled, tall and short, fat and thin'. Yet the people she cites in the book as authorities and inspirations are a strikingly homogenous bunch. Try some of them for size:

Europhile Tory Lord (Chris) Patten

Lib Dem grandee Lord (Paddy) Ashdown

Labour film-maker Lord (David) Puttnam

Financial Times chairman Sir David Bell

Ulster community worker Lady Blood

Civil liberties snoot Lady (Shami) Chakrabarti

A couple of Anglican bishops

Gay-rights activist Simon Fanshawe

Banker Dame Amelia Fawcett
'Queen of the quangos' Dame Deirdre Hutton
Restaurateur Prue Leith
Blairite ex-policy adviser Geoff Mulgan
Ex BP chairman Lord Simon
Serial waffler and quangocrat Lord (Adair) Turner.

Not many fiery Righties in that lot, are there? Not many audacious anti-Establishment voices or quixotic individualists or challengers of received wisdom. They're about as diverse as a platoon of tin soldiers.

> NETWORK – vb, intransitive, to mingle over canapés and warm white wine while swapping business cards and keeping half an eye on the rest of the room in case someone more interesting/useful/rich enters, in which case you can quickly dump the schmuck you have currently snagged.

One of Julia Middleton's chums, Dame Amelia Chilcott Fawcett (b. 1956), can probably lay claim to the title 'most successful networker in Britain and America'. Once you start looking into the various bins and dumps and silos of the British Establishment, that name Fawcett keeps appearing. Originally a law student and banker, she has been chairman of the Hedge Fund Standards Board, deputy chairman of Swedish investment firm Kinnevik, director of State Street Corporation, independent director of the Treasury, deputy chairman of the National Portrait Gallery, member of the council of the University of London, board director of Business in the Community, governor of the London Business School, chairman of the

Prince of Wales's Charitable Foundation, a commissioner of the US-UK Fulbright Commission, trustee of Project Hope, chairman of the London International Festival of Theatre, vice-president, managing director, chief administrative officer and vice-chairman at Morgan Stanley, chairman of Pensions First, lawyer at American law firm Sullivan & Cromwell, chairman of Guardian Media Group, non-executive director of Millicom International Cellular and director of the Bank of England. She bagged a CBE in 2002 for services to the finance industry and won the Prince of Wales's ambassador award in 2004. She has an honorary degree from the American University in London (Richmond) and is a governor of the London Business School where she has encouraged their teaching of 'thought leadership' (they think, their pupils follow). She once sailed the Atlantic in a 47-ft yacht with a crew of four to raise money for charity. In her spare time, she farms lavender and makes scented cushions at her 40-acre property in Wales. She is also the first Lady Usher of the Purple Rod, overseeing the investments and chattels of the Order of the British Empire.

Phew!

Left-leaning Dame Amelia, unmarried, is plainly a woman of boundless energy. But when she gives a head-girlish laugh and says anyone could do it, we may perhaps be allowed to demur. No matter how many networking seminars you attended, you would not match that sort of output. The Dame Amelias of this world are phenomenal exceptions and it is patronising baloney to suggest otherwise.

What a Gasbag

The chief scientific adviser
who got it entirely wrong

———————•———————

Let me through, I'm a scientist. Most of the time we are so touchingly obedient that we yield to experts. We accept that scientists are right. In the case of Sir David King there was even more reason to swallow his word. In his case, it was 'Let me through, I'm the government's Chief Scientific Adviser.' He was Boffin by Appointment, Whitehall's Man in a White Coat, an egghead with a Downing Street pass on that lanyard he wore round his neck like a stethoscope. King was a white South African who had opposed apartheid. He had been photographed shaking hands with US Vice President Al Gore. These things made him a Good Person, stamped as such by the approved news channels.

King was 'CSA' (scientists, like the military, relish acronyms) from 2000 to 2007. That coincided with Tony Blair's possibly slightly less sane years as prime minister. Not being a scientist, I hesitate to draw any connection between King's presence and Mister Tony's wildness of personality, his Messiah complex, his bulgy eyeball that used to throb and rotate like a lighthouse beam when he spoke of national dangers. I merely mention the dates so that you can recall the era, one in which official-dom, steered by such hygienic desk-bangers as Alastair Campbell, came to acquire a heaviness of moral insistence. It was a time when Blair and his cronies kept justifying policies on the grounds that 'it's the right thing to do'. They were right and anyone who opposed them was wicked.

David King was keen on genetically modified crops. That suited Blair and bad Al, just as it suited mega-spon-doolicks agrochemical firms pushing GM knowhow via their richly-rewarded lobbyists.

King was also gripped by climate change. After a hot spell in 2003 – in which some 2,000 people may have died as a result of the steamy weather – he declared that heat-waves were going to be a worse threat to the world than terrorism. The *Spectator* magazine was unhelpful enough to note that many more British people died as a result of *cold* weather. It was also pointed out that just two years earlier almost 3,000 souls died and another 6,000 were injured in the 9/11 attacks in the United States. Yet such atrocities were now to be considered secondary to climate change? Scientist King was clearly not the most sensitive of operators. His gloomstering was greatly appreciated by the politicians. He gave expert approval to their political desire to promote eco issues. After King stopped being CSA he was made (by William Hague) the Foreign Secretary's permanent Special Representative for Climate Change. More official policy sessions. More international con-ferences with close-knit consensualists. More lectures to young global ambassadors and tomorrow's leaders. More lanyards and more photocalls with Important People.

Before that, while still CSA, King said we should buy diesel rather than petrol cars. Millions of British motorists were soon doing just that, encouraged by taxation policies that made diesel-powered vehicles a more attractive option. We were told that this would be good for the environment. Diesel cars did more miles to the gallon than petrol ones and they emitted less carbon dioxide. So went the theory. As the driver of an ageing diesel-fuelled Renault Laguna at the time, I remember being surprised, because whenever I put my foot down reasonably hard to accelerate, a cloud of black smoke would pour out of the exhaust pipe and in my rear-view mirror I could see cyclists coughing and wobbling in the noxious cloud of filth. Once or twice I revved the car when in neutral and a deposit of soot would be left on the ground. Diesels, to my inexpert mind, seemed pretty grubby. But not being 'an expert', what did I know?

King, little prey to public doubt, was mightily pleased with himself. So were certain car makers (among them Volkswagen), who had invested in diesel engine plants and therefore made a fortune from all that switching by motorists. The rest of us were told that King was bound to know his stuff. At the age of thirty-four, he had become one of Britain's youngest university professors and his specialist subject was car-engine exhausts. How he managed to combine that academic research with all his political work – having once been suspected by the South African authorities of being a communist – we could not say. We simply had to accept that he was some sort of worthy genius. He was the government's Chief Scientific Adviser. You don't become that without having a sceptical disposition and the ability to resist pressure from politicians until the evidence has been fully tested. Do you?

But Houston, we had a problem. It turned out that the policy on diesel cars was wrong. Far from being good for the environment, they were a smoggy disaster. My Renault Laguna was not the only diesel car producing a plume of black gunk – or noxious nitrogen oxides, as they turned out to be. Volkswagen, one of the biggest manufacturers of cars on our roads, had been fiddling some of its emissions results. In 2015 Lord Drayson, a former Labour science minister, admitted that diesel cars were 'literally killing people'. He added: 'We now have a much better understanding than we did just a few years ago of what are the health effects of the products of diesel cars and they are literally killing people so it's clear that in retrospect that was the wrong policy.'

It would be another year and a half, just as he left his climate-change sinecure with the Foreign Office, that Sir David King coughed out his own admission that he had made a mistake. He claimed that he had been misled by car makers as to the dirtiness of diesels. 'It turns out we were wrong,' he said. Turns out! What masterly nonchalance. A Transport for London report found that as many as 9,500 people a year had been dying in our capital city owing to air pollution. *Pace* that remark of David King in 2003, you could almost say that scientific ineptitude – or even scientific arrogance, acting in the name of environmentalism – had caused more deaths than terrorism.

What really drove bungler King and the Blair government to push us towards diesels? Was it raw (and as we now see, wrong) scientific data? Or was it high-handedness, an insistence that they knew best, and that even if they cottoned on to weaknesses in the research, they should keep mum on the basis of *pas devant les enfants*?

The editor of the *Lancet* – never exactly eager to attack scientists – accused King of 'letting off blasts of hot and sometimes rancid air'.

News reports often use the magic words 'scientists say' or 'experts claim'. Since the days of the TV show *Tomorrow's World* these have brought a halo of authority to all sorts of scientific theories. The same happens in advertisements. In the old Anadin commercial – 'tense? nervous headache?' – a scientist with a white coat stared at a clipboard and then gave a decisive nod and a tick of his pen before moving on to another part of the laboratory. He embodied our hunger for expert reassurance. That is fine so long as the experts are alive to their limitations. They are well advised to steer clear of political egotism because that might prevent them admitting to mistakes.

King has been a supporter of a form of Hippocratic oath for scientists. This would bolster 'trust' between scientists and what they call 'lay people' (that echo of the priesthood is instructive). In 2007, King laid down a 'universal code of ethics' for researchers around the globe. Seven principles were identified and they included:

- Act with skill and care in all scientific work. Maintain up-to-date skills and assist their development in others.

- Take steps to prevent corrupt practices and professional misconduct. Declare conflicts of interest.

- Minimise and justify any adverse effect your work may have on people, animals and the natural environment.

- Seek to discuss the issues that science raises for society. Listen to the aspirations and concerns of others.

- Do not knowingly mislead, or allow others to be misled, about scientific matters. Present and review scientific evidence, theory or interpretation honestly and accurately.

Well, he said it!

Talk to My People

Everyone has a chief of staff
these days, darling

———————•———————

To have an entourage has always been a sign of grandeur. 'All the king's horses and all the king's men' may have been unable to repair Humpty Dumpty but they signalled the monarch's importance. In Shakespeare, King Lear erupts with rage ('thou art a boil, a plague sore, an embossed carbuncle') after his daughters tell him to dispense with his one hundred cronies. Lear was modest compared to Bolesław the Brave, ruler of Poland a millennium ago. When touring his lands, Bolesław took along one thousand five hundred horsemen. Catering nightmare. 'Darling, King Bolesław wants to come and stay at our castle for a few days. He says is it okay if he brings some friends?'

Our Queen, at the state opening of Parliament, is accompanied by a Ruritanian array of train-bearing page-boys, ladies-in-waiting, heralds and Herberts of the royal household. Some carry wands, others such essential appurtenances as the Sword of State and the Cap of Maintenance, which is a hat and not a contraceptive. The Duke of Edinburgh somehow puts up with them all.

Moses with his executive support team

When US President Bill Clinton travelled to China at his decadent zenith in 1998, he was accompanied by more than one thousand courtiers, so many that they filled four passenger planes, with transporter planes for their luggage and equipment. The Clinton retinue included security advisers, policy geeks, press handlers, stenographers, speech writers, doctors (both spin and medical), fixers, interpreters, protocol wallahs, lawyers (how American), Hillary's hairdresser, Bill's valet, six members of Congress, five cabinet members with their own secretariats, trade negotiators, two White House TV crews, snipers, sniffer-dogs, bodyguards and no doubt the odd bosomy intern.

Bolesław the Brave and Clinton the Concupiscent may be unusual in the size of their caravans but retinues, once the preserve of despots and commanders, have become a me-too must-have for our governors and greasers. Plutocrats, actors, bankers, bishops, quangocrats, ministers – all feel the need for advisers and aides. 'I'll get my people to talk to your people,' they drawl. Having so many polishers and lackeys allows them to affect a lofty vagueness about detail. They can distance themselves from mistakes and cruel oversights. They can say, 'I don't recognise that account of what happened,' or, when things become really sticky they can say, 'Obviously that shouldn't have happened but I'll have a word with my team to see if we can find out what went on.'

A few years ago the West End first night of a Michael Jackson musical called *Thriller* was delayed for several minutes. We soon learned that the curtain would not rise until a VIP member of the Jackson family arrived. Finally the VIP arrived – we were told it was one of Michael Jackson's brothers – and he was accompanied by a platoon of boastful twerps who took their seats in the stalls with affected languor. Were they chums, agents, bodyguards, general dudes? Hard to say. They were wearing baseball caps, mostly back-to-front, but they did not look fit enough to be sportsmen. In the interval, I found myself in the gents next to the late arrival and told him I thought he had been rude to arrive so late and thus keep the rest of the audience waiting. His companions became shirty with me. It had plainly been a while since anyone had spoken to their big buddy like that.

The Dalai Lama has a retinue, and he's meant to be an unworldly monk. He turned up at the House of

Commons once to give evidence to the Foreign Affairs Select Committee and in his wake there trailed about ten young male acolytes in sandals and orange robes. For a moment it looked like a claque of Liberal Democrats. Mr Lama, if that is what we call him, turned out to be a charming fellow, if hard to comprehend. He had a habit of uttering cryptic remarks and then giggling at them, whereupon his retinue would join in the laughter, turning to one another as they savoured the brilliance of their demi-god's repartee.

Whiny Russell Brand, comedian, brought a posse of helpers when he appeared at a parliamentary hearing on drugs policy. It is hard to become too vexed about a clown like Brand. He may have treated the whole parliamentary thing as a joke but who is to say, when his chief interrogator was Keith Vaz, that he was not right to do so? Actor Hugh Grant and Steve Coogan, two more comedians on a political mission, were a more formal prospect when they gave evidence to parliamentarians about press misbehaviour. Again, they arrived with various lobbyists and supporters but whereas Brand had worn Jesus-goes-to-Glastonbury garb of armless T-shirt and torn leather trousers, Grant and Coogan had poured themselves into funeral suits. In they strutted, tumescent with self-importance, Grant almost indistinguishable from Tony Blair on one of his more sainted days. He started to play the part of the thoughtful young Lochinvar, milking his pauses, his larynx handsomely checking itself before recounting the horrors of his privileged life. Behind him: the faces of his retinue, sympathy etched deep into their nodding brows. Richard Curtis could not have directed it better.

Top government ministers have something called a PPS, a parliamentary private secretary. These are junior MPs who act as a link between their ministers and backbench MPs. They are not paid for the work but it makes them feel important. They are expected to vote with the government in all divisions. Former Labour MP Chris Mullin described the PPS system – which swelled to a record size under Tony Blair – as a way of 'neutralising intelligent individuals who might otherwise make a rather more useful contribution to the proper functioning of Parliament'. Fair point. But monk-like Mullin, every sophisticate's favourite Leftie, gave up his own backbench independence to become a very minor cog in the Blair government. What a surrender to careerism and a ministerial salary by a man who might otherwise have made 'a rather more useful contribution to the proper functioning' of British politics.

Bank of England Governor Mark Carney, a regular visitor to Westminster for Treasury Committee meetings, invariably arrives with beetle-browed outriders, press officers, deputy governors and Bank grandees. We parliamentary sketchwriters have an old theory that the more subordinates a select-committee witness brings, the more evasive he or she is likely to prove. Meanwhile, parliamentary committees have themselves become loaded with researchers and staff members. Until a few years ago it would be rare to see more than one clerk sitting on the table next to the chairman. Many committees now have two clerks at the table. They seldom seem to do much. They just spend the time tapping keenly on computer keyboards, staring intently at the screens. Is their work vital to the furtherance of public scrutiny of the Executive, or are they there simply to make the MPs feel big?

Job-title inflation has seen the most humdrum back-bench MPs employing 'chiefs of staff'. Who do they think they are? General Eisenhower pushing through Europe in 1944 or the Hon. Member for Dullsville South on a wet Wednesday? The title 'chief of staff' was little known in British politics until Tony Blair appointed Jonathan Powell his chief of staff in 1997. The most important officials at 10 Downing Street had previously been the prime minister's principal private secretary and the cabinet secretary, both of them non-partisan figures. Under Blair, plainly, that would never do. And so he appointed Powell, all frown lines and Grecian curls and clipped sentences and contempt for old ways. One of his brothers, Charles, though an eggier character, fulfilled a similar function for Mrs Thatcher, being her foreign-policy adviser. What was it about Charles and Jonathan Powell that made them such successful courtiers? Was it discretion? A work ethic? Was it subtle poshness (Cathedral Choir School,

---

Job-title inflation works two ways: it strokes employees' vanity and means they will probably accept going without a pay rise, and it seeks to intimidate the public into thinking these people are executive aces. Railway ticket inspectors are 'revenue-protection officers'. Supermarket shelf-stackers are 'replenishment assistants'. Can it be true that petrol-pump attendants are 'fuel-injection engineers' and restaurant potwashers 'sub-aquatic ceramic technicians'? Possibly not. But dinner ladies have become SMSAs, or school meals supervisory assistants, lavatory cleaners are hygiene managers and ambulance men and women have become paramedics. Most ludicrously of all, Tracey Emin calls herself an 'artist'.

Canterbury, and Oxford), their murmuring, dry-chuckle seamlessness, an ability to enter a room as though on oiled castors, to remember foreigners' names and to swallow the worst excesses of realpolitik? Was it their disregard for molten patriotism, an eye for other men's flaws? Are these the requisites for a top political aide?

Charles, nowadays Lord Powell of Bayswater, did well out of his association with Thatcher. He has gone on to acquire more directorships than most of us have teacups. Jonathan, too, is unlikely ever to be poor. Apart from being a consultant to Tony Blair Associates, he has continued to schmooze the international politics circuit as an adviser and think-tanker and envoy and bank director. And yet he never conveys much warmth. He seems to have become weighed down by the business of being superior. Charles, married to an Italian eyelash-flutterer (the magnificent Carla), gives you occasional hints that he knows his life has its absurdities. Jonathan is more trapped by his exalted status.

Corporate Balls

The strange nonsense of mission statements

———————————————•———————————————

Somewhere in Corporate Headquarter Land, a div-isional boss is unhappy. She scowls at her staff. 'Where the HELL is our mission statement? Where's the stuff about how our corporate values, about how caring and sharing we are? I want pictures of old people, mixed race, silver hair, good teeth, clean cardigans, barefoot on a beach – now! I want stuff about sustainability and team-work and that modern slavery Act crap. You're not going home till it's done.'

She is only raging because one of the board directors enquired about progress on that front – an example of stress cascading down the executive organogram. And lo, the job is soon done, and looks splendid. The website gushes that the company in question – a law firm, bank, oil company – is a 'robust' believer in accountability, in shared work practices, speedy problem resolution, integrity, respect and modernity. Fostering creativity, too. Don't forget creativity. To be honest, the team nearly did but then they saw creativ-ity mentioned at the bottom of the rival firm's website, from which they were nicking most of their ideas.

Mission statements – often found on the 'our values' pages of company websites – would have us believe modern capitalism is staffed by souls so kindly that they make Winnie the Pooh seem a bit hard-nosed. Piety is laid on with a steamroller. Companies insist that they are propelled by the highest motives. You would never suspect that greed and profit are vital urges in business.

The word 'mission' should immediately place us on our guard. Does any modern business executive really feel a sense of 'mission'? This is a word to describe a nineteenth-century Christian's journey into darkest Africa or a parachutist's drop behind enemy lines. Most business executives work simply to earn some money.

British Telecom, that infuriating, leaden-footed, customer-averse company, says it is 'totally dedicated to customers, now and in the future'. Its retail arm is:

> A customer-centric distribution business that will grow shareholder value and deliver an excellent, continuously improving, customer experience . . . build new routes to market . . . excite and engage our people to maximise the value they create for themselves, our customers and the communities in which they work. Our vision paints a vivid picture of the future we are determined to create. It captures where we want our business to go, what we want to achieve and how we will contribute to the world by making it a reality. In so doing, it sets an audacious goal for all of us to rally around and pursue.

The use of the transitive verb 'grow' for anything other than fruit and veg is a portent of management baloney.

Audacity, goals, continuous improvement, striving: this

is the currency of mission statements. Passion, integrity, courage, independence, commitment, understanding can be translated as middle-management ennui, cynicism, risk-aversion. Beaten-down employees are doing the bare minimum to get through another working week, poor souls.

Coca-Cola, whose fizzy drinks have been rotting our teeth and making us fat for generations, has a mission statement 'to refresh the world . . . to inspire moments of optimism and happiness'. Sports-gear manufacturer Nike operates under the corporate rallying cry, 'bring inspiration and innovation to every athlete in the world; if you have a body, you are an athlete'. Did they never see the late Demis Roussos?

Business motivators will insist that mission statements are essential to corporate strategy, a boiled-down *jus* of communal endeavour. But there is a suppression of individualism here, too. Did the frontier-breaking agents of the seventeenth-century Hudson's Bay Company or the adventurers of the early East India Company have to sign up, first, to a corporate code of values?

British Aerospace is, among other things, a defence company – that is, an arms manufacturer. The whole point of some of its products is that they can blow human bodies to smithereens. 'Our vision,' murmurs this merchant of death, 'is to be the premier global defence, aerospace and security company. Responsible behaviour is one of the four pillars of our Company strategy, together with customer focus, programme execution and financial performance.' Could they not have avoided the word 'execution'?

The company's statement of values, having already referred to its four pillars, also mentions 'three Values which are fundamental to our culture'. These are trust ('we are honest'), innovation ('we empower teams and work together to turn our ideas and technologies into solutions') and boldness ('we constructively challenge and take the initiative, operating with tenacity and resolve – we accept challenges and manage risk and set ourselves stretching goals').

Bogus corporate mateyness has seen the rise of 'wackaging', packaging polluted by chattiness. Innocent, a fruit-drinks company, affects to be its customers' best friend. Its bottles are covered in fey little messages and its self-congratulatory website is a mixture of kiddies'-style games and sermons about poverty. Frijj milkshakes tell customers to 'get in fella! The stuff it's good to have . . . suitable for vegetablists'. Buff nuts calls its customers 'you naughty squirrel, you'. Pret a Manger says its drinks are 'best chilled (as indeed we all are)'. And let's not forget the lowercase crowd, who operate on the basis that capital letters are too daunting for their clientele. Soap makers chic&basic say their product is 'the cutest soap that you will steal from a hotel. enjoy it.'

oh get stuffed.

The crown princes and dictators of the world, leafing through BAE's latest brochure of weapons systems and seeing mention of the company's 'Values', must think, *Phew, that's just as well – I could not possibly have bought my weapons from a firm that did not respect community standards.*

Sir Philip Green is one of the more gamey faces of British business. Yacht-faring Sir Philip is not only a loadsamoney swank – waving his Lloyds chequebook in the air when he came to a Westminster select committee – but also a crafty operator who extracted himself from

British Home Stores shortly before the business went down the tube. When the receivers were called, 22,000 members of the BHS pension scheme were left looking at financial losses, even while Sir Philip was gadding about Monte Carlo in his deck shoes. Bearing that in mind, let us look at the mission statement of Sir Philip Green's Arcadia Group. 'Our team of people,' it begins, 'are at the heart of everything we do.' It goes on to talk about how 'professional, supportive and knowledgeable' Arcadia and its people are, and how 'when it comes to the things that unite us – strong work ethics and enthusiasm for fashion – we're one big team'.

Sir Philip's closest rival, both in British retail and in grotesquery, may be Mike Ashley, owner of Sports Direct. 'Our people are what makes the Sports Direct Group such a success,' says its mission statement.

> The Board is committed to ensuring that all of our people have the opportunity to be inspired, stimulated, motivated, and empowered. We believe that it takes every single team member to make a difference and drive performance, and we are committed to the development and rewarding of our people to enable the Group to achieve its future growth plans.

In 2016 a parliamentary select committee inquiry into one of Ashley's factories heard of its work practices as being worthy of a Victorian workhouse. Employees were treated 'as commodities rather than as human beings with rights, responsibilities and aspirations'. Union officials told a story about a woman giving birth in the lavatories at the factory because she was allegedly so worried about losing her job if she missed a day.

Why does Sports Direct bother with a mission statement? Unless Ashley wrote it himself (he does not strike one as a wordsmith), he must have had to employ someone to do it. Why waste the money, Mike? Hoard your readies, mate.

Wetherby, the London prep school attended by Prince George, claims in its mission statement to provide 'an environment that promotes educational excellence and tradition through a forward-thinking, holistic curriculum within which the needs of individual pupils are fostered'. Here's a lesson, children: when you see the word 'holistic', run. There is no surer sign the grown-ups are talking sausages.

Serial polluter ExxonMobil pumps out not just oil but also this rather soapier material: 'We commit to be a good corporate citizen in all the places we operate worldwide.' Cigarette makers Imperial Tobacco cough up:

Everything is possible. Together we win. Our positive mindset drives our success. We work together to find the best solutions and ensure that we are aligned to deliver them. There are always reasons why it's possible, not why it's impossible. It's not about achieving perfection, it's about finding a pragmatic approach and running with it, adapting as we go. And if it doesn't work first time, we'll work out why and then try again.

You could almost say they were addicted to success.

Burger King, perhaps with an eye on drive-in customers, says: 'Corporate responsibility isn't about a final destination; it's about an ongoing journey.' Talking of journeys, the Great Western Railway's mission statement says: 'From greeting you at the station, to friendly on-board teams, we make sure every smile given, every bag carried, every refreshment served goes towards making your journeys safe, comfortable and enjoyable.' If you said that to the dawn commuters riding in one of Great Western's crowded, uncomfortable trains, they would just stare back at you with exhausted incomprehension.

All right, all right, you wail, we get the idea. But the greater the litany of examples, the more we may understand how this epidemic has spread. Ernst & Young is just a firm of accountants and consultants – pretty boring, but rich thanks to all the money it shakes out of the government's purse. It talks about its wage-slaves having 'the courage to lead' and 'build relationships based on doing the right thing' (getting their sums right, perhaps).

Even lawyers have started using mission statements. Public Interest Lawyers – the firm whose founder, Phil Shiner, was struck off for dishonesty and lack of integrity after he pursued British soldiers for their conduct in the Iraq War – had the following declaration of intent:

Public Interest Lawyers provides a voice for the ordinary man, woman and child in Britain and beyond. We are living in a very challenging period in our history and we can expect to face a further number of difficult situations in which the executive will try to force a number of measures on a society that is already at breaking point. Our team is here to help you fight for your rights against the unfettered power of the executive when these situations arise, whether they arise on UK or foreign soil.

And from law to ice cream. Ben and Jerry's, no less, makes clear its political stance in its mission statement – 'leading with progressive values'. In ice cream? At £4 a pot? Ben and Jerry's says:

> Our Social Mission compels us to use our Company in innovative ways to make the world a better place. To operate the company in a way that actively recognizes the central role that business plays in society by initiating innovative ways to improve the quality of life locally, nationally and internationally . . .

That may not make you feel sick but the ice cream might.

Last word on mission statements goes to Charlie Mullin, who runs a London company called Pimlico Plumbers. 'Charlie had a vision then to remove the stigma associated with the plumbing industry i.e. plumbers with bad workmanship, who turn up late, rip off the customer, driving rusty old vans, not wearing uniform and arse's hanging out their trousers.' The unnecessary apostrophe is nicely authentic.

Theresa May made a fool of herself in the 2017 election campaign by repeatedly saying 'strong and stable'. When she failed to win a majority she looked anything but strong or stable. Her advisers thought that if she said the slogan often enough it would register with the voters. They were right up to a point – but once the voters did cotton on to it, they thought it was rubbish.

Conservatives have shown a terrible weakness for slogans in recent years: 'a brighter, more secure future', 'forward, together', 'an economy that works for everyone'.

This is politics as dog biscuits. But what do you expect when advertising agencies are involved in election campaigns? That is how ad people operate: product, packaging, slogan and sale. The process employs persuasion techniques to lure the gullible, plus corporate waffle – demographics pie charts, focus-group analysis – to placate the ever-panicky client.

No ad man is reckoned to have worked the politics trick more effectively than Lord (Maurice) Saatchi. To him and his peculiar brother Charles fell much of the credit for Margaret Thatcher's 1979 general election win. If you think 'peculiar' is unfair, Charles Saatchi once lost four stone by eating nine eggs a day – and nothing else, allegedly – for nine months. One dreads to think how long his morning constitutionals took.

Received wisdom has it that the Saatchis' poster of a long unemployment queue under the slogan 'Labour isn't working' clinched power for the Conservatives in the late 1970s. That theory implies that voters surrendered to a gimmick. But did they? Or was the real advertising mirage here simply the idea that ad men can win an election for a politician?

The 'Labour isn't working' poster was false on at least two levels. First, the queue of one hundred dole-seekers was faked because only twenty people from a London Conservative association turned up on the day of the shoot. Their image thus had to be duplicated. Second, the poster implied unemployment would drop with the Conservatives in office. It most certainly did not. Unemployment became a scourge of the early Thatcher years, creating in some parts of the country a generation's resentment against the Tory party. You can argue that job losses were an inevitable and necessary consequence of attacking inflation and remoulding the British economy but that is a different matter. Saatchi & Saatchi's poster sold voters a lie. Unemployment became hideously worse under the Conservatives in the early 1980s.

Maurice Saatchi has been a thoughtful member of the House of Lords. He wears great glasses. But as a poster-boy of political advertising he deserves a Roald Dahl-sized raspberry. Saatchi's model approached politics as retail activity. It took the responsibility for political instinct away from the politicians, making them less real as personalities. More by luck than merit, the ad men were seen as vital to success, even though Mrs T's original victory was surely down to public anger at James Callaghan's Labour government.

After 1979, many political leaders thought, *I need a Saatchi*, or at least, *I can get away with this if I hire a Saatchi to do my hard thinking for me*. Hang the expense. Hang the hyperbolic deceits. Slick advertising was going to win them power – if they could only find another Maurice. In 2005, on the advice of advertising dude Trevor Beattie, Labour ran adverts that used childlike graphics depicting Tory leader Michael Howard as a flying pig. Tory spending plans did not add up and if you believed them you might as well believe that pigs could fly, etc. The Conservatives claimed that the advertisements were anti-Semitic because Howard was Jewish and Jewish culture is averse to pig meat. Labour did win that election but the flying pigs were about as tasteful as dodgy frankfurters.

Sloganeering is slick exaggeration at the expense of truth, self-adornment without detail – the technocratic class trying to say to the voters, 'Don't worry about

On 3 May 2015, that giant of British politics, Ed Miliband, summoned the media to a car park in Hastings, East Sussex. What important announcement was he going to make? A new policy four days before the general election? Er, no. Miliband unveiled a block of limestone on which had been written six commandment-style pledges. He intended to erect his tablet in the garden of 10 Downing Street once he moved into his official residence as prime minister. The Edstone, as it was dubbed ('some weird commie slab,' said Boris Johnson), symbolised the vacuous Miliband and his campaign. Swing voters in the marginal Hastings & Rye constituency duly chose a Conservative MP. And the nation's gardeners surely thought any man who could propose to erect such an eyesore amid the flowerbeds must be a philistine.

the small print.' During the 2017 election campaign, Conservative candidates were laughed at when they started parroting the 'strong and stable leadership' and 'coalition of chaos' slogans. I even heard one person shout 'Full house!', as though playing bingo, when Chancellor Philip Hammond turgidly said 'strong and stable' for something like the sixth time in a few minutes. The Tories just made themselves sound robotic. They surrendered to Jeremy Corbyn's madcap Labour the vital idea of being bold outsiders. In the end, the voters narrowly decided not to give the plainly incompetent Corbyn a majority but it was a close-run thing. That showed just how much the people now hate their prosaic rulers.

Some slogans become awkwardly truthful. 'Britain deserves better,' said Labour when it sold Tony Blair to the public in 1997. Yes, we *did* deserve better than that ham actor Blair. Conversely, the Lib Dems' 'Winning Here' placards, waved at the TV cameras on the campaign trail, are usually pathetically wrong. If they only held placards saying 'Losing Here' – which is what normally happens to Lib Dems – more of us might vote for them.

'Vote for Change,' said David Cameron's Conservatives in 2010, when that party was markedly cautious and offered little difference from the Labour government that had gone before. 'One more heave,' said Jeremy Thorpe's Liberals in 1974. Nausea was certainly widespread when Thorpe was charged with conspiracy to murder Norman Scott not long afterwards.

Lib Dems have at various points used the slogan 'The real alternative', to which the rejoinder is 'Alternative to what? Strychnine?' Tony Blair's 'Education education education' cloned a line by Cassio in Shakespeare's *Othello* but thanks to the damage done to school standards by Blair's party in the 1960s and 1970s, few people got the reference. When George Osborne became editor of the London *Evening Standard* he attacked Mrs May for relying too heavily on one-liners; this from the man who for years spouted 'fix the roof while the sun is shining' and 'long-term economic plan'. Osborne even laced his Budget speeches with soundbites – 'we stand for opportunity for all', 'this is a Budget for Britain, the Comeback Country', and 'Britain is walking tall again'. Television producers like this sort of soundbite to fit their 'packages' but the result is bland news bulletins that tell the viewer almost nothing.

Politicians are also handed daily and weekly buzz-words to work into their interviews: 'the squeezed middle' from Labour, 'stronger economy in a fairer society' from the Lib Dems and 'hard-working families' from all of them. Ed Miliband tried to steal 'one nation' from the

Conservatives' Benjamin Disraeli. How clever, how cunning, how hand-rubbingly canny Miliband thought he was when he did that. The Westminster commentators, many of whom had, like him, studied PPE (philosophy, politics and economics) at Oxford, leaned back and clapped, hailing a master of strategy. The public didn't buy it for a moment.

How many times have we heard a variation of the claim that there are '72 hours left to save the NHS'? Is there a single voter who falls for this guff? 'We're all in it together,' claimed Conservatives. How much easier that would have been to believe had their party not been funded by multi-millionaires who at White Ball fundraising auctions would bid £160,000 for a game of tennis with Cameron and Boris Johnson. New balls, please. Even better, no balls. Just be straight with us.

Soft-focus sentimentalism is another sales technique used by political image-makers. In 1987, Labour's election campaign manager Peter Mandelson commissioned a ten-minute film from Oscar-winning director Hugh Hudson. This mini-biopic about Labour leader Neil Kinnock became known as 'Kinnock – The Movie'. It took British politics even deeper into leader-worship than the Conservatives had ventured with their idolisation of Mrs Thatcher.

It opened with footage of an RAF fighter plane, which segued into more placid, serene shots of a seagull gliding over a coastal vista. From war to peace, see? Cue some orchestral Beethoven (a version of 'Ode to Joy', now the EU anthem). Walking on clifftops beneath this bucolic scene was a middle-aged, bald chap with his springy wife: Neil and Glenys Kinnock.

While the music rose and fell like that seagull on the coastal thermals, Neil's lovely voice was heard saying, 'I think the real privilege of being strong is the power that it gives you to help people who are not strong. The real privilege of being fit and bright and young and strong is the ability that that gives you to give others a helping hand.' Hudson may have been an Oscar winner but he was not subtle. 'Strong' kept being nailed home and there was also repeated use of 'young' through the film. Yet his bald head and wrinkles showed that he was firmly in middle-age.

Much political advice is counter-productive. Tory strategist Sir Lynton Crosby devised a 2017 campaign that was built on Theresa May's character. Disaster! She barely had one. For years she had played the technocrat game, hiding behind small-print. She had never waded bracingly into oncoming electoral surf. Had there ever been a party leader with so little zest for campaigning? She hid from the public and the public went off her. Jeremy Corbyn is many things. He wants to tax us to Hades, is soft on terrorism, hates singing the national anthem and even wears a beard. But the one thing he is not is a patronising bastard. At that point, he stood outside the consensus, beyond the Centrist hub. No wonder he did much better than expected.

Mandelson admitted later that the film was intended not only to promote Kinnock's 'stock' as a leader but also to 'camouflage' the policies on which Labour was standing. This was classic Mandelson, taking voters for fools.

A cynic would say that for Kinnock's true personality to have been shown, he should have been filmed at a

Marketing aces in the Church of England have devised tag lines for diocesan websites. 'Loving Living Learning' goes the zippy trinity offered by the diocese of Leeds. 'Renewing Hope – Pray, Serve, Grow,' says Salisbury. At Southwell and Nottingham it is 'Growing Disciples Wider Younger Deeper'. They do love this modern-managerial use of 'grow' – Carlisle 'Growing Disciples', Hereford 'Proclaiming Christ growing Disciples', while Birmingham is 'Growing churches at the heart of each community' and Truro is 'Discovering God's Kingdom Growing the Church'. Durham opts for 'The Church of England from the Tyne to the Tees and the Dales to the Sea blessing our communities in Jesus' name for the transformation of us all'. They should have stuck 'Amen' at the end of it.

Exeter's slogan sits you down, holds your hand and says: 'I know the plans I have for you, says the Lord, plans for your welfare and not for harm, to give you a future with hope'. 'Generous engaged open,' says Newcastle, perhaps reaching out to dentists. Lincoln comes up with 'Faithful confident joyful'. Bristol seems to have borrowed 'Creating connections' from the city's Temple Meads railway station.

Take the linguistic equivalent of a food mixer. Buzz in a few bland words. Whirrrrrr. The Old and New Testaments of the Authorised Bible are 789,600 words long. But a whizzo consultant reckons the job can be done with one crisp slogan. Easy. Next!

Michelin-starred restaurant in Brussels, lifting a glass to the camera and saying, 'This one's on you taxpayers!' And yet, if you today watch 'Kinnock – The Movie' you may be reminded that in Parliament and at party conferences, not least when he took on Derek Hatton and Militants, Kinnock was a fine public speaker. The Kinnock seen in those moments was a better performer than anyone in current British politics – and a far more attractive personality than the bloke strolling the cliff with his missus, the two of them putting on all sort of hokum airs for the benefit of Hudson and his schmaltzy film. Had Peter Mandelson allowed that Kinnock, the impassioned orator, to shine more clearly than the soft-focus seagull clips, Labour might have done better.

Please Offend Me

The creamy delights of being a victim

———————————●———————————

Just as Colorado gold prospectors sifted through gravel for gold nuggets, modern politicians search for insults. *Grant me, O Lord, a grievance. Let someone abuse me, please!*

Labour MP Angela Eagle is just such an operator. No lizard's tongue darting out to seize a bluebottle was ever so speedy as our Angela if she senses an 'ism' in her orbit. ''E insoolted me!' she'll wheedle, and with that she is off, ventilating her eyeballs, playing the violated virgin. Defamation! Discrimination! Smelling salts, Petunia. Ms Eagle, sour as a cider apple, adopts a scowl that could sink a thousand ships.

What does one mean by 'ism'? Racism, sexism, anti-Semitism are the three biggies – the Premiership, FA Cup and League Cup of grievance politics – but other brands of prejudice are available. White supremacism, transphobia, ableism, colonialism, Islamophobia, sizeism, ethnocentrism, lookism – these and others are on the checklist, to be scanned for on the grievance radar.

Ms Eagle, a keen cricketer who bats for the other side,

is quick to discern 'homophobia'. Quite right, too. To tickle someone under the armpits over a matter as serious as sex? Tut! It is just as well she was not running the film studio United Artists in 1978, or *La Cage aux Folles* would never have been made. Commissar Eagle is also mustard-hot on class differentiation. She can sniff out toffs like a beagle. Yet our Angela herself is the product of the University of Oxford and its privileged quads.

Sunbeams must have been off the menu the day Angela and her twin sister Maria were conceived. The Eagle girls (as they are never called) glower at the world from under tugged-down, Oliver Hardy fringes. They pong of misery like wet polyester, like cold chips, like a rainy day at Formby.

One Wednesday in April 2011, Prime Minister's Questions was trotting along without much incident when David Cameron flashed a casual rudery at Labour heckling. 'Calm down, dear. Calm down, calm down,' said Cameron in jocular fashion. Whoosh! Instant recoil. Labour MPs started squawking. Cameron laughed. This only ignited further exaggerated disgust from the Labour side. The cause of their so-called anger? They claimed Cameron had called Angela Eagle 'dear'.

Had he? He had indeed used the expression 'calm down, dear' but from my gallery seat above them I thought he was possibly directing it at Ed Balls. The words were a catchphrase from a television advertisement (for Esure insurance) in which arch chauvinist Michael Winner told a woman, 'Calm down, dear, it's only a commercial.' Even if Cameron had aimed his remark at Eagle, it was hardly personal. He was using a line from modern culture in a humorous way.

Eagle, who is no fool, must have known that. Yet she decided Offence Was Going To Be Taken. The Labour press unit, which included an extremely rude man called Tom Baldwin, said Cameron's 'mask had dropped'. He was a sexist brute/misogynist/cur and worse. Angela Eagle, wearing an expression of white-faced disbelief, averred that 'a modern man would not have expressed himself that way'. Harriet Harman was wheeled out to defend Sister Eagle and say that Mr Cameron had made a 'contemptuous remark' that demonstrated his 'patronising and outmoded attitude to women'. Eagle added that she had been 'patronised by better people than the prime minister' (did she mean sketchwriters?) and that Cameron had 'annoyed 51 per cent of the population'. Caroline Flint, another Labour MP and in private perfectly sensible and rather good fun, claimed Cameron had 'put women down'.

The Mumsnet website, or at least some of its dottier contributors, had an attack of the vapours. Ed Miliband, spreading his legs to make himself look less tall, posed with a group of female Labour MPs. All this was leapt on eagerly by the BBC, which gave the story far more attention than it might the outbreak of war in central Africa. The *Guardian* spoke of 'Labour fury'. Fury? They were loving it!

Voters looked at the kerfuffle and concluded that Eagle and Co were humourless drudges with their priorities all wrong. As Theresa May was to discover a few years later, British voters can put up with most things but the lack of a sense of humour is not one of them. An experienced journalist on one of the big Sunday newspapers solemnly told me that she believed Cameron had just lost himself the next election with that remark. But the public saw what was happening and it was not some grotesque rudeness on Cameron's behalf. It was game-playing by silly Labour strategists desperate to mobilise a non-existent thing called 'the women's vote'.

Daftmanship

Prince Charles's heroic battle
with the 'ego-tecture'

———————•———————

Leading architects are sometimes asked what their latest
high-rise buildings represent or resemble. Is it a shard,
a cheesegrater, a gherkin?

A testicle?

Some of those names have stuck. But often the answer
to 'What drove this design?' is a simpler one. It's big, it's
bulbous, it's brutal – it's the architect's ego.

Stuff historical context. Stuff the people who will have
to live in or under or near this new skyscraper, or look
at it from a distance of several miles. I've got an idea for
an eyesore I intend to stamp on the city. My idea – mine,
mine, mine – is all that's important. National heritage?
Neighbourly considerations? Communal notions of line
and beauty? Budget constraints? Such matters, to the star
architect, are gnats on the windscreen.

Arrogance on a drawing board, imperiousness cast in
polished glass and steel, the architect has become a figure
of tyranny and petulant impatience. They think they are
doing such vital work modernising and 'challenging' the

public aesthetic (which is another way of saying 'ruining much-loved vistas'). Amid this self-regard, the default setting of architects is languid boredom, their loathing for lower mortals' taste barely disguised. Have you seen the human beings they tend to include in their drawings? They are tiny specs, even less defined than the stooped figures in an L. S. Lowry painting. These are people as weevils.

Architects may freight their utterances with egalitarian theory but they make big money. When Dame Zaha Hadid died in 2016 at the age of sixty-five she left some £70 million in her will – not bad for a patrician grump who for many years was famous for not having had a single project completed in the UK. Among her unbuilt designs was the 1995 Cardiff Opera House. When local authorities opted instead for a rugby stadium she drawlingly retorted that the knuckle-headed Welsh were not sophisticated enough to appreciate her design. Hadid's curved plan for the 2020 Olympics stadium in Tokyo, likened by some to a lavatory seat, was another non-runner. It was dumped in favour of a more traditionally Japanese-looking design costing about half a billion pounds less.

Baghdad-born Hadid, a mournful-looking podge who dressed in Issey Miyake black suits and lilo-puncturing heels, had more falling-outs than your average Parachute Regiment instructor. She was a Suprematist, which did not mean she thought she was a member of a supreme race, though given her off-hand manner you could have been forgiven for thinking that. She once despatched an underling from the Venice Biennale to her flat in London to collect a pair of shoes she had decided she must have. Suprematists place artistic feeling above functionality or utility or cost. That may explain why her drawings often won competitions but went unbuilt. Once the engineers and clients had a discussion, they realised Hadid was more interested in visual effect – the purity of her brilliance – than in whether or not the building would stand upright for the next one hundred years. 'I almost believed there was such a thing as zero gravity,' she once said of her younger self. Yet either by gravity or magnetism, or sheer force of haughtiness, she still raked in 70 million smackeroos.

Switzerland-based Lord (Norman) Foster – he lives in that tax-efficient country solely in order to be near his family, no doubt – is said to be worth £150 million. You don't get that rich by designing buildings for little people. You work for super-sized companies looking for a corporate statement – the likes of HSBC, Renault, Hong Kong Airport and Commerzbank – and you do not hesitate to charge top whack. Soon you become not so much an architect as a brand. One of Foster's best-known designs was the 1991 Stansted Airport terminus, swooned over for its clean lines and its 'romance'. Romance? What, that hellhole for delayed holiday passengers, pushed into a small, glass-lined, echoing box as they wait for their luggage to be checked on to the Lanzagrotty flight? It's not exactly *Brief Encounter*, is it? Meanwhile, the practice led by Labour peer Lord (Richard) Rogers also coins it in, its turnover in 2012 having been more than £28 million. That from a man who styles himself a socialist and was a great supporter of Ken Livingstone for the London mayoralty.

Fey Rogers, practically haloed by his continental sophistication, made a reputation with buildings such as the Pompidou Centre in Paris (1977) and the Lloyd's of London building (1986). Both were hailed as masterpieces for sticking much of their pipework on the exterior. The Pompidou Centre has aged badly. The Lloyd's building was an extravagant silliness by an institution that, shortly afterwards, fell into rank disrepute for various insurance-syndicate rip-offs.

When Rogers was a Labour adviser, chairing the Urban Task Force, he dispensed homilies about how 'great leaders delivered visions'. He opined that 'high-quality architecture' (he may have meant 'expensive architects') and 'social inclusion' could regenerate cities. When Ken Livingstone was standing against Boris Johnson for the London mayoralty I attended a rally of pro-Livingstone architects. The one matter they seemed interested in was easier planning permission for corporate skyscrapers.

Rogers's wife Ruth – Lady Rogers – is a Left-wing American restaurateur who runs the River Café in west London. One of their Barolos is £2,400 a bottle. Back in early 2016 her ladyship was one of those cosmopolitan neck-clutchers who allowed their names to be attached to a letter signed by 'leading UK women uniting behind the campaign to stay in the EU'. They included hotel designer Kelly Hoppen, theatre-owner Sally Greene and internet person Lady (Martha) Lane Fox. As Lady Rogers so poignantly argued, her River Café would be obliterated, ruined, driven on to the rocks by Brexit. 'We rely on the quality of the wine, olive oil, cheeses, vegetables and fruits from all over Italy.' Did she think that such delicacies would no longer be importable – that they would somehow be banned from Britain if we left the EU? Or did she mean she might have to pay another quid in duty on her £2,400 bottle of Barolo?

Both Richard Rogers and Norman Foster have lordly titles. Foster, who accepted a 1999 peerage from Tony

Blair and could have been an interesting adornment to our Parliament, hardly ever turned up and in 2010 he said he was quitting Westminster. Couldn't be fagged? Or had he never really been serious about being part of our legislature? Although he has resigned his seat in the House of Lords, he keeps his title, naturally.

Architects have not had it all their way. One person, in particular, has frustrated them and cost them millions of pounds in lost fees. Step forward Charles, Prince of Wales and, er, voice of the masses. The Prince has repeatedly attacked modern architecture for being ugly and brash. Architects still shudder when they think of the May 1984 dinner at Hampton Court Palace held to celebrate the 150th anniversary of the Royal Institute of British Architects. Some seven hundred darlings of the design world were there, initially in a shivery frisson at having bagged the Prince to make a short speech and present a gold medal for architecture to Charles Correa, an Indian architect who was a dab-hand at hideous tower blocks. Their pleasure soon turned to horror when Charles stuck it to them in spectacular fashion. He started by saying how important it was 'in human terms, to respect old buildings, street plans and traditional scales' and to enjoy 'facades, ornaments and soft materials'. He was very clearly attacking his modernist, minimalist, hard-material audience. He took aim at elitists who gave insufficient thought to tenants, particularly the disabled, and to 'the feelings and wishes of the mass of ordinary people' but seemed more interested in pleasing their fellow architects.

One of the big public developments at the time was a planned extension to the National Gallery, which Charles described as 'a kind of municipal fire station, complete with the sort of tower that contains the siren ... a monstrous carbuncle on the face of a much-loved and elegant friend'. He also took a swipe at designs for a twenty-one-storey Mies van der Rohe tower at Mansion House, calling it 'a giant glass stump, better suited to downtown Chicago than the City of London'. By now the assembled guests were practically chewing their fists. 'Why,' continued Charles, 'has everything got to be vertical, straight, unbending?'

The architects were hopping mad. *Who the bloody hell invited that big-eared fool to come and talk to us?* they asked. *Er, we did*, they had to admit. They had fawned to royalty and royalty had skewered them.

The Prince has so far torpedoed at least two Rogers designs. First was a scheme for Paternoster Square next to St Paul's Cathedral. Charles compared it to the damage wrought by German bombers in the Blitz, though he said at least the Luftwaffe had left behind nothing more offensive than rubble. Then came a 2009 rumpus when the Qatari royal family was about to commission a Rogers design for a multibillion-pound redevelopment on the site of Chelsea Barracks. The initial design was for sixteen close-built, ten-storey pavilions made from steel and glass. Lovely was not the word. Charles, alerted to the 'Gucci ghetto' plans by concerned locals, had 'prince-to-prince' words with the Qataris. They had another look at the design and decided Charles might have a point. Rogers was off the job.

Think of all those fees he lost! The kudos! The royal Qatari connections! Rogers went on the warpath, demanding a public inquiry into the constitutional validity of the Prince's eructations not only on architecture but also medicine and farming and climate change. Various grandees took his side, signing letters of protest and doing everything they could to soothe and sympathise with the indignant Rogers. Among these allies were Lord Foster, Renzo Piano, Frank Gehry, Jean Nouvel, Sir Nicholas Serota, Sir Anish Kapoor – my dears, *le tout d'architecture, le tout d'art.*

Lady Rogers, the £2,400 bottle of Barolo gal, quivered sorrowfully beside her husband saying that friends and allies had telephoned to say, 'It's you today but who is next?' Her ladyship continued: 'The prince's actions are akin to calling up a publisher and saying "I want all books to have a happy ending."'

'Charles knows little about architecture,' raged Rogers, deploying the classic attack of experts toppled by popular taste. In the *Guardian* in 2005, the same Rogers wrote that it was 'dangerously irresponsible' to consider that architectural quality was merely down to subjective opinion. 'There are well-established criteria and standards for judgement,' he wrote. 'Understanding and appreciation come from education, experience, the fine-tuning of our senses and, perhaps most importantly, good professional leadership. And yet we have miserably failed to put the best architects at the heart of the decision-making process.' He was enraged by the lack of democracy in the Prince's behaviour over the Chelsea Barracks site. A Labour life peer – who was given a place in our legislature for the rest of his days – was cross about lack of democracy!

Prince Charles has been known to call it 'egotecture'. He ain't far wrong.

Last word on architects: in November 2016 a speech was made to the World Architecture Festival in Berlin by

Patrik Schumacher, director of Zaha Hadid Architects. In a forthright eruption, Schumacher called for civic planning laws to be sharply reduced and for constraints on land use to be abolished. Instead the naked market should prevail. He wanted to abolish the setting of housing standards, scrap zonal protections, scrap the imposition of quotas for 'social and affordable housing' (these were 'trying to paralyse us with bad conscience'), stop government giving housing subsidies to certain people, abandon rent controls and privatise entire streets, squares, parks and maybe even entire urban districts. The architectural world rushed to distance itself from Schumacher. He defended himself by saying that he had been speaking 'as an intellectual, theorist and polemicist'. Prince Charles should try the same line next time the egotects moan about him. As for Schumacher's peppery polemic, extreme though it was, and politically unrealistic, was it not more honest than the democratic posturing of Rogers, his Mistress-Mark-Up wife and their ilk?

Peak Arrogance

Liberal elite's annual *concours d'élégance*
at the Davos Forum

———————●———————

For Muslims it is the Hajj pilgrimage to Mecca and for European Christians it may be Santiago de Compostela in Holy Week. And for patronising corporate swanks, there is one shrine above all else: the Swiss ski resort of Davos Klosters, third week of January. That is when the schmoozefest of the World Economic Forum (motto: 'Committed to Improving the State of the World') takes place. Book me in, Miss Bingo. I'll need a superior suite with mountain rooms and privileged-partner accreditation.

Out on the pistes, skiers shuss and slalom. In the World Economic Forum's efficiently carpeted conference halls, moguls of a different sort grimly go about the business of networking. For seven days and seven canapé-laden nights they pose and preen. They haven't a clue how terrible they look.

This is capitalism at its most condescending, senior snowflakes in their Alpine fastness. The plight of the world's masses may be on the official programme – all 150 pages of it, detailing meetings and seminars and power brunches – but the unspoken agenda is of professional self-advancement, business cards being palmed and emails exchanged. Even better, the whole thing may be tax deductible.

No satire would dare depict such paradoxical excess as is found at Davos. Billionaires draw their lips into bows of concern to give lectures about poverty. Rock stars mix with dictators to discuss democracy. Such a regrettable thing, populism. Cocktail parties are held to mark world hunger. Another caviar-topped quail's egg, ambassador? It's a long time till the black-tie fondue. At the Hilton hotel a corner of the foyer has been roped off for an exhibition that shows how the poor live. This museum-style display features freezer bags of rice, sad little rolls of bedding, meagre tents, crumpled water bottles. Refugees live in rough conditions? You don't say!

The trustees of this high-octane freebie (admission £22,000) range from Christine Lagarde, disgraced boss of the International Monetary Fund, to Peter Brabeck-Letmathe, who used to run rapacious multinational Nestlé. Davos philosophy sessions often dwell on diet and world food dilemmas: sessions about sustainable and healthy food, a talk on heart disease at the health hub, a Malaysian health minister discussing 'human-centric health' and a panel of mass-produced food industrialists chewing over 'advanced healthy food systems'. How do Nestlé's Kit Kats, Carnation condensed milk and Herta farty-farty frankfurters fit into all that? That last panel on 'advanced healthy food systems' included a board member from, my goodness what a surprise, Nestlé.

Maybe the world's health would improve if globalised companies like Nestlé did not force so much synthetic pap packed with sugar and saturated fats down our gullets. When Marie Antoinette said, 'Let them eat cake,' at least she was envisaging something freshly made without E numbers. The peak troughers of Davos would have looked at Marie Antoinette and given their most pitying smiles. Did she not have a strategy for blame evasion? Could her 'people' not have reached an accommodation with the *sans-culottes* and 'cut a deal'? She should have positioned herself better and bought some Third Sector favours to dilute the mob's fury.

Davos cable cars whisk fur-booted tax accountants, bankers and lawyers, lawyers, lawyers to James Bond villain-style lairs atop a distant peak, there to discuss public-health shortfalls or sustainable development. *Perhaps a glass of gluhwein,* meine Damen und Herren, *before we watch the next video about clean water supplies in the Third World?* The fur-booted brigade later clamber back into the ecologically incorrect cable car (ski lifts are horrendous polluters) to admire the Davos nightscape and all those twinkly lights wrecking the night sky.

Davos's World Economic Forum identifies 'Young Global Leaders' – professional thrusters (aged under forty) who are going to rule the world. They are 'pushing boundaries and rethinking the world around them'. The latest lot included: a psychologist of altruism, a spin doctor from Sweden's foreign affairs ministry, a women's-underwear designer from Canada and, good grief, footballer Rio Ferdinand. Nice chap, Rio. But a global leader?

As each year's Davos forum begins, private jets whine into St Moritz's Samedan Airport, disgorging passengers into 7-Series Beemers that convey these pashas of liberalism the last few miles to their five-star destination. Climate change will again dominate proceedings but the Learjet class long ago worked out that environmentalism was an essential look. Global-warming bore Al Gore has a carbon footprint the size of a yeti, his house in Nashville using twenty times more electricity than the average US household. And yet he zooms all over the world to finger-wag about greenhouse gases. Al is one of the Davos trustees. Good old Al.

Last year actor Leonardo DiCaprio was summoned to Davos to receive the Crystal Award (correction, 'the prestigious Crystal Award'). DiCaprio, hair greased, his film-star bod poured into a suit, delivered a homily in which he spoke about his own foundation, the generosity of philanthropists like him and repeated well-worn theories about how the planet was doomed unless mankind became less extravagant. 'Our planet cannot be saved unless we leave fossil fuels in the ground,' he said.

DiCaprio has done great things for his reputation in Hollywood by remoulding himself as an environmentalist. He has made such a song and dance about his green views that it is almost as if his helicoptering and yachting lifestyle belonged to someone else – perhaps a character he was playing. Actors sometimes have difficulty identifying which part of their lives is real. In May 2016 DiCaprio flew by private jet from Cannes to New York in order to collect another award for his climate-change campaigning. Having attended the glitzy event he had himself flown back to Cannes, a return trip of 8,000 miles that guzzled oodles of those very fossil fuels he believes should be 'left in the ground where they belong'.

Newspapers occasionally point out such blatant double standards. Does it have any effect? No! Celebrities do not embrace this climate-change thing to impress the little people. They do it to plug into the network, play the game, show agents and publishers and studios and Academy members that they acknowledge the political tides. A few Tweets to the fanbase along the lines of 'Humbled to accept prestigious Crystal award @wef for my foundation's climate change work' soon bypasses any scurvy paragraph in a Fleet Street gossip column. Principles are worn as baubles, political affiliations as jewellery. If a star is expected to follow the mantras he spouts, come off it, the worthy messages would soon decline and how would that help the thousands of consultants and charity executives and fundraising professionals whose lives depend on these campaigns? Do you want to create MORE poverty, for heaven's sake? I think not!

Back in Davos, as the shivering bellboys sweep fresh-fallen snow from the hotel steps and bodyguards and police snipers keep watch for protestors, the Great Lie continues. Canada's boyish prime minister, Justin Trudeau, a man quite possibly elected on the strength of those delicious little licks of hair at the nape of his neck, comes out with the killer argument. 'Poverty,' he declares, 'is sexist.' The World Economic Forum hails him for this discovery and notes that pretty Pierre has thus joined '86 leaders' who signed a letter making this important assertion. These 'leaders' include Melinda Gates, of whom we would never have heard were she not married to the world's richest man. They also include someone called Sheryl Sandberg. This Facebook executive – basically a glorified advertising sales exec – is paid some £13 million a year and has a

fortune in excess of a billion pounds. Such sums are com-
monplace at Davos.

From its foundation in 1971, the Davos forum was
originally little more than a niche jolly for liver-spotted
bankers and out-of-power politicians. They would analyse a few philosophical trends, have a couple of spanking
dinners with cigar and schnapps and agree to meet the
following year ('but maybe see you at Bayreuth in the summer, Helmut'). Slowly, barnacles adhered themselves to
this sodality. Around the turn of the millennium, as baby-
boomer social democrats took command of the European
chancelleries and the White House, Davos hit maximum
swank. It is now this grotesque gymkhana for the globalised elite, a week-long knees-up with the company
credit card when they can parade their social consciences
at high altitude. The Forum – a word dusted by an unwar-
ranted suggestion of public legitimacy – has become for
management consultants and multinational bankers what
Cannes is for film-makers.

Hollywood's Stars With A Social Conscience attend.
Toppled statesmen are invited – last year George Osborne
(in training shoes) and David Cameron mixed with
wooden George Clooney and that frighteningly lacquered
wife of his. Bono is a Davos favourite, his pink spectacles
raising the tone at the Hawaii-themed booze-up thrown
by a Californian software billionaire, Marc Benioff. Is it
possible to have a conversation about artificial intelligence
and advanced robotics while wearing a grass skirt and
swaying to the beat of ukeke hula music?

Later in the week perhaps they will attend that BBC-
sponsored talk on 'populism' and the 'rebellion of the
forgotten' (do they mean all those middle-aged women the

Beeb has dropped for being too wrinkled?). The Beeb has sent along Zeinab Badawi to present the discussion. Few narrow their eyes with quite such commanding superiority as Badawi. After lunch at the Congress Centre, multi-millionaire chef and businessman Jamie Oliver is giving an 'Insight' talk about healthy food for poor people. This *amuse-bouche* is chaired by scary Arianna Huffington. Teeth like a piranha, accent from a food-mixer, seemingly power-fixated Arianna once decorated the arm of poor Bernard Levin, as strange a pairing as tequila and pork pie.

'The Future of Consumption' is chaired by Baohong Sun, Dean's Distinguished Chair Professor of Marketing at the Cheung Kong Graduate School of Business in the People's Republic of China. A communist state having analysts of consumer choice might be odd enough, but since when has any have you ever met a truly 'distinguished' marketing person?

Davos Klosters is itself not for the poor. A plate of pasta bolognese in the local bistros can set you back 40 Swiss francs – the monthly wage, give or take a few strands of spaghetti, of a Bangladeshi textile-factory worker. And yet these creeps, these frauds, these patronising plutocrats take it upon themselves to identity the concerns of 'the poor' – and to tell them how to behave. Where's an avalanche when you need one?

Dress Code: Haloes

The self-polishing possibilities
of foreign aid

———•———

When a Whitehall permanent secretary (a 'Sir Humphrey') gives a celebrity-style interview with macho photographs, it may be a sign he has gone power mad. Civil servants are mere functionaries, servants of the public. If there is any vanity to be shown, let it be displayed by the taxpayers who fund the whole shebang. Sir Humphreys should hover in the shadows.

There was certainly something pushy about an interview Mark Lowcock gave to *Civil Service World* magazine in April 2016. There he stood in a trendy white shirt, no tie, arms crossed as he glowered at the camera like some tycoon. In another shot he was shown with hands in pockets, a sideways angle catching him against the wall of what looked like one of those nineteenth-century warehouses that have been turned into swish offices. Magazines use such photographs to indicate corporate despatch. Power. Personal heft.

Lowcock? Name or pendulous medical complaint? The man in question turns out to be a pigeon-chested specimen, weedy, weak-voiced. If you gave him a moustache he could be the skinnier of the two Chuckle Brothers. And yet, in the *Civil Service World* photographs, he was presented as a figure of substance.

Mark Lowcock was until recently Permanent Secretary at the Department for International Development (DfID), the government outfit that spends £13.3 billion a year of our money – not his – on helping foreigners. The Lowcocks of this world seldom put it quite like that. 'Foreign' is the sort of word from which the bureaucratic elite will shy like horses from a rattlesnake. Consider how we may no longer talk of 'TEFL' (teaching English as a foreign language). It is now TESOL (teaching English as a second or other language). It is a wonder Whitehall has not yet changed the name of the Foreign and Commonwealth Office.

The *Civil Service World* interview with Lowcock dwelt on his visionary qualities and his 'strategy'. It described the battles he had fought to overcome public scepticism and establish foreign aid as a political inevitability. 'Increasingly people don't want to debate whether we do development or not,' he claimed. 'I worry much less than I used to about making the case for development.' He looked to the horizon and expressed the hope that there might come the time, in some distant day, that DfID's work would be done and there would be no more waifs in the world. 'My objective is to see the world advance to such a point that DfID isn't really needed,' murmured the great man. But while there were still babies in the Sudan with flies crawling round their eyes, while Yemeni tribes continued to blast the bejaysus out of each other, well, sigh, the British workforce, from Walsall garage mechanics to Bangor hairdressers, would have to carry the world's burdens. Such are the duties of being superior mortals. And by the by, the continued need for aid should at least see out Mark Lowcock's continuing public-sector career. After his eventual departure from DfID he bagged a job at the United Nations as Under Secretary General at the Office for the Coordination of Humanitarian Affairs. Did he win the job on merit or was it spooned to him as an act of mercy?

The magazine carried a proud boast from Lowcock that international aid was 'the most amazing success story in human history'. (What, bigger than the spread of Christianity? The Industrial Revolution? The discovery of penicillin?) The interview ended with him expressing quiet satisfaction that he will one day be able to dandle his grandchildren on his knee and tell them that he did something worthwhile with his life, saving billions of people and helping to 'eradicate' poverty. That 'eradicate' is a favourite cliché of our ruling class.

Mark Lowcock (b. 1962) worked at DfID all his Whitehall career. Having studied at Oxford and trained as an accountant and economist, he began at what was then called the Overseas Development Administration in 1985. Foreign aid was good to him. He was a high-ranking mandarin for several years and was on some £165,000 a year as permanent secretary, plus pension entitlements and other perks. Furthermore, his wife worked for the department as a senior economic adviser. No poverty for the Lowcocks! Although they were paid a lot of money, it was a mere handful of sand compared to the billions Sir Mark got to spend on our behalf.

The simple figure '£13.3 billion' may go in one eyeball, out the other. Who among us can envisage a billion quid?

It may help a little if we see how many noughts that entails – £13,300,000,000 – but still our minds may struggle to comprehend the sum. Millions are a bit more graspable, so let us say that this represents about £256 million a week, or £36 million a day. Every day of the year. Every year for the past decade or so. And that money is coming from the British taxpayer. A JCB with a big bucket would struggle to shift that many pennies in the time.

Consider foreign aid against the budgets of other government departments. It is roughly a third of what we spend on defence. It is about half of what our government spends on industry, agriculture and employment aid combined. It is just under half of what we spend on public order and safety. Those spending departments must jockey for their budgets every time the Chancellor is reviewing the nation's books. Yet foreign aid, having been set in law at 0.7 per cent by David Cameron's coalition government, is protected from cuts unless the economy shrinks. Meanwhile, the British government's debt interest payments run at £39 billion a year. A more moral course might be to clear our enormous debts before giving away so much money.

Why did David Cameron place such emphasis on foreign aid? As a church-going Anglican he was no doubt aware of the parable of the Good Samaritan. The Samaritan is a generous man. But his giving of alms was a one-off. He did not go on giving the victim billions of pounds every year. DfID has at times resembled the firemen on the *Flying Scotsman*, shovelling banknotes into the boiler at double-speed, frantic to get the loot spent on time in case the government did not meet its annual spending requirement. Billions of pounds have been sent to obscure

World Bank trust funds, incurring millions of pounds in administration fees of up to 10 per cent. Administration fees are a polite way of saying 'a cut taken by the clerical/ professional/lawyer class' – the very sort of people who are so keen on development spending in the first place.

David Cameron calculated the politics of his 0.7 per cent aid provision. He wanted to make the Conservative Party look kind and thus nullify the tiresome attacks on the Tories as 'the nasty party'. Is it too cynical to wonder, too, if he hoped to parade his own, personal conscience (as in, 'I, Cameron, am doing this in the face of complaints from the Right of my party')?

Emergencies aside, there may be a case for the British government supporting good works in foreign lands. If that reduces the number of unhappy refugees coming to our country, if it wins us political favour in countries vulnerable to Islamisation, if it supports a regime that is well disposed to Britain, even if it bribes a local despot: in such cases, aid could make sense. But the scale of the spending is amazingly high, particularly when our own social-care budgets are in trouble. It should not be wicked to say that.

Perhaps the very name of DfID gives the game away. A. C. Capey, a correspondent to the Prayer Book Society's *Faith and Worship* magazine, has pointed out that 'development' is 'a particularly Whiggish word, the philistine-ostrich's word – an optimistic, positive gloss on the neutral "change" or the pessimist's "decay"'.

What do foreign-aid enthusiasts want from the spending? To reduce human suffering, presumably. But there may be other desires. Do they seek a buzz of altruism, even if the money belongs to other people? A sense of power over the recipients? Here you are, you wretches of the world, come and peck crumbs from our hands like December songbirds: is that what drives it? There may be the desire to make our own country less rich. That would atone their feelings of guilt. The egalitarian often operates not so much by trying to raise others as seeking to lower himself – look at the way rich Left-wingers dress down, have tattoos and mockney-fy their accents.

'Development' may also be a euphemism for 'make them more like us'. Look at the stated responsibilities of the Department for International Development on its website. These single out 'improving the lives of girls and women and a greater choice of family planning'. As a husband with two daughters, I am in favour of being kind to women but such emphasis on women's rights is odd from a department that the public associates with emergency relief. Should Third World countries not come to feminism by their own means, rather than via a foreign power's Department for Handouts? Might that not create resentment?

> In domestic politics, government ministers insist that 'arm's-length' principles prevent them passing comment on art that is state-funded. No such scruples apply at DfID, which gave £9 million to an Ethiopian girl-band, Yegna, described as Ethiopia's answer to the Spice Girls. This was done to 'empower women in Ethiopia'. It no doubt empowered the women of Yegna to go and have a blowout at the shops.

The DfID website also focuses on 'hand-washing campaigns, vaccination drives and gender equality advocacy'. Hand-washing may be a practical response to hygiene problems but there is something of the primary-school

Staff at DfID are the highest-paid in Whitehall. Their average wage has been put at £53,000, twice the national average.

The department's executive organogram shows an array of titles. In addition to five directors for the main geographical areas, there is a director general of policy and general programmes, a director of the policy division, a director of the research and evidence division, a chief scientific adviser, a chief economist, a director of the international relations division, a director of the conflict, humanitarian and security division and a director of the stabilisation unit. Add a director general of finance and corporate performance and a director general of economic development. Under them toil a director of the human resources division, a director of finance and corporate performance, a deputy director of the strategy unit, a deputy director of trade for development, a director of the international finance division and a director of the communications division. Phew! And that is without even touching on the executive management committee that sits alongside the ministers – Vivienne Cox, Tim Robinson, Sally Jones-Evans and Richard Keys.

For a flavour of those four Solomons, take an interview Sally Jones-Evans gave to an inclusive-leadership psychology campaign called 'The Glass Lift'. Describing herself as an 'avid people-watcher', she preached about the importance of 'honing leadership skills', 'focusing on being your best self' and 'the importance of building a network before you need it and being savvy about the occasional terrorists you come across pursuing their own agendas'. Just the person to deal with Third World tyrants.

mistress here, checking pupils' hands as they come into lunch to make sure their fingernails are not too grubby.

'Did you wash your hands after going to the lav, William? Good boy.' Wetwipes for west Africa.

What must adults in drought zones think when these Westerners lecture them like this? Is the Bangladeshi grandmother or the Iraqi refugee-camp matriarch or the Nepalese earthquake survivor expected to accept this advice, lowering her eyes with grovelling gratitude to the DfID sahibs? Is she not likely to think, quietly, *How the bloody hell dare these condescending white bastards tell me when to wash my hands? Do they think I was born yesterday?*

International development, as practised by the Mark Lowcocks, may be less about handing out food and medical supplies to people in dire need; it may be more about moulding attitudes, impinging on political views, persuading non-Western cultures to adopt our codes of conduct. Yet this is done by a political class that throws up its hands in horror at Christian missionaries who link handouts to evangelism. It is endorsed by an elite that cringes from 'judgementalism', even while it lectures the Third World on women's rights. Old seadogs had a word for such behaviour: rum.

Shennan D'oh

The campaign to destroy our
heritage of hymns

———————•———————

This may sound uncharitable but when BBC radio
executive Bob Shennan dies, what will they play at his
funeral? It is unlikely to be hymns. Thanks to Shennan,
hymns are not so well known these days. As Bob is borne
on his last, doleful journey and his bereft friends lift
hankies to their eyes, some technician may have to press a
button to play a Cat Stevens song or 'Kumbaya My Lord'
or some such horror. Simon and Garfunkel's 'The Sound
of Silence' might suit, for silence is what the Bob Shennans
of this world have imposed on our once world-conquering
culture of hymns.

Have you been to a wedding recently where the congregation included non-regulars? You will have noticed they
were mumbling. 'Singing' is not the verb. The sound will
have had more in common with what happens at the den-
tist's before the cotton wool has been removed. You want
to say, 'Yikes, that hurt,' but all that comes out is 'Hrmpfff
ghrrph brrrrfwwwmrp,' and the fang bandit replies, 'I'm
glad you think so.'

At too many church services now, the following happens when the organist plays the opening bars of an old standby such as 'Hills of the North, Rejoice' or 'Ride on! Ride on in Majesty'. The church's musty air reverberates as the bottom notes sound from the pipes. That magnificent parp is enough almost to loosen the moorings of your skull. Deep breath, team, it's time to fill the lungs and let rip, even if your voice is rough as an emery board. Big moment of expectation. Drum roll. In we go! . . . Oh. All that comes out is a tiny, reedy, embarrassed *wheee*, so feeble it might have been whispered through a woollen sock.

Hymns used to be for everyone. They were liberatingly democratic. Droners and groaners could mix with perfect-pitch choristers. Tiddlers piled in, grannies warbled, the tone-deaf honked away, confident they had finally cracked this music lark. Hymn-singing was a Grand National of noise.

You can see why the community-minded Methodists loved hymns. They had catchy tunes, got the blood circulating and gave a beat to churchgoing. Dogma came second to congenial music. Some hymns had dicey rhymes ('hearts' were forever being chimed with 'imparts', 'immortal' with 'portal') but occasionally the writing was high-grade. Cardinal Newman's 'lead, kindly light, amid the encircling gloom' caught the despair that can close in on us unless we have hope to hand. John Bunyan's 'hobgoblin nor foul fiend can daunt his spirit' had alliteration, euphony, enjambment, half-rhyme, rhythm, assonance, syncope and more. Samuel Crossman's 'My Song Is Love Unknown', sung to the sublime John Ireland tune, had a dramatic third verse to make you blink back tears: 'Then "Crucify!" is all their breath, and for his death they thirst and cry.'

Then the Anglican hierarchy, in a decade or two of egalitarian itchiness, decided the old favourites were an affront to modernisation. The BBC (which is where Bob Shennan comes in) went along with that *de haut en bas* approach and engineered the near-obliteration of hymns. And so, from church pews nowadays, there often simply comes the sound of tongue-chewing as forty-year-olds struggle to negotiate tunes that everyone would formerly have known and loved.

You can rely on most people over fifty to know such classics as 'Praise, My Soul, the King of Heaven' but if the worshippers are any younger than that you may draw blank expressions. Sporting fixtures have kept alive 'Guide Me, O Thou Great Redeemer' (sung at Wales rugby matches) and 'Abide with Me' (FA Cup finals). Christmas carols have kept going because they are linked to that great December retail festival of Mammon. Thanks to the revival of Remembrance Day, 'Jerusalem' and 'I Vow to Thee, My Country' are widely known, despite whinge-ing from peaceniks twitchy about nationalism. Stephen Lowe, a former Bishop of Hulme, Manchester, said he thought 'I Vow to Thee, My Country' was 'heretical' and stoked 'a wish for a white-dominated, simple world of Englishness'. 'I won't sing it,' piped Bishop Lowe. If he did sing it, perhaps he would see there is no mention of England anywhere in the hymn. There is no reason that, say, a Guatemalan could not sing that hymn and feel patri-otic. Lowe was just being intolerant.

What damage such attitudes have done. If you ask younger friends to hum 'All People that on Earth Do Dwell' or 'Crown Him with Many Crowns' or 'Jesu, Lover of My Soul' to the turbulent, rhythmic tune 'Abergavenny', you will be met with incomprehension. Two generations ago, hymns were a great British cultural achievement. Now children are leaving school without knowing the basics of Anglican hymnody. This is even true of Church of England schools and many of the once-great independent schools. I know the chaplain of one public school who insists on slipping babyish happy-clappy hymns into ceremonial services, just to spite the school parents.

Our hymns were Britain's answer to Italian opera or African-American gospel. They had key changes or harmonic chord progressions that caught the mellow softness of our countryside. They had a way of expressing deeper-rooted emotions, which the British, by and large, were not terribly good at putting into words. How do you explain in sentences that mixture of pride and sadness when a family member has died? Hard to do, isn't it? But if you sing 'The Day Thou Gavest, Lord, Is Ended' and you reach the final verse, you may feel a tingle down your spine and the emotions will somehow feel expressed:

> So be it, Lord, thy throne shall never,
> Like earth's proud empires, pass away;
> Thy Kingdom stands, and grows for ever,
> Till all thy creatures own thy sway.

The organist, if skilful, can bring a growl to the music in the second line of that verse. A final-line rallentando milks extra feeling. Agnostics, doubters and lapsed churchgoers could gain inner comfort, provided the hymn was familiar and had grown within us, acquiring the patina of years. That deep marbling of hymns enriched us. Hymns made us fuller, bigger, more linked to one another.

The Bob Shennans of the world did not like that. They perhaps regarded hymns as addictive, sentimental and too much of a throwback to the days when ladies wore hats to Sunday evensong.

During the 1960s, the Church of England introduced 'The Peace' to communion services. There is no surer way of emptying the pews. As the service approaches the climax of the bread and wine, things are interrupted so congregants can exchange a sign of God's Peace. Paradoxically, this is noisy. People shake hands and kiss, leaping from pew to pew to share lovey-doveyness. The celebrant will bear down on you, robes flowing, gaseous smile pinned to goaty lips. 'The peeeees, the peeeees, the peeeees.' Double-clasp handshakes. Cloying pity. The Peace has put more people off church than any number of pederasts. I am a Protestant. At church I like to confront my smallness before God without interruptions from other members of the congregation. If they must say 'hallooo', let it be after the service. Over a large sherry.

'The Day Thou Gavest' was particularly popular on a Radio 2 programme called *Sunday Half Hour*, which went out in the evenings and consisted of recordings of favourite hymns. There was something reassuring about *Sunday Half Hour*, which had been part of BBC radio's light-entertainment schedule for seventy years. The first episode on 14 July 1940 had been broadcast from St Mary Redcliffe in Bristol to boost morale with some 'community hymn singing'. It did that exceedingly well and continued to attract a solid if unexceptional audience. The show was once presented in a straightforward manner, allowing the audience to listen without distraction. The BBC suits decided it needed to be 'more accessible'. New presenters were found. They included an Irish Roman Catholic priest, Brian D'Arcy (simpering, twee delivery), and an Anglican parson, Roger Royle (golly-gosh wonderment with a horsey laugh). They were eventually replaced by Diane Louise Jordan, once a presenter of *Blue Peter*, with all that that entails. She treated her listeners – average age north of sixty – as though they were kiddywinks. Audience numbers fell. Of course they did. 'Ha!' said Radio 2 Controller Shennan. 'See? It's unpopular!'

Many of us loved *Sunday Half Hour*. As the weekend creaked to a close, grand old hymns would drift through the house: maybe 'Rock of Ages, Cleft for Me' or 'O Worship the Lord in the Beauty of Holiness' or 'Fight the Good Fight' (a cousin of mine had that at her wedding – the marriage was nonetheless a success). The programme's audience may not have been young or rich, which is what advertisers like, but this was the BBC, so that should not have mattered. The corporation knew that the show was enjoyed. Then Shennan struck. The programme was shifted from Sunday evening – when the shadows were lengthening and people were starting to contemplate the coming week – to six o'clock on Sunday mornings.

Now I may be doing £271,000-a-year Bob Shennan an injustice – I have never met him, and probably just as well, for I might punch him – but I suspect he is seldom up and about at such an hour. Sunday is the day for a lie-in. We must hope that Brother Shennan was not resorting to the oldest, dirtiest trick of schedulers: if you want to kill a programme, first give it a different presenter, then move it to an unholy hour.

Complaints were brushed aside. 'Let them listen to it on the iPlayer,' said the BBC, no doubt aware that many of *Sunday Half Hour*'s ancient listeners would struggle with computers. It was argued that the new programme would be a whole hour long. It has not quite turned out that way. Much of the time is filled with (to my critical ear) inane chirruping from Diane Louise Jordan, who addresses her audience as 'you lovely people', in the sort of voice certain nurses address care-home inmates. 'All right, Doris, have you finished your milk pudding like a good girl?'

The programme now is not solely about hymns. It offers 'spiritually uplifting and inspiring music with hymns, gospel and choral classics'. It was also placed into the BBC's PC food-mixer. They had a special episode for International Women's Day. Is that now to be considered a religious festival, the camera focusing tight on a stained glass window showing St Harriet of Harman? Thirteen pieces of music were played for that event. They ranged from the Gateway Singers's 'Immaculate Mary' to Mahalia Jackson rippin' out 'Jesus Met the Woman at the Well'. The Salvation Army band played a number. There was a Katherine Jenkins version of 'Down in the River to Pray'. The playlist contained just two up-and-down hymns, both of them from the saccharine pen of Mrs C. F. Alexander ('All Things Bright and Beautiful' and 'There is a Green Hill Far Away'). Muscular Christianity was turned into a beach weakling.

Ambulances wait until we dial 999 on our telephones. Militant atheists are more interventionist. They barge through the crowd, nee-nawing scepticism, wailing 'disbelieve! disbelieve!' They rail against a God in whom they do not believe. You might as well chase rainbows. They dismiss religion as an 'opiate of the people' – and yet many of them are liberal about drugs.

Richard Dawkins and Lewis Wolpert and other leading secularists claim to be motivated by their superior appreciation of evidence-based argument, proof, reason and the deity of science. This has become the accepted position of the public sector. Officialdom looks down on religion. Church people are considered a bit below the salt by government agencies. In the Labour Party, once rooted in Methodism and Roman Catholicism, it is now unusual to hear activists affirm Christian belief. Judaism is sharply out of favour on the Left, which sees more virtue, or at least votes, in Islam, despite that faith's attitudes to women. The Lib Dems are probably the party most supported by the Anglican priesthood. It is almost a surprise, when watching the Church of England synod, not to find the wetter-looking archdeacons holding orange, Lib Dem-style placards saying 'Sinning Here'. And yet Tim Farron quit the Lib Dem leadership because his evangelical beliefs clashed with his political positions.

The National Secular Society campaigns for the separation of religion and state. Its members are happier attacking Christianity than Islam. Do you blame them? Muslims are big, bearded blokes with tempers. Muslims can play the race card, too. Equality and 'tolerance' is much prized by the National Secular Society, even though their whole purpose is to expunge. But, hark, what is this on their website? It is a list of 'Honorary Associates': a gallery of 'distinguished supporters in politics, human rights, science, philosophy, the arts, journalism and broadcasting'. How do we know they are 'distinguished'? Because the National Secular Society tells us.

Into the comradeship of atheism has thus been inserted a hierarchy – we could almost say an episcopacy – of unbelievers. That's not very egalitarian! The distinguished secularists range from 'professional footballer and philosophy student' Joey Barton to theatre director Jonathan Miller. Dearly beloved, we already have our York and Canterbury. Oh, to be in attendance were the bookish Miller ever to meet his colleague Barton, a twice-convicted thug. What a convocation of intellects. 'Well, Joey, tell me why you have these reservations about the Nicene Creed.' 'Yer wot?'

Other princes of the National Secular Society include: Tuscany's Polly Toynbee; Labour dullards Kerry McCarthy and Nick Brown; writer Philip Pullman; 'Geoffrey Robertson QC' and 'Lord Taverne QC'; Dan Snow, the leggy telly historian who married money; cross-patch David Starkey; a Left-wing cartoonist called Martin Rowson and food writer Jonathan Meades; life peer Lady Kinnock and her MP son Stephen; hater of newspapers 'Dr Evan Harris'; comedian Ricky Gervais; playwrights Michael Frayn and Edward Bond; higher education snoot Lady Blackstone; pro-EU peer and sometime Tory Whip Lord Garel-Jones; and a University of Oxford chemist, Prof. Peter Atkins.

Fervid fulminator Atkins says:

> I regard teaching religion as purveying lies. To assert 'God did it' is no more than an admission of ignorance dressed deceitfully as an explanation. To say that 'God made the world' is simply a more or less sophisticated way of saying that we don't understand how the universe originated. A god, in so far as it is anything, is an admission of

ignorance. Religion's inwardly directed sentimental glow reflects on issues privately, exchanges information by assurance and assertion, discusses awkward points by warfare, terror, and coercion, and builds up a network of conflicting ideas that conceal ignorance under a cloak of high-flown yet empty prose.

There is so much anger in that outburst you wonder if Atkins should seek help but the most striking thing about it is his anger at the thought of ignorance. Is ignorance not a fact of life? Are we not ignorant of a great deal more than we know about?

Keats was 'certain of nothing except the holiness of the heart's affections and the truth of the imagination' yet science seeks to colonise the concept of truthfulness. There may be deeper truth in a page of the Book of Common Prayer than there is in a whole issue of the *British Medical Journal*. Science once assured us of the theory of the humours. Science gave us medieval phlebotomy, with its wooden lances to 'air the veins' and its leeches to suck blood from our bodies. Science has given us pollution and waste and arrogance and the Sinclair C5. Secularists need not have a monopoly on scepticism. Atkins, so quick to call religion 'evil' (he says so with a giggle) and worshippers 'foolish', was asked once by Rod Liddle if he was not being a little arrogant in his certitude. Atkins replied: 'What's wrong with arrogance if you're right?' He is on his third marriage.

The National Secular Society can be seen as the provisional wing of the British Humanist Association, which at least aspires to a code of ethics. It markets itself under the message 'How can I be happy?' accompanied by an

Our village church (regular congregation *circa* twenty) generates £8,000 a year for a diocese that has an annual deficit of £740,000. That £8,000 is in addition to what our church must raise for the building, insurance, graveyard maintenance, organ, music, candles, books, wine and wafers. How do dioceses spend the cash they are given by parishes? The Church of England has been woodwormed by the professional class, fee-charging experts who are paid more than the hard-worked priesthood. The sits-vac column in the *Church Times* advertises openings for refugee-welcome coordinators, grants and relationships directors, directors of mission, child safety officers, health and safety directors, research directors, communications enablers, evangelism enablers, ecumenical officers, community workers, youth evangelists, parish giving champions and qualified family workers. Parish congregations are treated as scurvy supplicants, told what prayers they may not utter and what they may not do with their brass rubbings. Friar Tuck lives.

image of Stephen Fry, one of the country's better known manic depressives. Go to church, dear Stephen, and say the Prayer Book's 'A General Thanksgiving'. That might cheer you more than humanism ever will.

The Humanists, who also cleave to equality, go in for a similar list of prominent supporters. All men and women are born equal but some become celebrities. Well, semi-celebrities. Quite a few on the list are obscure young comedians. Why are they there? Some may genuinely be Humanists. But I can't help suspecting others may simply have let their names be added to the list: a) to increase its street cred; b) to give them some publicity. Other prominent supporters include former *Blue Peter* presenter Janet

Ellis (what IS it with *Blue Peter?*), scruffy comedian David Baddiel, 'Sir Geoffrey Bindman QC', *Crimewatch* presenters Nick Ross and Sue Cook and hot-air balloonist Don Cameron. From his suspended wicker basket has he really never looked down and thought, 'How can all this be here?' Transplant surgeon Sir Roy Calne is on the list, as is Simon Le blinking Bon and comedians Tony Hawks and Ed Byrne. Snoozy Lord Foulkes, the Labour peer who was caught kipping in the House of Lords by the BBC's cameras, has lent his name to the enterprise. Ditto the Left's favourite sculptor Sir Anish Kapoor, former government scientist Prof. Sir David King, film director Ken Loach, Alastair Campbell's girlfriend Fiona Millar, Dame Jenni Murray (or what's left of her after her drubbing over transsexuals), slim-wristed Sandi Toksvig, *Star Trek* actor Sir Patrick Stewart and former civil servant Lady Whitaker, who explained that she was once a churchgoer but she found religion's emphasis on sin and virtue to be 'uncongenial'. The poor dear.

To belong to a church is a grand thing, as good as any London club. You get to know some neighbours, blast out a few hymns and in time develop a relationship with the priest who may help you stagger through the coming vicissitudes. Vicissitudes there most certainly will be, with or without science. Peter Atkins would scorn the expression but life hurls thunderbolts at us. It is a bold creature who reckons to face them alone.

At its best, church-going helps us to find quietness. From the highest in the land to the lowliest tramp, we can quiver before the thought of our ignorance. Even if we find it hard to believe in deity, the possibility of its presence may check our arrogance. Actively to oppose religion and its comforts seems an odd thing. You might as well protest against country walks, or puddings, or holiday-making, or love, or the tinkle of a courtyard's fountain on a summer's day.

Elders Whine

Richard Branson, bounteous bwana
to the world's little people

———————●———————

D o you remember the Man from Del Monte? He appeared in 1980s advertisements for Del Monte juice and tinned fruit. The commercials would show a farm in some dusty country. A rich hombre in a white suit approached in a sea plane or fancy car. Impecunious locals became nervous as the visitor alighted and went inside the farm building to squeeze an orange or slice a pineapple. Tension mounted and straw hats were wrung. What was the verdict from *el jefe*, this *señor muy important- ante* (who was quite possibly from one of those Western supermarkets always seeking to screw extra profits out of suppliers)? Eventually the visitor vouchsafed a curt nod. The locals were ecstatic. Hats were thrown in the air, children clapped and a donkey brayed. Up went the exuberant cry: 'The man from Del Monte. He say yes!'

You wouldn't get away with that sort of advert these days. Insufficiently egalitarian. So what made rich whitey Sir Richard Branson think he could get away with a scheme called 'The Elders'?

The man from Virgin, he say 'yes'!

Elders Whine

Bearded box-wallah Branson makes out he is a caring, sharing guy but is in fact a tight-biting businessman with an interest in globalised pay rates, international commodity prices and the Western banking system. Please don't call it exploitation but this is certainly capitalism in the raw. Branson's Virgin trains are expensive. They are airless, cramped, have stinking khazis and, like other railway operators, flush away billions of pounds in public subsidies. If any other company ran such a foul service at our expense we would pelt it with cabbages but because it is run by Branson, and because Branson has groomed his reputation even more assiduously than he does that frightful beard, Virgin is somehow given a comfortable ride. If only the same could be said for its passengers.

Branson has created for himself an image of laid-back dude, the ordinary guy, your baby-boom groover next door. He portrays himself as such an anguished altruist, open-collared and long-haired, you wonder that he even knows phrases such as 'mark-up' or 'bottom line'.

Over the years he has run his companies with flinty acumen and grabbed a packet for himself. He lives on his own Caribbean island and is a remorseless collector of phone numbers of the fashionable and mighty. When it comes to climbing, he is in the clematis league, a name dropper of the first water, vain, self-important, a prize specimen of that genus *Bastardus (patronisingae)*.

Broadcasters would normally regard the knighted boss of a public-contract transport business with suspicion. A mate of prime ministers and presidents who lands beefy government contracts yet lives abroad? *Hmm*, they'd think, *we'll give this bloke a bit of blowtorch treatment.*

He would be subjected to scrutiny on BBC2's *Newsnight*, be empty-chaired on telly's *Have I Got News for You* and mocked on Radio 4's not-so-funny *News Quiz*. When he left his luxurious home of a morning or glided in to some swanky awards dinner, he would be monstered by a Michael Crick or Louis Theroux or some such gadfly asking tricky questions. 'Three billion pounds of public subsidy for your rail business, Sir Richard – why does an alleged entrepreneur of your calibre need such handouts from the state?' we can imagine the gallant Crick shouting, trousers flapping and that cheery leer on his chops before being stiff-armed by bodyguards.

Branson is treated by many broadcasters as some sort of guru. Is it because they think he is a liberal? Yet he is no great democrat. Five days after the British people voted to leave the EU, Remainer Branson was given an easy hit on ITV's breakfast television to demand a second referendum. The electorate had not understood the gravity of its decision, we were informed. The stock market had slumped. Bank shares were in crisis. We were going to go into recession and jobs were doomed. Branson did his trademark shake of the head – a gesture that seems to say 'these things are inevitable, you fools' – and the camera dwelt on his custardy-blond fringe, teased up like pampas grass, Gloria Hunniford in a breeze.

Branson's post-referendum gloomstering made big news yet the stock market bounced back strongly, bank shares rose, growth increased and employment reached a record high. He was so comprehensively wrong, you wonder how this booby ever made a bob on investments.

Why is he so esteemed? The Beeb included him in its '100 Greatest Britons' poll – he came eighty-fifth, one behind steam-engine inventor James Watt, one in front of U2's Bono (not even British). He is frequently asked for his opinion about addiction, the media and politicians hailing him as an authority on drugs policy. Why? Because Branson sits on something called the Global Commission on Drugs, a self-appointed body of has-beens and wannabes and second-division nabobs. He is an expert because he says he is!

This commission is classic Branson: a gathering of passé meddlers, who get promoted as 'highly respected' and are set up as dispassionate authorities senior to national government. They may in fact be engaged in a campaign to liberalise drugs. Personally, I have a measure of sympathy for that – that gives away my own roots in the liberal elite – but it is so sensitive an area of public policy that it should not be decided by some drifty-minded ex record-company boss and a posse of dud ex-presidents (Switzerland, Portugal, Colombia, Malawi, Poland, Brazil, Nigeria, Greece), 'public intellectuals' (Mario Vargas Llosa, the late Carlos Fuentes) plus that nincompoop Nick Clegg.

The commission describes itself as 'a key international reference' on drugs control strategy. Key/international/reference: three meaningless words. The commission adds that it proposes 'innovative and effective policy recommendations that protect human rights, scale-up harm reduction and promote development'. Again, this means anything you want it to mean. It also says the commission 'is composed of 23 political leaders and leading thinkers from across the political spectrum'. Branson is not a 'political leader'. Is he a 'leading thinker' or 'public intellectual'? Public school O-level thicko, more like. He left Stowe at sixteen and did not attend a university.

A self-acclaiming global coterie presumes unearned moral superiority and imagines itself to stand above democratically elected politicians. Here, riddled with jargon, is what the commission says about its work:

> Using informed advocacy and quiet diplomacy, the Global Commission has redirected the conversation away from prohibition and legitimized a more balanced, comprehensive and evidence-based debate on drugs, privileging human rights, safety and public health. The Global Commission carries out this role through the yearly publication of a comprehensive, detailed, evidence-based policy report including the commission's positions, as well as other targeted reports, opinion pieces, and interviews with government officials and intergovernmental organizations, in collaboration with civil society leaders. Since its inception, the Global Commission has produced six major reports and three documentary films with visibility in thousands of news outlets around the world.

Translation: we pump out propaganda, schmooze civil servants and journalists, and hope they fall for our output.

A 'global commission' sounds important but is, again, meaningless. Its output is swallowed by editors and officials who are eager to suck up to a rich man who did a few ballooning adventures a quarter of a century ago and now brings the same egomaniacal energy to his political views. To me, the commission just looks like a bunch of desperadoes anxious to increase their brand virtue.

Branson was once given a slightly tricky time by Jon Snow on *Channel 4 News*. Snow was asking him about the safety precautions on Branson's pie-in-the-sky spaceship project. Branson, pushing his prominent muzzle close to the camera on a video link from his private island of Necker, became most indignant and told Snow he did 'not respect him' for asking such questions. My my! Sir Richard Touchy! It was an illuminating moment but Channel 4 did not pursue the matter. It might well have done had Branson been a Rightie.

Anyway, back to 'The Elders'. In 2007 Branson hit on another wheeze to promote himself and associate himself with some of the big names of international 'thought leadership'. He went to Nelson Mandela and, having observed that they shared a birthday (18 July), proposed that they mark the great day for perpetuity by creating a group called The Elders. What a greaser. Had Mandela

---

Another Branson effort was Best for Britain, a crowd-funded political movement that 'educated and empowered' people to vote tactically against Eurosceptics in the 2017 general election. It was fronted by Gina Miller, the City investor who took Theresa May's government to court over Brexit. Behind the scenes, Branson was the sugar-daddy, giving the venture £25,000 and office space. Best for Britain came to little. Miller is that remarkable thing, a person with an even bigger ego than Branson. 'I have a huge sense of responsibility,' she said at the launch of Best for Britain, throwing her hairdo from side to side for the benefit of the cameras. Miller later campaigned in Vauxhall with the Lib Dems and staged a photo opportunity, which was meant to re-create Nigel Farage's Thames flotilla before Brexit. Alas, Miller and her Lib Dem friends could find only a beached dinghy. On election night in Vauxhall, Labour Eurosceptic Kate Hoey romped to victory.

been younger he might have told the bearded creep to get lost.

Just as tribal societies had village elders who were repositories of wisdom and experience and who would from time to time guide the society into following certain directions, so, thought Branson, the international community cried out for the same. The world needed a group of gnarled Solomons who could be consulted at moments of dilemma or difficulty. The world needed him, the benevolent, blessed Branson. The Elders would be given a seat and the global population would sit at their feet, look up to their walnut-lined faces and wait, expectant, until words of sage advice croaked from their parchment-dry larynxes. The Elders have spoken. The Elders (like the man from Del Monte) say yes!

Who was going to elect these Elders? Foolish question. They would be selected – by Branson and his friend Peter Gabriel, a faded pop singer. What do you call someone who selects world authorities? The Almighty? That may be how Branson sees himself.

Branson and his angel Gabriel soon came up with a list of Elders that included former UN secretary-general Kofi Annan (he's on the Global Drugs Commission, too), ex-US President Jimmy Carter, Irish ex-President and interminable windbag Mary Robinson, Mandela's wife Graça Machel and Marrti Ahtisaari, the Finnish ex-President whose aperçus include 'wars and conflicts are caused by human beings.' Gold star for Marrti, please. The Elders were presented as an answer to global problems. They issued an annual review, which 'expressed concern' (about things such as climate change, and more recently Donald Trump) and painted their 'vision' (usually for 'cooperation' or 'solidarity' or 'safeguarding civil space' or for 'bold and decisive action', provided that decisiveness did not include anyone with non-liberal views). They were served by a clever young secretariat, which created a website encouraging activists to make their voices heard in the 'global village'.

So much effort, so slickly presented. And the world paid them almost no attention.

Poop-poop!

Toadish Ian McEwan and his desire to drive
an entire generation off the road

———————•———————

Next time they are staging *The Wind in the Willows* and looking for someone to play road-hog Mr Toad, they should audition Ian McEwan. Novelist McEwan may not be much of a stage performer – at public events he is a mumbler who rocks on his feet and plays pocket billiards – but he has the necessary arrogance. *Poop-poop!* Right up close in your wing mirror he comes. *Poop-poop! Outta my way, slowcoaches! Get off the road and milk it, you oldsters! Zoooooooom!*

It is a pity, really. Ian McEwan is in some ways a fine writer and an agreeably cerebral figure. But he showed his Toadish side with a malevolent, gleeful little speech in which he looked forward to hundreds of thousands of old people dying. He wanted them out of the way because he disagreed with them over Brexit. Let the deluded fools who voted Leave in the EU referendum die and die sharpish, he argued, so that the country could soon hold another referendum and this time reach a different verdict. He, McEwan, as a Europhile, was superior to such fools and wanted rid of them.

Poop-poop!

Aggressive driving was seen as an eccentricity back in 1908 when Kenneth Grahame wrote *The Wind in the Willows*. Rat and Mole are walking along a country road when they hear what they mistake, initially, for the drone of a bee.

> In an instant (as it seemed) the peaceful scene was changed, and with a blast of wind and a whirl of sound that made them jump for the nearest ditch, it was on them! The 'Poop-poop' rang with a brazen shout in their ears, they had a moment's glimpse of an interior of glittering plate-glass and rich morocco, and the magnificent motor-car, immense, breath-snatching, passionate, with its pilot tense and hugging his wheel, possessed all earth and air for the fraction of a second, flung an enveloping cloud of dust that blinded and enwrapped them utterly, and then dwindled to a speck in the far distance, changed back into a droning bee once more.

Road hogs are less amusing today. They sit on your tail, gun their engines and in slow traffic or at junctions glower at drivers who are delaying their progress. They want you off the road. They consider themselves superior.

When we think of road rage we probably imagine the culprits as young men with buzzcuts, some furry dice hanging over the dashboards, go-faster stripes down the side of their chariots. Or do we think of that surly young woman who gave Radio 2's Jeremy Vine such a hard time on his bicycle in the streets of London? We do not expect such cars to be driven by eggheads who have won international prizes and contribute high-brow articles to Left-leaning journals. Naively, we regard novelists as civilised bods who will take a languid approach to life. Their daily craft, after all, moves at glacial speed. The stereotype has novelists as brainy snails but it is wrong.

So it has proved with the outwardly urbane McEwan, supposedly wry observer of humanity. He is not some John Osborne or Evelyn Waugh or Anthony Burgess, raging against the powerful. Far from it. He is part of the Establishment, invited to all the best parties, his attendance being a stamp of intellectual respectability.

Has McEwan become been soured by acclaim? Or has he been spoilt by becoming too close to an elite he should be satirising? Has he made too much money? Is he too keen to be liked?

Maybe it was the end of his first marriage, a messy affair that became luridly public when the former Mrs McEwan gave her bespectacled ex a bit of what-for while he was giving one of his lofty talks at the Cheltenham Literary Festival. What a cracking event that must have been – much more entertaining than McEwan's normal homilies.

McEwan certainly made little attempt to be objective about the EU referendum result. Having watched the campaign with elevated detachment, he felt stung when the result went against his ilk. He wailed that Britain had been 'changed utterly' by the outcome. Yes, a 'progressive' novelist was railing against change. McEwan sneered against the Boris Johnsons and Michael Goves of this world. Could a novelist not just have seen it as an incredible story and a fascinating tale of ambitions and betrayals? Instead, McEwan complained that leading Brexiteers had become 'intolerant of dissent', and said he was reminded

Poop-poop!

'I'm with Jon Snow – f*** the ruling class!'

Wrapped up in Ian McEwan's hatred of the old may have been his own generation's refusal to acknowledge the years. Channel 4 newscaster Jon Snow, sixty-nine, hardly acted his age when he hurried down to the Glastonbury Festival in June 2017 to pose alongside crowds of twenty-somethings protesting against, well, anything and everything. 'F*** the Tories!' they screamed, with would-be hippie Snow allegedly joining the taunts (although he later said he had no recollection of the events). And he the son of an Anglican bishop. A top news anchor who joined a UKIP rally and snarled 'F*** Labour!' would not have been tolerated but the authorities seemed eager to turn a blind eye to Snow. Perhaps that shows who the Establishment is these days. For the record, 'radical' Glastonbury can nowadays be more expensive than 'posh' Glyndebourne. If you go in for the sort of glamping (deluxe camping) that the Snows of this world do, you can easily drop thousands of pounds. Rock on, dudes.

of politics in Germany in the 1930s. Moan, moan, wheedle, wheedle, infamy.

These foamings found an eager audience at the *Guardian* newspaper. It approves of McEwan. He is a proselytising atheist. He chants the religion of climate change. His second wife was for many years a *Guardian* journalist – she is also a judge of literary prizes. McEwan's books are regularly chosen for A-level syllabi, school pupils plopping out fealty to the 'isms' of the day, plop plop plop, like little piles of sheep droppings. Round and round our civilisation spins, in a self-enriching, self-regarding vortex, until eventually the whole bloody thing will be sucked down the plughole.

The Establishment artist is expected to man the barricades when something interesting like Brexit happens. She or he must be heard to defend the powerful, even as all this fascinating change is unfolding, change that may well upend the ruling caste. The novelist, particularly one who (so we are told from all those prizes) is so brilliant, might keep his distance from the powerful. He might also wait a year or two to see how the thing shook out, and see which leaders of society made the ripest fools of themselves.

He had been asked to speak at a gathering of concerned snoots called the Convention on Brexit, co-organised by Henry Porter, a journalist so suave he could be George Clooney's older, cleverer brother. My dears, they were all at the convention: Nick Clegg, Gina Miller, Will Hutton, Anatole Kaletsky, Alastair Campbell, Boris's loopy sister Rachel Johnson, Jonathan Freedland, Afua Hirsch, Andrew Rawnsley, Anne McElvoy, Hugo Rifkind, Evan Davis, Neal Ascherson, Frances O'Grady, Rosie

Boycott, Mariella Frostbite, Helena Kennedy, Comrade Paul Mason, Labour MP Lisa Nandy, veteran Leftie wonk Ann Pettifor and a couple of token Righties such as Kwasi Kwarteng and Michael Gove (who can never resist a fight with metropolitan Lefties). John le Carré had been persuaded to give the convention a plug. So had little Alain de Botton, a deliciously absurd self-creation – a media philosopher with a personal fortune. He said Brexit had thrown up 'large and agonising questions' and there was 'a desperate need to ask ourselves what we're trying to achieve and what the right strategy might be'. By 'we', Baby de Botton may not have meant the wider electorate of Britain who have to park their cars outside their common little houses and eat processed food from Aldi. He may have meant the elite. He may have meant the sort of people who buy avocados.

This was the event addressed by Ian McEwan; he proceeded to speak balls. When it came to Brexit, he said he was 'a denialist'. 'Almost a year on, I am still shaking my head in disbelief. I know it's not helpful, but I don't accept this near mystical, emotionally charged decision. How can it be that in a one-off vote, a third of the electorate have determined the fate of the nation for the next half-century? A gang of angry old men, irritable even in victory, are shaping the future of the country against the inclinations of its youth. By 2019 the country could be in a receptive mood: 2.5 million over-18-year-olds, freshly franchised and mostly Remainers; 1.5 million oldsters, mostly Brexiters, freshly in their graves.'

Er, what was that about 'angry old men'? Here was a sixty-nine-year-old member of the elite raging that a national election had gone against him and his ilk. His response to that loss was to relish the prospect of mass deaths among Leave voters. How did the audience of elitists react? Why, with cheers and applause.

Another person at the event demanded non-violent direct action to 'stop the Underground, stop the buses'. Serial charmer Sir Bob Geldof said that he had loved McEwan's 'rejectionism', adding: 'Anger is a great animus.' Indeed it is. Just look how it animated the country's electorate to tell the Brussels bloodsuckers to fling their fishhooks.

Where did it go wrong for Ian McEwan? Was it his friendship with the late Hitchens, a lyrical reactionary against low taste? Had Hitchens made that speech, it would have been no less provocative but it would have been entertaining and colourful. McEwan's approach was no funnier than a *Daily Express* editorial.

Was his work undone by all the prizes he kept winning, with the attendant trips to splashy dinners, with plunging necklines and the whiff of candlewax? Oh, the need to say something exciting to make good copy and impress the doe-eyed hackette. These things can corrode a writer by making him too cocky. Nothing is worse for writing good fiction. Or for driving.

He pulled the lever and swung the car round the yard and out through the archway; and, as if in a dream, all sense of right and wrong, all fear of obvious consequences, seemed temporarily suspended. He increased his pace, and as the car devoured the street and leapt forth on the high road through the open country, he was only conscious that he was Toad once more, Toad at his best and highest, Toad the terror, the traffic-queller, the Lord of the lone trail,

before whom all must give way or be smitten into nothing-
ness and everlasting night.

Foundation Coarse
The rise of boastful giving

———————•———————

The Apostle Matthew might not have thought much of Tony Blair or Michael Milken or George Clooney. They are just some of the trainee saints who have set up their own charitable foundations. The purpose: to do good works. But why do they need to publicise it so assiduously?

St Matthew's Gospel, chapter six: 'When thou doest thine alms, do not sound a trumpet before thee, as the hypocrites do . . . that they may have glory of men.' Don't parp your own cornet. Don't brag about being a good person. A modern philanthropy consultant would tell Matthew to get real. Donors today want some bang for their bucks.

To create your own foundation was once an activity limited to a tiny number of statesmen. Retiring US presidents would establish a library and that usually entailed an eponymous charity. Supporters might wish to show appreciation for the departing president as he left office. A donation to, for instance, the Harry S. Truman Presidential Library and Museum in Independence,

Missouri, or the Richard Nixon Library and Birthplace in Yorba Linda, California, would thus be in order. In due course, the late president's bones would be taken to these places and dibbled in with reverence and tasteful publicity, to attract scholars and keep the late president's ideas in circulation among academics.

Libraries look quaint next to some of the celebrity foundations found in recent times. Actor Brad Pitt started the Make It Right Foundation, helping 'communities in need' to build eco-friendly houses. Private jetter Brad and his most recent ex-wife Angelina Jolie – not so eco-friendly, they – had at least five large homes, one of which was a thirty-five-bedroomed affair in France.

Lady Gaga (popstar, m'lud) founded the Born This Way Foundation, which is devoted to helping youngsters create 'a kinder and braver world'. American television presenter Oprah Winfrey has spawned the Oprah Winfrey Foundation and the Oprah Winfrey Operating Foundation and the Oprah Winfrey Leadership Academy for Girls and more. Stand, stand, you nations with huddling masses, and ululate to Jesus for the blessed munificence of Oprah. Sometime *Dallas* actress Victoria Principal started, among other things, the Victoria Principal Foundation for Thoughtful Existence. She's deep, that Victoria. One of the Principal Foundation's prime recommendations might be 'Don't watch pap on the goggle box.' Ms Principal – and yes, she does spell it that way – also embraced the Hollywood Pledge movement in which actors and actresses affirmed their commitment to the community and to charity. Such was this movement's devotion to the common people that it organised 'an exclusive VIP launch party and beauty retreat at a private mansion in Beverly

Hills' in 2011. The New Hollywood pledge, a spin-off of that original pledge, allows young actors and lawyers to assert their inner beauty by agreeing to the following statement:

> I intend to lead by example by being the best version of myself. I am aware that I am a work in progress and I allow space for that. I strive to be a positive, loving, supportive person who is mindful of my impact on those who cross my path, intending for my accomplishments to inspire others. I also know that others' successes do not diminish my own. I continue to learn and grow, to set goals for all areas of my life so I am empowered. I strive to match my words with my actions. I am respectful of others' viewpoints and differences. I speak up for my truth, my values and for justice. I give back to my community knowing that my passions are part of my purpose. I am a shepherd, not a sheep.

Baaaaaaaa!

In some cases the linking of a cause to a well-known person makes sense. The Elton John AIDS Foundation has made it easier for Aids to be discussed sensibly and humanely in African countries that might otherwise have tried to ignore people with that disease. Sir Elton's charitable involvement comes across as genuine. But where that connection isn't there, the suspicion is that philanthropy is being used as just another form of PR.

Former footballer David Beckham puts himself about on the charity circuit. What is his motivation? Is it pure altruism? Or is it a calculated trade in which he hopes to exchange his much-publicised benevolence for a knighthood? Oh-so-'umble Becks was a likeable lad, despite those tattoos, that World Cup sending-off and a rather canny approach to his tax arrangements. He was moistly attentive to his finger-crooking memsahib, the dainty 'Posh'. Her David often spoke about his modest background, his pride in skippering England, his respect for that brute Sir Alex Ferguson ('the manager') and the adoration he felt for his children, whom we must resist regarding as cost centres in the Beckham corporate empire. All of that was sweet. Yet Becks's reputation took a hit when a newspaper published emails allegedly giving his reaction to not being given a knighthood. Raging about the committee that considers people for honours, and had apparently given him a red light, boy-next-door-wouldn't-hurt-a-flea-me-I'm-just-a-poor-ragamuffin-from-Essex Beckham apparently wrote: 'They r a bunch of c***s. I expected nothing less. Who decides on the honors [*sic*]?? It's a disgrace to be honest and if I was American I would have got something like this 10 years ago.'

Is that 'to be honest' not the cherry on the cake?

The leaked email made Beckham's 'charidee' work look like a self-serving fake. But is he the only one? The trio mentioned at the start of this section, Blair, Milken and Clooney, all have their own foundations. They may not be in the market for knighthoods – two of them, being American, would not really qualify, and Mr Blair seems to be sitting out the dubbing process or to have been omitted. But they are certainly in the market for public attention.

Michael Milken was a big shot on Wall Street and in the City of London in the 1980s. In that era of red braces and Bolly-popping and 'greed is good', junk-bonds supremo Milken was the number one pocket-stuffer – and he went to prison. The same Milken, having served his porridge, is now pushing himself round the upper-tier social circuit in the United States and Europe as a Mr Generous. He runs the Milken Family Foundation, which attempts to 'advance collaborative solutions that widen access to capital, create jobs and improve health'. How wonderful, you may think, that such a malefactor has seen the error of his ways and is now trying to do good in the world. But is the Milken Family Foundation in part designed to place Michael Milken back at the apex? Is he still, in effect, driven by a greed, this time for acclamation? Every year the Milken Family Foundation holds a 'global conference' at which top speakers from around the world are invited to take the pulpit and preach to a hall of paying customers. It is in some ways an American version of the Davos economic forum. At the last Milken global conference, entitled 'Building Meaningful Lives', speakers included Lord Mandelson and Tony Blair. The days began with yoga classes, 'to decrease stress and tension'. Over the years I have found that one way to decrease stress is to keep well away from Blair and Mandelson.

Was it Live Aid in 1985 that changed our approach to charity? Until then, giving tended to be discreet. Bob Geldof put paid to that. His Wembley concert, raising money for famine victims in Ethiopia, was a worthy cause. But it also did wonders for the performers, and for gobby Geldof himself. Comic Relief and Children in Need, similarly admirable in their original aims, have also become career-boosters for the celebrities who take part. How much are they driven by altruism? How much by desire for fame?

For one of Milken's events, attendees (who paid $50,000 a person to attend the conference) were invited to wear 'jetsetter cocktail' fancy dress and revel in a nostalgic evening about pre twenty-first-century airline travel. A donation from the evening's takings went to some cause approved of by Michael Milken. Another event offered advice to 'ultra-high-net-worth individuals' on how to teach their children about money. In the Beverly Hills Ballroom, a 'fireside chat' was held for conference ticketholders keen to be told about 'the new investment landscape' by the likes of J. P. Morgan's Jamie Dimon, Rupert Murdoch's son Lachlan, Milken himself and the president of the World Bank. Journalists, industrialists, bankers and politicians, including governors of US states, paid court at this gathering of magnificoes. Mandelson spoke at an event discussing the EU – 'How did the EU become an endangered species?' it wondered, and they certainly had the right witness in the dock for that one. Blair moderated at an event entitled 'Populism: Passing fad or new political era?' in which he made a rather subdued speech saying how ghastly it was when politicians leapt on voters' concerns and created unrest. This from the man who took us into the Iraq War. And all this was being done, please, in the name of one of capitalism's most notorious crooks, Michael Milken, all fake smiles and self-esteem, quick to tell people that a magazine had called him 'a genius'. His biography on the Milken Family Foundation website is a work of ferocious self-adoration, yet oddly it bears no mention of the fact that he went to prison.

Such an event should make a terrific target for satirists, should it not? It should be roasted by the supposedly fearless liberal newspapers of the West. But no. The Milken 'Global Conference' was reported with hushed respect.

When Tony Blair quit 10 Downing Street he did not stay in Parliament to continue to serve the people of Sedgefield. He did not go to the House of Lords to lay his experience at the use of the Upper House and its committees. He went into business, making millions from PR work and speeches and doing a few business deals on the side. He set up the 'Tony Blair Faith Foundation' (cue some plainsong, please), which aimed to 'provide practical support to combat religious conflict and extremism'. The foundation promised to 'generate new solutions' and it stated its 'values' thus: 'We are empowering, pioneering, focused on impact, resolute and independent'. He had not been so independent when it came to crawling up George Bush's back passage and staying there, the instruction allegedly given by his chief of staff to the British ambassador in Washington, DC before the Iraq War, but hey-ho, perhaps the sinner has repented.

Or had he? The Tony Blair Faith Foundation, which never did quite 'generate new solutions' to the Middle East's many religious tensions, now has its 'work' carried out by the Tony Blair Institute for Global Change. Brace yourself for more waffle. The institute aims to 'help make globalisation work for the many, not the few. We do this by helping countries, their people, and their governments address some of the most difficult challenges in the world today.' Blair is presenting himself as a mentor to the world, a paternalistic superstar who can hold the hand of Third World governments and solve their problems. What sort of egomaniacal freak thinks himself so important?

> Tony is not the only Blair with a foundation. The Cherie Blair Foundation for Women has a long list of corporate donors, both capitalist enterprises and public-sector contract bidders. The foundation's website has a photograph of our Cherie grinning manically, surrounded by black people – the memsahib dispensing largesse to People of Colour. The website, which lists a large team of employees, hails Cherie for 'generously and tirelessly giving her time and resources' to the cause. Did she write that herself?

Which leaves us George 'Clunker' Clooney, film actor but a stranger to the stage – it would be interesting to see if he was up to it. Pretty George has been paid big money to present television commercials for coffee, cars and vermouth, raising his eyebrow with aplomb. So far, so blameless. Yet he has set himself up as a figure of intellectual substance and talismanic virtue – even of political radicalism. With his lawyer wife Amal he has set up the Clooney Foundation 'to advance justice in courtrooms, classrooms and communities around the world'. It intends nothing less than to 'empower a generation' of Syrian refugees by enabling them to return to school, create an international network of 'trusted journalists, lawyers, diplomats, parliamentarians and human rights activists' to monitor trials round the world, and also to resettle Syrian and Yazidi refugees in the United States. How realistic are these projects? Are they remotely achievable? Or will they simply create a good vibe for 'Clunker' and his feminist-lawyer wife Amal, all dollied up like a baby giraffe in a frou-frou skirt?

Clooney has also set up two other charities, Satellite Sentinel Project (spying on Sudanese warlords from space

– little to report so far) and Not On Our Watch, which wrings its hands about Darfur and was set up with Brad Pitt, Matt Damon and a few other Hollywood dudes. All this altruism may give George a lovely buzz. It may also allow Amal to improve her standing in the legal world and tell Western politicians to accept more refugees. From her four luxurious homes around the globe, how can she really comprehend the anxiety influxes of refugees can cause in crowded cities?

Good works extend the Clooneys' celebrity shelf-life. They mean Amal gets to speak at the United Nations, uxorious George holding her hand. It wins the Clunkers gooey praise from *bien pensants* and – though of course this was never their intention – it wins them entrées to elected politicians, and that can't be bad for Amal's legal work, either. If you're not careful, George, she'll overtake you in the fame stakes.

But might St Matthew not have thought it all a touch blowy on the brass section?

Dismal Dons

Material greed besmirches
our college cloisters

————————•————————

You seldom hear 'ivory tower' these days. Maybe that delicate soul Prince William has banned it as part of his campaign against *objets* made from elephant tusk. 'Ivory tower' was once said about scholars, as in 'those professors in their ivory towers know nothing about real life'. The towers served a happy function, mind you: the eggheads kept to themselves rather than pushing their snouts into public affairs and showing us what chumps they were.

Why are certain profs so prominent these days? Money. The government dispenses university research funding according to various criteria, one of which is 'impact'. How much publicity has a don's work had? Has he/she had a book or article published or been on telly and has the work helped to 'influence public policy'? When classicist Mary Beard appears on BBC1's *Question Time* she may be doing so not just because she is vain but because it helps her faculty's 'impact' ratings.

The 'impact' test has become a charter for busybodies and blowhards. It discriminates against exactly the sort of academics we should be encouraging – the ones deep in their study-burrows. More money is now given to pushy soundbite artists who can get themselves on telly or flog an article to the papers or be summoned to Westminster to give emphatic evidence to a select committee. Often those engagements are engineered by universities' publicity departments, which have grown like mint – another bank of administrative jobs sucking money out of the education sector.

The public forum demands vulgar certitude, preferably expressed in words of three syllables, or four in the case of 'absolutely'. Thus is scholarship's subtlety lost and every redbrick droner tries to come up with Brian Cox soundbites. The reasonable is forced to become trenchant and demotic to create 'impact'. Dons who quietly get on with teaching undergraduates go uncherished, even though they are probably doing more for our society.

Many taxpayers, when asked to consider the point of universities, would say 'teaching youngsters'. Not Lord Stern, the technocrat who was asked by the government to review universities' Research Excellence Framework. He thought 'influence on public engagement and culture' was as important. Stern also wanted 'a new institutional level assessment to foster greater cohesiveness between academics and reward collaboration on interdisciplinary activities'. Your eyes throb when the English language is used like that.

For the Lord Sterns of this world the most important thing is 'assessment'. Each time officialdom assesses institutions it costs oodles of money, most of which goes to the swollen inspectorate/managerial class. What fun they have sucking the air between their teeth and reaching grandiose conclusions, couched in a language all their own. When more money is spent on assessments, less is available for teaching. Shrug-your-shoulders time. Teaching schmeaching. It is such an inegalitarian concept, really.

No one ever seems to question the bureaucracy when its solution to an alleged problem is 'more assessment'. Pen pushers have taken command. Scholarship has been colonised by procedural dullards in hock to 'process' and they are on astounding money. The average pay of university vice chancellors is now above £275,000 and has recently risen at 10 per cent a year. Dame Glynis Breakwell, originally a scientist, was paid £451,000 to be vice chancellor of the University of Bath (she was also on the Economic and Social Research Council – motto 'Shaping Society' – which dispenses taxpayers' money to universities). In 2009, Southampton University paid its vice chancellor £227,000. Seven, austerity-affected years later, had the salary gone down? Had it risen by the 1 per cent of many other public-sector jobs? Had it, hell. It had risen to £350,000, the current lucky recipient being Sir Christopher Snowden, whose pay is set by a senior salaries committee on which he himself sits.

A third of universities gave accommodation to their vice chancellors. Why? Could they not afford to buy their own houses? Vice chancellors were also cossetted when they went on work trips, Dame Julia Goodfellow of the University of Kent managing to spend an average of £494 a night on her hotels. Not one for Premier Inns, Dame Julia? The £269,000-a-year vice chancellor of Bedfordshire University is Bill Rammell, formerly a stodgy Labour MP and minister, Rick Stein without the flair. Rammell pocketed pay rises even while imposing cuts on his university and extracting fees from students. Furthermore, he was having a tango on the side with his Professor of Dance (she herself was trotting along on a six-figure salary); they went on international business trips together, executive class, for such perks are written into bonking Bill's, er, package.

Returning to Lord Stern's report, the second big word in his strategy document is 'cohesiveness'. As a busy-busy organiser, Stern wanted the college caste to congeal and to become something more identifiable and united. Managers love synergy. But are such things wise for university dons? There is a growing tendency to speak of them as a group – as 'academics'. This makes it easier to try to craft them into a political force, as in 'should academics boycott Trump's America?' or 'why Brexit is bad for academics'. But it may run counter to their proper instinct, which is to be single-minded and competitive scholars. Mind you, 'scholar' is now heard as seldom as 'ivory tower'. It is considered elitist.

University professors used to be notorious for their eccentricity, their singularity, their scabrous disdain for conformity. Think of Frank Bryant, the professor in Willy Russell's play *Educating Rita*, a drunken, lecherous bully but, equally, an inspiring teacher who made high demands of his students. Think of Maurice Bowra, the unpredictable, bitchy, lascivious, brilliantly well-read supremo of English literature at the University of Oxford in the middle of the twentieth century. Bowra was the one who observed that 'buggery was invented to fill that awkward hour between Evensong and cocktails'. He was also said to have been one of several dons frolicking one day at Parson's Pleasure, a nude-bathing area by the

Cherwell, when a boat of respectable ladies came rowing into view. While the other men covered their whatnots, Bowra covered his face, saying, 'I don't know about you, gentlemen, but in Oxford, at least, I am known by my face.' Can you imagine a professor doing that today? They'd be marched off to Paddington Green nick by officers from Operation Yewtree.

Bowra was a gin-addled tartar. And yet he exemplified self-pride, an independence of mind, a defiance of fashion that is crucial to scholastic achievement and sets a far better example to the young than some groover who swallows the latest trends. When I was at Trinity College, Dublin, in the 1980s, the English faculty was far from over-burdened by sanity. One lecturer held tutorials in a pub. Another was addicted to Benylin cough syrup, a third wore mad-Goth clothes, a fourth strode around the campus shouting Old Norse to the wind and at least three had barely concealed romantic hots for their undergraduates. The place was a riot. The QAA – the Quality Assurance Agency, which regulates higher education standards on the British side of the Irish Sea – would freak if it encountered such goings-on. But those English dons in Dublin inspired great affection. We looked at the offbeat spirit of those intellectual buccaneers and we were captivated. They were 'experts' but not in the modern sense, in which expertise is caged and defined, becoming tame and procedure-obeying, complying with protocols.

In the early 1980s there was still enough cavalier verve in British universities for historian Norman Stone to write a withering obituary of a possibly over-vaunted colleague, E. H. Carr. Stone's signed article in the *London Review of Books* was a humdinger, accusing appeaser-turned-quasi-Marxist Carr of numerous flaws. It was written with characteristic Stone brio – plus the odd factual inaccuracy – and it was naughty, exciting, crackling with intellectual energy. Can we imagine today's drably orthodox *London Review of Books* allowing a Right-winger such as Stone to fire torpedoes against a revered sage of the Left? There was also a time when Cambridge professor Eric Griffiths could earn the admiration of Fleet Street diary columns by being peppery to his fellow collegians. English don Griffiths is said to have wandered into a feminist consciousness-raising meeting at Trinity College to enquire, 'Is there anyone here who can sew on a button for me, please?' Griffiths, in his heyday, was known for blasting opera out of the windows of his rooms in college and encouraging undergraduates to drink gin and tonic from pint mugs. Good for him. A don who tried that today would soon be disciplined. In 2015, Prof. Tim Hunt, septuagenarian biochemist and Nobel Prize laureate, was forced to resign from University College London after attempting some bumbling, mildly chauvinist humour during a speech to science journalists in South Korea. His ill-advised but innocuous remarks created a stir on Twitter and in this age of executive paranoia he was doomed from that moment. The complaints had nothing to do with academic malpractice. The rumpus was driven simply by political correctness, UCL oozing satisfaction afterwards that Hunt's departure was 'compatible with our commitment to gender equality'. A top don had stepped an inch on the wrong side of the 'commitment to gender equality' line and that was the end of him.

Another busy day at the annual conference of the
National Union of Teachers

As they become this homogenised blob – the 'academic world' – so have their politics conformed. For years it has been plain that the National Union of Teachers is the *Guardian* letters page made flesh. And the Adam Smith Institute recently found that 80 per cent of British university lecturers were Left-wing. So much for the diversity that almost all universities say they wish to encourage.

We are losing something of the notion of pure learning, which is now called 'research' (that word has a more utilitarian flavour). Value is something which bureaucrats such as Lord Stern think they can measure. Mind you, they first need to understand his instructions on doing that measuring. His report stated:

In order to gain an appreciation of impacts across all disciplines, we propose that institutions should be required to submit a minimum of one impact case study in each Unit of Assessment (down from a minimum of two in REF2014). We considered that the institution could have a modest amount of flexibility to vary where case studies could be submitted – between 10 and 20% of their total submissions – by transferring impact case studies between Units of Assessment. However, our main recommendation is that all institutions submitting to the REF should be required to submit some 'institutional' level impact case studies which arise from multi- and interdisciplinary and collaborative work, which could cross several Units of Assessment. Institutional level case studies would be evaluated by a specialist institutional assessment panel, discussed further below.

No wonder universities need so many administrative staff – they are all trying to work out what central officialdom wants. This is a power grab not by scholars but by administrators, compliance officers, hoop-jumpers, form-fillers, squeezing the fun out of universities and strangling initiative and spontaneity and intellectual zest. The result is fewer Bowras, more Rammells. This is not progress.

Did impact assessments encourage an Oxford physicist, Prof. Joshua Silver, to report Home Secretary Amber Rudd to the police for a 'hate incident' after she gave a speech at the 2016 Conservative Party conference? Silver, who is apparently well regarded in the field of spectacle lens research, was already angry about the EU referendum result. When he heard that Rudd might ask firms to publish details of their non-British workforces, he decided to stand on his hind legs and balance a beach ball on his nose. As it turned out, the pre-speech report of Rudd's speech, which Prof. Silver saw, was inaccurate. Her actual speech contained no such passage and Rudd merely said that she hoped we could reach the point where foreign workers were 'not taking jobs British workers could do'.

Prof. Silver was in such a rush that he did not watch the Home Secretary's speech. That did not stop him proceeding with his complaint to West Midlands police who, having been told (by Home Secretary Rudd!) that they should list every allegation of a hate crime that came their way, duly licked their stubby pencils and made an official note of the academic's complaint.

This Oxford professor, in some ways a very clever man, put his stupidity beyond doubt when he agreed to go on the BBC's *Daily Politics* programme to be interviewed by Andrew Neil. Presenter Neil duly dismantled him, as a skilled diner will remove a cooked prawn from its jacket. Few who watched the interview will have afterwards thought, *Gosh, the University of Oxford must be an impressive place if it has dons of that calibre.* Quite the opposite. But it will have all been good for the prof's impact assessment.

The 'hate crime' gambit was turned on its head when another professor, Nicholas Boyle from the University of Cambridge, wrote a shrieky article for the *New European* website – and duly found himself reported for racial hatred. Prof. Boyle, Emeritus Schröder Professor of German, wrote that:

The referendum vote does not deserve to be respected because, as an outgrowth of English narcissism, it is itself disrespectful of others, of our allies, partners, neighbours, friends and, in many cases, even relatives. Like resentful ruffians uprooting the new trees in the park and trashing the new play area, 17 million English, the lager louts of Europe, voted for Brexit in an act of geographical vandalism.

This provoked Robin Tilbrook, leader of the English Democrats party, to report the Boyler to the police in Essex for a 'hate incident' (logged under hate-crime reference 42/17384/17). Tilbrook claimed that there was 'no doubt he was meaning to be offensive to the English nation. As an Englishman I am offended by such a tirade by a person who is supposed to be and is paid to be a role model for students. Attacking the English is just as much "racist" as attacking other groups.' You may not be entirely surprised to learn that Mr Tilbrook never heard any more of the matter.

> The British Academy is officially a charity although it is bunged some £30 million of public money a year. It acts as unofficial trade union of humanities thinkers and does so from swish offices on Carlton House Terrace, near Whitehall. You don't see many elbow-patched jackets and bicycling bluestockings there. Its staff are very much members of the technocratic lobbying elite.
>
> Where once the academy might have administered college exchanges, run a few overseas institutes, acted as an umbrella club for scholars and generally settled for a bookish existence by organising symposia about Milton or Shakespeare, now it immerses itself in politics and public affairs. It waffles about 'creating frameworks for international networking'. It has its own 'strategic framework', which talks,

among other things, about 'delivering global leadership in research'. Naturally, it is in a lather about Brexit. The academy has its own 'foreign secretary', Ash Amin from the University of Cambridge, who put out an official statement making various demands of the government to prevent Britain losing 'international influence'. Here was an organisation, which is given millions of pounds by the government, using some of that money on . . . lobbying the government.

Amin's devotion to the continuance of British influence abroad must be taken for the principled internationalism he would no doubt tell us it was. But we can note from the academy's biographical notes that

> Professor Amin is known for his work on the geographies of modern living: cities and regions as relationally constituted; globalisation as everyday process; the economy as cultural entity; race and multiculture as a hybrid of geopolitics and vernacular practices. He has held Fellowships and Visiting Professorships at a number of European Universities.

One of British intellectualism's fishier items is A. C. Grayling, a mane-topped oddity who is the poor person's Richard Dawkins. Grayling is a virulent atheist and pro-European. Those things often go together. God-hating Euro-zealots recoil from the mystery of religious worship but kneel down before the altar of Brussels. Perhaps they like the certainty of cold, legal print. Perhaps it is a sense of their own higher calling, Europe's clerical Brahmins seeing themselves as demi-gods. Yesterday's Jesuits are today's Europhile professionals.

Grayling is a staunch Labour supporter, compulsively tweeting to kick out the Tories and get in that nice Mr Corbyn. I doubt Corbyn would like the man. He is, after all, both a user and provider of expensive private education, which Momentum would happily obliterate. The product of Falcon College, Rhodesia, he has sent children of his own to independent schools and now runs the New College of the Humanities, which charges undergraduates £18,000 a year, twice the rate of most British universities. The college is based in Bloomsbury, that central London area haunted by pioneer patronising bastards Virginia Woolf and J. M. Keynes; not that rationalist A. C. would ever admit to believing in wraiths. New College has the flavour of an American private college and attracts rich kids from the Continent. Grayling thus has a financial interest in fighting Brexit, because it has placed uncertainty over the numbers of foreign students who will be admitted to Britain. New College created a stir when it was founded because it was so nakedly a competitive presence in the universities sector and was funded by various investors including venture capital, opulent private funds and a backer from Switzerland. Guardianistas gasped that a Leftie such as Grayling should be extracting such large sums from students. His big draw was a line-up of celebrity lecturers who included Dawkins, Christopher Ricks, David Cannadine and token Rightie Niall Ferguson. They would only make occasional visits but they would be feted and garlanded and lauded and, most of all, PAID! The great redistributionist Grayling was up to his oxters in capitalist competition – naked, red-clawed evolution.

Grayling has been called 'the brains of Remain'. Letters, articles, broadcast interviews and learned polemics have all been fired off to proclaim his opposition to Brexit. *It's a 'coup'! It is all going to go wrong, just you see! Pleeeeease let it go wrong! Let it take a generation,* he declared, *but we would have to return to the bosom of Mother Brussels.* At one point he was so angry about Brexit that he said the nation might well have to go on a general strike to ensure that the government saw sense.

Grayling is the author of many books, including one called *The Future of Moral Values.* Since you ask, he has been divorced once and is currently separated from wife number two.

Gimme Gimme

The professionalisation and
diminishment of charity

———————•———————

There used to be the Poppy Appeal and Alexandra Rose
Day and maybe a collection for the local hospital
friends group. That was pretty much it for the year. Rattle-
rattle went the collection tins. Genteel folk would invite
passers-by to donate a few bob. In the evening, they might
go door-to-door, making it a neighbourly activity. The
money was only part of the point. Charity days reminded
us that some unlucky souls were in trouble and needed
our solidarity.

Those flag days were special occasions and people thus
responded warmly, volunteering and giving. That helped
to create communal bonds. If you hold a charity day
every other week, helpers will eventually have to be paid.
Charity will stop being something that seeps upwards
from a community. It will become professionalised and
just another job. Which is what happened.

At some point in the last couple of decades, professionals barged on to the charity turf and started to designate
this day and that for particular 'good causes' (often with a

political flavour). Not just days, either. Soon we had weeks and months being fenced off – it was the charity world's equivalent of the Enclosure Acts. The word 'charity' started to be replaced by 'Third Sector'. Causes acquired chief executives, as though they were profit-making concerns. Trustees became directors. The volunteers who used to shake those rattling tins became tabarded chuggers and instead of creaky Private Godfreys they were now energetic youngsters paid the minimum wage on zero-hours contracts to operate as a hit squad on high streets. They waved their clipboards in your face and said, 'Buddy, can I grab a second of your time to ask you a few questions?' My son did charity fundraising for a while. It was high-pressure sales work; few recruits lasted more than a month.

Charity has lost its sense of community – comradeship, if you like. It has become less about getting to know the people on your road and more like double-glazing salesmanship. Where once we might have stuffed a tenner into the tin, now we are asked to sign up to a 'giving plan' via direct debit. After an encounter with chugging gangs, few of us feel positive about the charity they represent.

Occasional charity fundraisers were eclipsed by 'awareness days'; 4 January became World Braille Day, 7 February Safer Internet Day, 27 February the start of Fair Trade Fortnight and 26 April Take Our Daughters (and now Sons, too) to Work Day. The causes were often designated 'International' and tended to be as much about political education as old-fashioned alms. Awareness days are exploited by hangers-on: public relations advisers, charity careerists, journalists. Lazy news editors can jump on an awareness day and fill a programme or a few pages with uncontroversial puffery for the cause in question.

A radio programme linked to Deaf Awareness Week? Maybe not such a great idea. But International Dawn Chorus Day (1 May) – yes, let's tweet that, ho ho. And how about World Thinking Day (22 February)? Um, anyone got any bright ideas?

Awareness days are popular with press officers because they can pump out press releases, thus justifying their salaries. Companies with a reputational problem can serve public penance by sponsoring an awareness-day reception at somewhere like the Houses of Parliament, just to Show How Much They Care. It will cost a bit but shriving has always involved handing over a few crowns. Third Sector executives can point to drinks receptions as evidence of the networking thrust they have brought to their charity. And the politicians, oh the politicians, they love awareness days. They can hashtag like maniacs. They can present themselves as having a soft side. Moral one-upmanship soon follows. During broadcast interviews they can pause and say, 'Today, of all days, my opponent should hang his head in shame . . .' Awareness days are made for single-issue vote chasers.

The United Nations has set itself up as the arbiter of awareness days. It lends its imprimatur to numerous days that have taken the seed of charity and, in some examples, made it nakedly political. Others are just odd. Here are just a few 'International Days' designated by the UN:

22 February – International Mother Language Day, to promote cultural diversity.

29 February – World Day of Social Justice.

1 March – Zero Discrimination Day.

24 March – the snappily entitled International Day for the Right to the Truth concerning Gross Human Rights Violations and for the Dignity of Victims.

22 April – International Mother Earth Day.

21 May – World Cultural Diversity Day.

21 June – all say 'ohm' now, it's International Yoga Day. Twang go a million hamstrings.

30 June – International Asteroid Day (are asteroids not 'interplanetary'?).

1 July – International Day of Cooperatives.

16 November – International Day for Tolerance.

21 November – World Television Day.

29 November – International Day for Solidarity with the Palestinian People.

11 December – International Mountain Day, to raise awareness of people who live in mountains and of the role of mountains in providing food and water, etc., etc.

International Women's Day in March leans on world leaders (the sort who are already feminists, usually) to 'pledge gender parity'. Other worldwide promotional efforts include World Wetlands Day (2 February), World Orphan Week (begins 6 February), World Kidney Day (8 March), World Poetry Day (21 March), World Down Syndrome Day (21 March also) and World Theatre Day (27 March). Clear your throats on 3 May for World Asthma Day, give a puff to World No Smoking Day on 31 May and raise your left hand for International Lefthanders Day on 13 August. Try to remember 21 September's World

Alzheimer's Day, and, laydees and gentlemen, the big one, the glamorous one, the one you've all been waiting for, World Town Planning Day (8 November). So many days, so much to 'be aware' about that it becomes quite exhausting.

Westminster Hall, an offshoot of the House of Commons, has endless debates about these various issues and other Days or Weeks or Months that have been marked out by some grievance front. Lobbyists descend, wine-and-nibbles receptions are held, press conferences arranged. Frenetic activity keeps hundreds of Third Sectorites in their congenial jobs. What good it does to the unfortunate people who suffer from the relevant diseases or disadvantages, one knows not. Awareness days and weeks are run for the convenience of the elite that organises them.

Quite apart from the United Nations commemorations, Britain has its own special days and weeks. These range from the noble to the commercially opportunistic and include:

28 January – National Storytelling Week.

 7 February – National Marriage Week.

20 February – National Chip Week.

 1 March – National Bed Month, organised by those bright sparks at the Sleep Council.

 1 March – Start of Vegetarian Month.

26 March – National Salt Awareness Week.

April – National Pet Month.

12 May – National Doughnut Week.

15 May – British Sandwich Week.

18 May – Be Nice to Nettles Week.

16 May – Walk to School Week.

23 May – Noise Action Week.

16 June – Day of the African Child

18 June – Recycle Awareness Week

25 June – National Incest Week. Sorry, let me type that again. National Insect Week.

6 July – Children's Art Day, when we can all stare hard at some splodge and say, 'Well DONE, Jemima!'

September – National Organic Month. Total rot.

13 September – Roald Dahl Day.

October – Black History Month.

7 October – not only National Poetry Day but also World Smile Day, though World Simile Day might be more apposite.

9 October – National Curry Week; also Seed Gathering Sunday, organised by the Tree Council.

17 October – Child Poverty Day and the start of both National Parents' Week and National Baking Week.

2 November – National Stress Awareness Day. Organisers v frazzled.

21 November – Anti-Bullying Week.

30 November – Computer Security Day.

2 December – Abolition of Slavery Day.

There are ribbons and wristbands to be had. Each cause has its colours. Ace birdwatcher Bill Oddie might find his feather-spotting talents tested by the multiplicity of charity awareness liveries. A triple-striped blue, white and pink wristband or ribbon signifies that the wearer is rooting for those suffering parental alienation syndrome. A blue paisley ribbon is for thyroid disease. Plain blue can be alopecia but it might equally be for those struck down by gout, hurricane damage, rectal cancer or those keen on Save the Music. A magenta ribbon may indicate an active feminist or an active pro-lifer. You don't want to mix up those two. Grey ribbons are for brain tumours or for mental illness or Parkinson's, among others. Green may mean anything from Save Darfur to manic depression or recycling. Someone wearing an orange ribbon may be showing that they support racial tolerance and cultural diversity, or that they support Jewish settlements in the Gaza strip.

The JustGiving website describes itself as a 'tech-for-good company'. It channels donations to good causes, allowing people to support a charity at the click of a button, but what they may not realise is that some 6 per cent of the donated value is pocketed by JustGiving. 'We charge a fee,' conceded JustGiving, but 'all of this fee is re-invested into building innovative new tools to make giving better for everyone.' Is it? In one year alone, JustGiving spent £10 million on staff costs on some sixty-five employees, the head of the company being paid roughly £200,000.

The enterprise, founded in 2001 by lawyer Zarine Kharas and Anne-Marie Huby, charity director, not only creams off millions a year from altruistic giving but also charges charities to be part of its operation.

Wolff at the Door

Design is politicised

———•———

London's Olympic Games were terrific. The stadium was built on time. A forlorn part of east London was revitalised and the country pulsated with patriotism. After Somali-born Mo Farah won two gold medals in the athletics, Brits of all persuasions and none felt a prickle of pride as our national anthem was played. Even British National Party miseries may have felt a tear lurk at the back of their tattooed skulls as the camera moved from Farah's fine, serious face to the swirling Union flag.

One or two Righties grumbled about the opening ceremony written by Frank Cottrell Boyce and directed by Danny Boyle. The four-hour show, 'Isles of Wonder', was a pottage of history, music and hammy humour. It included Mr Bean, 'Abide with Me', the Queen apparently parachuting into the stadium and a messy theatrical tribute to the National Health Service. Tory MP Aidan Burley attacked the ceremony as 'multicultural crap'; Burley is no longer an MP.

For the fortnight of those Olympics, Britain was a happy place. It felt sated, not so much by all the medals our Olympians won as by the sportsmanship; there was neither a terrorist atrocity nor some administrative cock-up. If you had to describe the mood of the country you might have reached for something like 'ripe'. There was a contented, tubby, summery plumpness in the air. Curvaceous. Globular.

All of which made Wolff Olins, designers of the London 2012 official logo, look a bit daft. Five years earlier, in exchange for £400,000, Wolff Olins devised a design that was jagged and edgy – that being their idea of the Olympic spirit. The four digits of the 2012 date were cut-outs that had been jumbled together at weird angles. Some said it looked like Marge Simpson engaged in what tabloid newspapers call 'a sex act'. Others felt it resembled a chopped-up swastika. There was certainly a troubling hint of the old Waffen SS badge. The competence of the draughtsmanship seemed a bit dicey. Did the shadows behind the numbers conform to a single light source? There was a lack of generosity, an absence of *give* in its art. The only curvy thing was the time-honoured symbol of the Olympic Games, five linked circles. Everything else was so sharp, angular, aggressive – ostentatiously ugly.

The public went 'yuck'. The logo was greeted with mockery and raspberries. Several people with epilepsy had nasty turns after watching an animated version of the logo. Ken Livingstone, then mayor of London (and a man normally quite interested in swastikas), said he wouldn't have paid the designers a penny. Parliamentarians called for the logo to be scrapped. Petitions were signed and petitions, of course, were ignored. Petitions! They're even more vulgar than plebiscites.

Brian Boylan, chairman of Wolff Olins, ducked below

the radar, dodging journalistic enquiries. Brother Boylan, a member of the New Labour quangocracy and a chum of Sir Nicholas Serota, was very much an Establishment aesthete. He was a founding board member of Tate Modern, involved with the Whitechapel Gallery and the Serpentine Galleries in London, and associated with Herzog & de Meuron, the Swiss architects who turned the Bankside power station into Tate Modern. For years this bespectacled, designer-T-shirted baldie had told us what was cool and what was not. He had been involved in the branding of 'Cool Britannia' at the start of the Blair Terrors and he had been on the board of the Commission for Architecture and the Built Environment. Suddenly he found himself exposed to public criticism. Nasty, burning populism: it was like taking a chef's blowtorch to marshmallows. Oucheroo, Brian didn't like that. Dive, dive, dive!

It was left to the Games's supremo, Sebastian Coe – looking faintly seasick – to insist that the logo was 'a brand we genuinely believe in'. Coe's commercial director, Chris Townsend, said that 'the key thing is our sponsors love it, our staff love it, our stakeholders love it'. Clock those priorities. The 'stakeholders' plainly did not include the British public whose taxes were paying more than £9 billion for the Games. They thought the logo was horrible.

There was puzzlement that Coe & Co. on the Games organising committee had approved the logo. Should they not have told the creatives at Wolff Olins to clean their red spectacles and come up with something better? How many cans of super-strong cola had the designers downed when they came up with that bonkers symbol? Had they been sleep-deprived for a week? But maybe the compliant attitude of the committee should not have been a surprise. Wolff Olins, remember, had been paid £400,000 for its logo. If the sum had been closer to £4,000 or even £40,000, the committee's non-designer members might have felt readier to say, 'Hang on a moment, that's rubbish'. But Wolff Olins were too posh to be pushed.

Marketing people love to patronise us with silly mascots. Think Gaz and Leccy, those not so adorable japesters who publicise Smart Energy. The London Olympics and subsequent Paralympics also had two mascots, characters called Wenlock and Mandeville. These were long, sausage-shaped and had a single eye in their large heads. There is no easy way to say this: they looked like penises. They were designed by a company called Iris, selected unanimously after a bidding process that started with hundreds of firms (Lord knows how dreadful their ideas were). Iris allegedly worked on the design for twenty months. The public had a chance to buy Wenlock and Mandeville toys – but ran in the other direction. Toymaker Hornby over-ordered so many that prices were slashed by 85 per cent in an effort to shift the merchandise. A profits warning followed and Hornby shares slumped by a third.

It is the same in restaurants. Diners are more likely to complain in a greasy-spoon café ('Can you make these baked beans hotter, Marjorie?') than they are at the Savoy Grill ('Waiter, this Dingley Dell pork tenderloin, braised pork cheeks, spiced apple and baby carrots doesn't contain enough adjectives'). There is something innately condescending in costliness. The condescension is in the vendor, who thinks his product wildly chi-chi, rather than the customer, who may simply be having a splurge. Take those expensive wristwatches found at Swiss airports – tens of thousands of pounds for a Breitling or a Rolex or whatever. How can any wristwatch cost more than a Porsche? Yet manufacturers claim 'our brand is worth that'.

'Brand' once referred to the marks that were sizzled into the rump of a cow to help farmers identify livestock. Now it is used to describe the name of some overpriced product.

Back at the London 2012 Olympics, commercial director Townsend claimed that he was happy with Wolff Olins's jagged logo. 'We knew it was bold, we knew it would get a reaction.' Ah, 'bold': that defensive trigger word means 'too daring and high-falutin' for you plebs to appreciate'. Designers are people who Know Better than the little people. And if you are designing the logo for an Olympics committee that is partly dependent on a Labour government that fancies itself as radical, well, clever old you. You have played the game. You have flicked a V-sign at ordinary taste and have made the Volvo-socialist minister feel she is living the cultural sub-Marxism dream. Screw the bourgeoisie. And where shall we send the VAT invoice?

Brand-design company Wolff Olins operates under the promise that it is 'firmly on the side of the individual', an ingeniously meaningless phrase. 'The individual' could well be the designer and not the client. Olins was founded in 1965 to 'help organisations shake off their corporate camouflage and take their place in the world', which again is artfully waffly, given that their place in the world might be a lowly one. As for 'corporate camouflage', that is precisely what brand managers such as Olins are creating.

In the event, the London Olympics logo was not seen as 'slightly off centre' but as plain messy, ineffective, adolescent and nasty, both by the public and by design professionals. *Design Week* readers' comments ranged from 'unforgivable abomination' to 'atrocious, exceedingly cheap', 'too clever by half' and 'it all smacked of politics'.

London's Design Museum opened in 1989 to examine problem-solving in manufacturing. It was hijacked by ideologists. In 2004, industrialist James Dyson resigned from the trustees, no longer able to stomach the dumbing-down of the museum's noble purpose. Early shows looked at the work of people such as Victorian railway builder Isambard Kingdom Brunel and geodesic dome inventor Buckminster Fuller (d. 1983). The focus was on serious engineering. With the arrival of Alice Rawsthorn as curator in 2001, that changed. Rawsthorn, a former media editor at *Campaign* magazine, was more gripped by the design of glossy-magazine typography, film credits and Constance Spry's flower-arranging. She mass-marketed the museum and got in sponsors. Dyson argued that 'the museum has become in thrall to making design inclusive – an awful, trendy mantra for which the only measure is visitor figures'. Rawsthorn was only in charge until 2006 but the damage was done. Recent Design Museum exhibitions have been about women's fashion power, Christian Louboutin shoes and photographs of urban Africa. Rawsthorn went on to become a trustee of the Arts Council, a trustee of the Council-funded Whitechapel Gallery, and a judge of the Turner Prize, BAFTA's awards, the PEN history book prize and the Aga Khan Award for Architecture. She was a member of the government's advisory panel on BBC charter renewal and has also spoken at the World Economic Forum in Davos.

*

This obsession with ugliness: where does it come from? Fashion designers (like architects) are weirdly attracted to the harsh and the miserable. They go out of their way to slash and offend – you can even now buy jeans that are pre-ripped. We should hardly be surprised that our fellow citizens are so aggressive: they are mirroring the aesthetics thrust on them by top-dollar stylists.

To possess beauty in the past you had to be young or rich. The young had their looks. Older people, if rich, could buy objects or clothes that were beautiful. This offended the baby-boomers' sense of egalitarianism, and so it became fashionable to flaunt grunginess.

High fashion often seems exactly that – high – when magazines run heroin-chic photo-shoots. Skinny models are told to adopt glum expressions in poses that make their legs look wonky. There is an active effort to project awkwardness. One example: the *Sunday Telegraph*'s *Stella* magazine of 23 April 2017 had a robotic-looking model showing off clothes in an empty swimming pool and on a tennis court. 'Off duty for relaxed weekends,' ran the copy. Relaxed? The poor woman just looked zoned out, exhausted, wearing the sort of clothes you might find on a hobo. The Home Counties matrons who read the *Sunday Telegraph* must have been perplexed. Open *Vogue* magazine and you are likely to find models with dark rings under their eyes, anaemic complexions and the haunted look of underfed whippets. Where is the joy? Is it too much to ask people parading fiendishly expensive clothes to look just a little bit chuffed with life? During catwalk shows at London Fashion Week the front-row dahlings – with that sunglassed misery

Anna Wintour in their midst – pout and scowl almost as much as the models. Is this angst an affectation or are they really so spoilt that they cannot see how lucky they are?

Socialist fashion designer Vivienne Westwood first won fame for her bondage-chic designs for the Sex Pistols – chains and safety pins and nose rivets. For years she made big profits from a Left-wing shtick, creating clothes and jewellery – some of it modestly spelling out her name – associated with political movements such as nuclear disarmament and climate-change control. Punk queen Westwood, so-called anti-Establishment doyenne, accepted a gong from the System and became Dame Vivienne. On the day she went to Buckingham Palace to receive that honour she omitted to wear any underpants. Accept the Queen's hospitality, but then let it be known you were ventilating your pudendum. Sorry about the swarm of bluebottles, your Maj. Ah, there ain't nothing like a dame.

The Westwood image as a virtuous Leftist was mottled in 2011 when she had to pay £350,000 to the Inland Revenue after it was found that she had underestimated the value of her brand. It could happen to the best of us. She also has an offshore company in tax-efficient Luxembourg. Perhaps she was designing a range of grey socks for all those tax-avoidance lawyers who live there. And yet, as a noisy supporter of the Green Party, she wanted the rest of us sentenced to life in a higher-tax Britain.

Dame Vivienne once wore a T-shirt saying, 'I AM NOT A TERRORIST please don't arrest me'. For greater accuracy she should perhaps wear a T-shirt saying, 'I AM A CAPITALIST, TAX-AVOIDING, STINKING

HYPOCRITE please don't take my Left-wing posing seriously'. The Greens, to their credit, told the gurning termagant to hop it.

Boutique hotels, likewise, suffer from this aversion to gorgeousness. Boutique hotels are for people who consider themselves too good to stay in 'ordinary' four-star hotels. They have ill-lit corridors down which you stub your toes and clonk your bonce when you head to bed. They place a premium on design, not comfort or cosiness. Cosiness! The very word 'cosy' is sneered at by the high-falutin'.

Boutique hotels have bullet-hard sofas and beds, bars where it is impossible to read a newspaper, desk clerks who think they are on the catwalk and bathroom-tap controls so hard to master, you end up burning your bottom in the shower. Juxtaposing bare brickwork and untreated or salvaged wood with over-the-top velvets and baroque chairs: that's the boutique-hotel look. Some find it eclectic. The rest of us think 'what a mess'.

The first boutique hotel was Morgans in New York. Co-owner Steve Rubell claimed it was going to be as different from a normal hotel as a boutique was from a department store. Got you, Steve: it was going to cost more. Rubell's partner, Ian Schrager, liked to fill his hotel lobbies with pouting luvvies who would sit there, wearing black, looking bored but superior. Did they never go and do a day's work? Only little people have routine jobs, perhaps. The Rubell–Schrager formula was soon being copied in London and elsewhere. London's Bayswater had a place called the Hempel, named after designer Anouska Hempel (Lady Weinberg to you and me). It was minimalist chic, white walls, sliding doors, gizmos at every turn, as friendly as cold steel. A friend of mine stayed there on his wedding night. The marriage lasted a year.

Boutique hotels claim to offer guests individualism – we are all so deserving of exceptionalism, darlings. How exhaustingly they strain for effect, be it the impala-pelt rug on the floor or the of-the-moment sound system so convoluted you can play the latest acid house music and get the lights to throb in time to the beat – but blow me if you can find Radio 3 or a packet of custard creams to keep you going at elevenses.

In the early 1990s I lived for a few months at the Gramercy Park Hotel, New York. Wonderful place. It hadn't changed for decades. Its concierge was as bulbous-nosed as W. C. Fields and called everyone 'Mac'. The bellboys were into their sixties, with accents from a Capone film and a knack of palming tips without anyone noticing. Its restaurant served club-style grub served off silverware from the 1920s. My suite had a deep, oatmealy sofa and chairs, a telly in the corner, windows you could open, a deep bath with ocean-liner taps, proper writing paper and a fridge for my own beers. The corridors were plain, utilitarian, calm. I went back recently. Disaster. The place had been boutiqued with a Renaissance-revival refurb. W. C. Fields and his creaking bellboys had gone and the concierge was now some unguented, twenty-something dandy who kept admiring his jawline in a mirror and knew the square root of nothing. The old bar, once a fine place to sink your snout into a dimpled tumbler of bourbon, was all sawtooth chandelier, poncy nibbles, prices that seemed to be three times what they had been and a clientele more keen to be seen than to sink consoling wets. Warhols polluted the walls. Designer Julian Schnabel

– schneery Schnabel – had even left his own fingerprints imprinted on some of the brass fittings. I fled.

Boutique hotels abjure cosiness, regarding that as bourgeois, twee, way below them. They want constantly to challenge your aesthetic and assert their trendiness. All you probably want to do is flop into bed for a decent night's kip. Ring down to the front desk and ask a boutique hotel to send up a Horlicks and they'll think you're asking for an East European tart.

And not a Corby trouser press in sight.

What a Comedian
Steve Coogan, not so jovial funny-man

———————————•———————————

Money, money, money: Steve Coogan loves it. He poses as a striver for the poor but old-fashioned spondoolicks also motivate libidinous, Tory-hating Steve.

Before Coogan claims this is another intrusive slur by the press he so loudly detests – he was prominent in the Left's 'Hacked Off' campaign against Fleet Street – he admits to this money fixation. His autobiography, *Easily Distracted*, keeps detailing how much he is paid, how rich he is, how well he has done for himself with his Aston Martins and other gleaming roadsters and his television fame and his success with the 'birds' (as he calls them). He reports that one evening, in his desire to be both rich and rebellious, he double-booked himself. He agreed to do a 'corporate gig' at the start of the evening – a comedy routine for private clients for which he would be paid thousands – and later that same night a 'left-wing, right-on gig'. When the first event kept being delayed he realised he was not going to be able to do both. 'I had to make a choice,' he says, 'so I went with the people who were paying me the big cheque, not the trendy lentil-eaters.'

The young Steve Coogan waits for his school bus

Another time, this Thatcher-detesting, Reagan-hating Mancunian was wrestling with his conscience. Should he follow his political beliefs or seek a career in London in the entertainment mainstream? 'I had to go where the money was,' shrugs Coogan, the man who fronted a 'For the Many Not the Few' Labour rally days before the 2017 general election.

There is no need to invade Coogan's privacy to analyse his character. He does that himself in *Easily Distracted*. It starts with eighty-five pages of narcissism as he takes the reader through his successes, dropping the names of comedy associates we are presumably meant to recognise. I hadn't heard of half of them. In addition to *Spitting Image* and Alan Partridge, which was partly the creation of Armando Iannucci and Patrick Marber, Coogan worked on Iannucci's news-bulletin spoof *On the Hour*. More recently he co-wrote and co-starred with Dame Judi Dench in *Philomena*, a film about a mother's search for a child she was forced to adopt. Dame Judi receives just six mentions in the entire book.

Dwelling on the importance of 'total honesty' in comedy, Coogan says he no longer cares what people think of him – unless, presumably, they are journalists. The fifty-two-year-old declares: 'I've learned late in life to understand the beauty of thoughts and reflections. I've taught myself to formulate sophisticated thoughts and it's taken a long time. I'm trying to find truths that are under-represented on screen, to embrace nuance and

> Brexit has made life tricky for alternative comics, so many of whom took the Establishment view that the EU was wonderful. Mockney Marcus Brigstocke, well-concealed patrician and stalwart of BBC Radio 4's *Now Show*, was amazed when non-London audiences started booing his anti-Brexit routines, some walking out in protest.

ambiguity.' Good old 'nuance'. It never fails.

Stephen Coogan was born in October 1965 to a church-going, Roman Catholic family in Middleton, Lancs. He describes his family as 'lower middle-class' but they seem to have been reasonably affluent. His father, now retired, was an IBM computer engineer and member of the local Round Table. He drove a Morris Oxford, later a Volvo. Stephen's mother did not go out to work. The Coogans were careful with their money, as any family with six children might be, but in 1977 they splurged £500 (£3,000 in today's money) on an *Encyclopaedia*

Britannica. They holidayed abroad most years. They owned a large house, which had a garden with mature plants and a bird bath. Is that 'lower middle-class' or middle middle-class? Search me.

The Coogans seem to have been stalwarts of Middleton's bourgeoisie, becoming foster parents with all the selflessness that entails. Reading of Coogan *père*'s DIY skills and his solid morals, I was reminded of my late father-in-law, who was brought up in working-class, Roman Catholic Birmingham. Yet my father-in-law was not remotely attached to the Labour Party. Mere circumstance does not explain Coogan's insistent hatred of the Right.

Although the Coogans disapproved of selective education, they sent their children to grammar school. We learn that Mrs Coogan wanted Shirley Williams (who destroyed many grammar schools) to become prime minister in 1976 after Harold Wilson's resignation, in part because Mrs Williams was a Catholic. The family was supportive of a united Ireland but not in favour of the IRA violence that cast such a pall over the 1970s and 1980s. Steve's father left Labour at one point to join the breakaway SDP but he never liked Margaret Thatcher on account of 'this appalling "I'm all right, Jack" mentality which means they only care about themselves'. Would that be the same 'I'm all right, Jack' mentality that leads a comedian to cancel a right-on gig in favour of a corporate booking?

Young Stephen, a bedwetter until the age of eleven, had to be pushed to get into the grammar school and he makes it sound like something from Dickens with its corporal punishment and manly muscularity. Perhaps he exaggerates. He claims first that his people were so poor he could not have Matchbox toys but later he writes of his memory of Matchbox toys landing through his home's letterbox. Perhaps he is as fanciful as the red-top reporters he helped put out of work when the *News of the World* was closed.

He claims that when working as a petrol pump attendant he diddled money out of racist comedian Bernard Manning after Manning drove up in his Rolls-Royce and told the boy to fill the tank. It sounds a good story. There are pages about what television programmes he watched. He knew the young Damien Hirst but we are given no more than a couple of lines about that encounter with the shark-pickling artist in his pre-fame years. Perhaps Hirst took one look at Coogan and concluded, not unfairly, that he was a dork.

This book, pseudish and prosaic, no doubt netted him another fortune. There is an uncritical market for the memoirs of stand-up comedians. Peter Kay made some £10 million with his. BBC Radio 2 and *Blind Date* presenter Paul O'Grady, who in 2015 said he would emigrate to the south of France if the Tories got back into government, made more than £7 million from his book. He has yet to leave our shores. Showbiz Lefties Dawn French and Julie Walters have made packets out of their memoirs, as has Russell *Booky Wooky* Brand. More than any Booker Prize nominee, these are today's power authors, making a fortune for themselves, their sleek agents and, quite possibly, their accountants. Yet still they pose as soldiers of serfdom.

Perhaps Armando Iannucci will one day satirise hypocrites in the comedy Establishment. Steve Coogan would no doubt happily appear in it, provided the money was right.

We, the Undersigned Snoots . . .

Everyone who is anyone signs group letters

———————————————●———————————————

Sometimes you will see a mass-signed offering in the letters column of the newspapers. They are often published on Monday mornings, slow for news, and they tend to be sent to the two main Establishment titles, *The Times* and *Guardian*. It does not matter if the paper in question has a small circulation. What matters is that the letter is noticed by the right sort of reader.

The basic message is this:

Dear Sir – we the undersigned are Important People. The world should Heed and Do What We Say. We send this in full expectation that you will give us a puff on your front page. If you fail to do that we will take this sort of letter to your rivals next time – and then you'll be sorry.

Yours,

Various top bods in commerce, the law, public administration and the media, quite possibly including Sir Richard Branson, Richard Dawkins, Stephen Fry, Jon Snow, Lady Chakrabarti, whoever happens

257

to be Poet Laurate and Children's Commissioner, Alan Rusbridger, A. C. Grayling, Sir Sandi Toksvig, Alastair Campbell, Jo Brand, the current head of the CBI, Sir Tom Stoppard, Hugh Grant, Benedict Cumberbatch, Steve Coogan, Michael Mansfield QC, Adair Turner, Dame Gary Lineker, Bob Geldof, Kathy Lette, Ena B. Maxwell, etc., etc.

Such letters preceded the Scottish independence referendum of 2014, the general election of 2015, the EU referendum and the American election of 2016.

We can trace this sort of purpling self-grandeur to the early days of Mrs Thatcher's premiership. Sneering at Mrs T became the default position for intellectuals. Some say Friday the 13th can be unlucky. It certainly proved so for Cambridge economics professors Frank Hahn and Robert Neild who on Friday 13 March, 1981, wrote to fellow economists, asking them to sign a group letter (to *The Times*), which was going to attack the Thatcher government. Three days earlier the Chancellor, Geoffrey Howe, had delivered a Budget raising taxes to tame inflation. Howe was adopting a monetarist approach at odds with received theory. An elected politician was disagreeing with the experts. Plainly that was intolerable – to the experts.

Profs Hahn and Neild contacted fellow economists with the injunction that 'for the sake of the country – and the profession – it is time we all spoke up'. Savour that inclusion of 'the profession' in their call to arms. They saw themselves as a body of opinion, almost a union; the National Amalgamation of Economics Wonks. When dons start to swallow the idea of communal loyalty, their usefulness may shrivel a little. Should a proper scientist (are we not often told that economics is a science?) not be devoted primarily to the truth, even if it conflicts with what colleagues are saying? Does groupthink have a place in our universities? Discuss. And no extra marks for originality.

The Hahn/Neild letter to *The Times* stated that the undersigned believed the Thatcher government's economic policies were wrong. It said:

> We, who are all present or retired members of the economics staffs of British universities, are convinced that: (a) there is no basis in economic theory or supporting evidence for the Government's belief that by deflating demand they will bring inflation permanently under control and thereby induce an automatic recovery in output and employment; (b) present politics will deepen the depression, erode the industrial base of our economy and threaten its social and political stability; (c) there are alternative policies; and (d) the time has come to reject monetarist policies and consider urgently which alternative offers the best hope of sustained recovery.

At that point in 1981, Mrs Thatcher was fighting for her political life. The cognoscenti suspected it would not be long before 'the men in suits' of Tory high command ushered the little woman gently to a waiting ambulance and Ted Heath was reinstated as leader of the Conservatives. It would be another six months before Mrs T felt strong enough to sack prominent wets from her government, among them Sir Ian Gilmour who departed in a high temper drawling that she was 'steering full speed ahead for the rocks'. Sir Ian, like the EU Remainers who would follow him thirty-five years later, did not manage to conceal the glee with which he predicted ruin for our country. He would spend the last twenty-six years of his life looking thoroughly cheesed-orf.

Hahn and Neild's letter was signed by 364 academics, including 76 professors, a majority of the chief economic advisers to the government since the Second World War and the president, nine vice presidents and the secretary

---

Prof Neild would later admit that the letter was partly motivated by personal distaste for Milton Friedman, Mrs Thatcher's monetarist guru, a vigorous debater who irked the heck out of Establishment economists. Prof Neild, who had worked for the Callaghan government, later had an adulterous affair with Jim Callaghan's daughter, Margaret Jay (later Lady Jay, leader of the House of Lords in the Blair years). If he wrote Margaret love letters they must have seemed very flimsy with just the one signature.

---

general of the Royal Economic Society. Professor Tom Cobbleigh and all. The sages included two Nobel laureates, one future Bank of England governor (Mervyn King) and two future prime ministerial advisers (Julian Le Grand, later knighted, and Anthony Giddens, a 'radical Centrist' visionary who would come up with the Blairite 'Third Way' and was ennobled).

Off the letter went. It made a splash. News bulletins led with the story. The government was challenged for its response. Alarums. Hype. General jibbering. For the letter's eager signatories, as they relished the impact of their mighty missive, there was just one problem. Immediately after Geoffrey Howe's Budget – almost overnight – blood started to flow back into the British economy. The growth statistics, on which economists place so much emphasis, started to lift. The recession was ending. Could it be that those 364 eggheads were wrong? It most certainly could!

To this day some of the signatories of that letter maintain that they were right. They argue that unemployment in the Thatcher years could have been kept lower had their advice been followed. But Neild has grudgingly accepted that he was wrong and Mrs Thatcher has gone down as the premier who (with her obdurate chancellor) rescued the British economy. Those 364 know-alls, those snooty Joes with their superior airs, were left looking the most frightful fools.

Bearing in mind this cautionary tale, let us leap to August 2014, when London's club-class elite belatedly woke up to the possibility that Scotland might vote to leave the United Kingdom. The Scottish independence referendum had generated little interest for months but with the vote just a few weeks away, opinion polls were narrowing – and sphincters in Westminster were tightening. People who for years had mocked the Union Jack and had inveighed against Britishness and national institutions now pushed themselves to the fore to say what a terrible thing it would be if the Scots believed the siren lurings of Alex Salmond's Scots Nationalists and opted for self-rule. The *Guardian* ran a group letter aimed at Scots voters. It said:

> The decision on whether to leave our shared country is, of course, absolutely yours alone. Nevertheless, that decision will have a huge effect on all of us in

the rest of the United Kingdom. We want to let you know how very much we value our bonds of citizenship with you, and to express our hope that you will vote to renew them. What unites us is much greater than what divides us. Let's stay together.

Signatories to this billet-doux included: newspaper columnist David Aaronovitch, sailor Sir Ben Ainslie, runner-turned-motivational-speaker Kriss Akabusi, actor Roger Allam, 'property porn' telly presenter Kirstie Allsop, BBC TV's *Pointless* quiz presenter Alexander Armstrong, Sir David Attenborough, spear-chucker Steve Backley, Lady (Joan) Bakewell, *Wombles* theme-tune composer Mike Batt, drag impersonator Stanley Baxter, hairy Mary Beard, historian Antony Beevor, retired cricket umpire Dickie Bird, Cilla Black, a playwright called Ranjit Bolt, untidy actress Helena Bonham Carter, young chinstroker Alain de Botton, Lord (Melvyn) Bragg, Jo Brand, Gyles Brandreth, actor Rob Brydon, Simon Callow, ex-rugby player Will Carling, actress Michelle Collins, sometime royal crumpet Susannah Constantine, comedian Steve Coogan, Ronnie Corbett, disc jockey Sara Cox, film-maker Richard Curtis, diver Tom Daley, Richard Dawkins, Dame Judi Dench, loudmouth artist Tracey Emin, explorer Ranulph Fiennes, hunky Ben Fogle, Bruce Forsyth, dead MP's daughter Emma Freud, conductor Sir John Eliot Gardiner, ex quiz-show presenter Bamber Gascoigne, pop impresario Harvey Goldsmith, David Gower, A. C. Grayling, actress Tamsin Greig, Field Marshal Lord Guthrie, sculptress Maggi Hambling, black-hole bore Stephen Hawking, Gloria Hunniford, Eddie Izzard, Sir Mick Jagger, Griff Rhys Jones, artist Sir Anish Kapoor, *EastEnders* actor Ross Kemp, dead billionaire's daughter Jemima Khan, living millionaire's daughter India Knight, writer Kathy Lette, Lord Lloyd-Webber, sports presenter Gabby Logan, Dame Vera Lynn, Old Haileyburian actor Stephen Mangan, James '*Top Gear*' May, SAS writer Andy McNab, author Michael Morpurgo, Dame Esther Rantzen, astronomer Lord Rees, Sir Cliff Richard, Baldrick actor Sir Tony Robinson, telly presenter June Sarpong, head-wobbling historian Simon Schama, former *Blue Peter* presenter Helen Skelton, telly historian Dan Snow and his swingometer father Peter, *Star Trek* actor Sir Patrick Stewart, Sting, sour Lord Sugar, Alan Titchmarsh, David Walliams and actors Dominic West and Kevin Whately.

At which you may say 'phew'; and 'how did Corbett, Brandreth, Bird, Gower and Dame Vera get enmeshed with that lot?'

Did the *Guardian* letter have any effect on the way Scots voted in the referendum? Who can say? But what made Tracey Emin, to choose just one of those peaches, think her plea would make a wavering Scottish voter think, *I was going to vote Yes to independence but I am changing my mind because Tracey is such a brilliant artist*? What was the reasoning that led an actor with as slight an artistic pedigree as Stephen Mangan to think, *I am loved! I am gorgeous! My voice is bound to carry some sway on the housing estates of Dundee*?

Before the EU referendum, George Osborne's Treasury encouraged business bosses to add their names to letters that urged voters to side with the Remain camp. On 23 February 2016, *The Times* ran a letter from 197 executives. Little more than a glorified slogan ('Britain will be stronger, safer and better off . . .'), it argued that being in the EU would boost the economy. Those sticking their names to this masterpiece included: Jacqueline Gold of the Ann Summers sex shops, Sir Roger Carr of arms dealers BAE, PR man Sir Alan Parker, Sir Mike Rake of BT, Lady Lane Fox of lastminute.com, stonkingly high-paid Dame Carolyn McCall of EasyJet (previously in charge of the *Guardian* newspaper), scandal-spattered banker Stuart Gulliver, John Holland-Kaye of arch lobbyists Heathrow Airport, Sir Stuart Rose of Ocado (who was in charge of the Remain campaign), Warren East of Rolls-Royce, Gordon Brown's friend and former fixer Lady 'Shriti the Shriek' Vadera, budget airlines loudmouth Michael O'Leary, Juergen Maier of Siemens, Rupert Soames of Serco, chi-chi London restaurateur Lady Rogers, Tom Mockridge of Sir Richard Branson's Virgin Media, new Tory peer Lady (Karren) Brady of West Ham United FC, Dido Harding of Talk Talk, blowhard ad-man Sir Martin Sorrell and various other multinational types.

While I apologise for these lists of names, they may illustrate the multiplicity of little plays in hand, the cat's cradle of strings and levers and connections. Voters may

---

Rupert Soames, boss of outsourcing company Serco (which makes millions from the government and the EU), wrote to David Cameron to suggest ways that big business could be used to make pro-EU noises during the referendum campaign. He said he would persuade them to include Brexit risk scenarios in their pre-poll annual reports. We must take it on trust, as best we can, that Soames never for a moment thought that giving Mr Cameron this discreet assistance would help Serco win government contracts.

have had little idea, for instance, that bondage-gear vendor Miss Gold – awarded a CBE for services to Women in Business (as opposed to women in the business) – was a Tory party supporter and 'bessie' of Lady Brady.

The innocent may not have realised that Parker once employed Gordon Brown's wife Sarah and that Mr Brown was godfather to his son; or that David Cameron in 2007 attended Parker's second wedding. The plain name 'Dido Harding' was less than fully informative; she was £2.8 million-a-year telecoms executive Lady Harding, daughter of a hereditary peer who was made a life peer in her own right by David Cameron two years earlier, and also married to Tory MP and minister John Penrose. So many links, threading like the blue veins on an alcoholic's nose, yet so few hours in our naive days in which to notice them all. Were these business people pushing for a Remain vote simply out of their private beliefs or were they schmoozing a Downing Street gang they presumed would be there many a moon more?

In October 2016, seventy Nobel Prize winners signed a letter supporting Hillary Clinton's candidacy for the US presidency. 'The coming presidential election will have profound consequences for the future of our country and the world,' they wrote. Profound: it is a word used, often, by people who consider themselves to be profound. Did those Nobel types put their names to the letter in the spirit of democracy, namely that every vote is of equal weight? Or did they imagine that their opinions were worth more than those of the morgue orderlies, the burger chefs and road-toll collectors of America?

Another group letter came just after the EU referendum and was signed by 1,054 lawyers who demanded that the British withdrawal process from the EU should not start until a royal commission had looked at the 'benefits, costs and risks' involved. Happily that letter, organised by one Philip Kolvin QC, was ignored. But if such a royal commission had been agreed to by the government, it might well have taken years to report. Still, the stunt made Mr Kolvin prominent enough that a few months later London's Labour mayor, Sadiq Khan, made him chairman of the city's Night Time Commission. See how group letters can help your political ambitions? Start one today!

In March 2017 the heads of nearly all of the University of Oxford's colleges and halls wrote to *The Times* demanding that Parliament force an amendment to the Bill starting our withdrawal from the EU. The college principals complained that their dons could face uncertainty about residency rights in Britain. The letter was signed by the likes of Will Hutton, a Blairite journalist (and, inter alia, one of the dullest chisellers of prose in the English language) who has washed up as principal of Hertford College. Honorary fellows at Hertford include anti-Brexit lawyer Lord Pannick and, God help Hertford, that low-wattage lightbulb of a former home secretary, Jacqui Smith. Others to sign the Oxford letter included: political scientist Sir Ivor Crewe, long sceptical of the need for Labour to heed the working-classes; Alan Rusbridger, *Guardian* editor turned Principal of Lady Margaret Hall; Oriel's Moira Wallace, a former Whitehall permanent secretary who was paid half a million pounds when she quit the Energy Department; Wadham's Lord Macdonald, a former Matrix Chambers barrister friend of Cherie Blair; Brasenose's John Bowers QC, a race relations hot-trotter who is described by Brasenose as 'an employment law rock star'; New College's Miles Young, formerly in the advertising business. The more one looked at the list on the Oxford letter, the less one worried about post-Brexit residency rights. All I could think was, *They seem to appoint any old dobbin an Oxford college chief these days.*

No Conferring, Please

Business conferences,
plague of the executive age

———————————•———————————

Business conferences are an opulent folly, a job-creation beano for hired wafflers who promote capitalism as high-minded communal endeavour rather than the profit-chasing, customer-screwing rat-race it is.

Conferences are held for the benefit of their organisers who acquire political clout plus fees worth hundreds of thousands of pounds. They acquire fancy titles ('director general', 'chief of staff'), prance around on bright-lit stages and speak into head-mikes about 'the new economy'. Along the way they may also meet politicians and chief executives who could help them in future.

Conference-goers tend to be middle-raters whose loyalty to their companies is at best tenuous. Why spend a day at head office, compiling the monthly audit of paper-clips, when you can be in the Great Room at Grosvenor House, snoozing through a motivational speech by an Olympic oarsman? The conference-goer looks forward to an easy day with a fusion-cuisine lunch. There should be a chance to mop up a bottle of Chablis at that little wine bar

In the afternoon session conference delegates broke out
into useful workshops

next to Paddington station before the first-class train ride
home. It beats having to work. Put your business card in
the vase for a chance to win a weekend for two in Prague.
Here, have a goodie bag with a Parker pen and a designer
notepad. Madam, how about another of those dinky chocolate mousses served with tubular Italian wafers – indulge
yourself before the afternoon session. Talking of afternoon sessions, where *have* Bruce and Sara gone? Answer:
upstairs to Sara's queen-sized suite, for an adulterous
quickie before the 'riding the recession' workshop.

The Olympic oarsman claims there are parallels
between top-level sport and office life. It is all to do with
'pulling together as a team' or 'charting a course for success'. Sporting demi-gods who deliver such can-do speeches

have, lucky devils, never been salary-ants at a City law firm, stapling and proof-reading mergers and acquisitions documents of the most balls-aching tedium. They have not spent years going to work on a grotty industrial estate at the back of some Thames Valley conurbation where a globalised pharmaceuticals firm has its regional headquarters and where the one frisson of the day is the arrival of the sausage-roll van in the company car-park at elevenses. The Olympic oarsman claims that 'if you believe in yourself, anything is possible' – a demonstrably false assertion. The redundant steel worker in Redcar, the zero-hours contract worker in Montgomeryshire, the exploited minicab driver in Plymouth: such people may have plenty of self-belief but they are never going to be Bill Gates. Yet self-belief has worked for the Olympic oarsman, given that he has charged £5,000 for this half-hour of claptrap.

Conference delegates feel they belong to a superior caste. When they talk to counterparts of 'hooking up' for a meeting, they mean doing each other a good turn, to ensure that they both retain their place on the executive ledge. We once spoke of 'the officer class'. The idea persists in expressions such as 'leadership unit' and 'executive team'. These are the goodie-goodies whose social media pages boast that running mini-marathons is their hobby and that they live in Hampshire with their organically reared llamas and their super-talented sprogs. They see they are part of a supervising clique and if they speak the right language and conform to blether, they will remain in that group.

When a manager says, 'I'll be away at the start of next week at a conference,' what do colleagues think? Do they say, 'Oh, bad luck, boss, I imagine that will be hard work as you toil for the greater good of our company, filling our

order books and securing jobs for our tight-knit community'? Or do they think, *Lucky bastard – all that wine, all
those canapés and a night at a posh hotel with a chance
of meeting some headhunters?* Recruitment firms are often
sponsors at big conferences. A manager keen to attend conferences is often a manager who wants to leave the firm.

> The March 2016 British Chambers of Commerce conference:
> Sajid Javid, Jeremy Corbyn, George Osborne and German
> finance minister Wolfgang Schäuble were there to promote
> a Remain vote. Mr Cameron sent a video message. City
> analyst Stephanie Flanders (ex-squeeze of both Ed Balls and
> Ed Miliband) flicked her fringe around like Jomo Kenyatta's
> fly whisk. Even Lord Rose, hapless leader of the In campaign,
> made an appearance. Poor Rose. A fine Captain Peacock
> floorwalker, flogging Marks & Sparks jim-jams, but hopeless
> at politics. Anyway, it had been one-way traffic for In. Then
> the Chambers' director general, John Longworth, made a
> speech. No one had checked his text to make sure he was
> on-message. The boss class simply assumed that, because
> he was their host and 'spoke for business', he would share
> their view. He didn't. Soft-spoken Longworth said he had
> weighed the evidence, reckoned it a close call but, on
> balance, he was pro-Leave. Less than a week later he was out
> of a job. Three months later, so were Cameron and Osborne.

Executives heading for a conference these days seldom
pack anything so vulgar as product samples or brochures.
Modern conferences are not about selling goods. They
sell an idea of business managers as a priesthood, with
orthodoxies and silent understandings. Instead of theo-
logical college ordinands, this world has internships,

secondments, leadership courses. Its archdeacons are the compliance officers and human resources directors. Its canons and prebendaries are the slim-waisted divisional managers in the multinationals. Its bishops are the FTSE-100 chief executives.

At last year's CBI conference, the docile delegates put up with an hour-long symposium on 'disruption'. The blurb explained that 'disruption is taking place across all sectors with businesses breaking the mould and re-imagining the way they do business with fascinating results'. Disruption was being presented as a thing that could be tamed, subsumed into the corporate maw. Their instinct is to copy and smother. They hate Brexit and Momentum equally. Conferences are wreathed by so much forced enthusiasm and arrested scepticism, it's enough to turn you into a screaming Corbynista. The stage screens carry rolling tweets from delegates. 'Typically brilliant speech from Sec of State fascinating #conference today' or 'insights aplenty from our panel this morning #conference'. With my fellow Fleet Street sketchwriters I ping off less obliging Twitter messages – 'what a crasher the Sec of State is #conference' or 'usual tosh #conference'. One year my colleague from the *Guardian* got one of these comments posted on the screen over the stage. We all thought it wonderfully funny. Childish, I know, but when you have been forced to listen to a half-hour of interminable verbiage by Business Secretary Greg Clark or a flat tyre such as David Sproul, 'UK Senior Partner & Chief Executive Deloitte', you do become a bit hysterical. Deloitte are the chumps who in December 2016 withdrew from pitching for UK government contracts after one of their consultants was caught pitching for Whitehall business by slagging off Britain's ability to cope with Brexit.

At the CBI last year, attended by 1,000 suited schmoozers, the morning session brought a 'keynote address' from CBI president Paul Drechsler, an Irishman distinctly grumbly about Brexit. Throughout the EU referendum campaign, the CBI and many of its bigger members had been vociferously on the side of Remain. Were they representative of the wider CBI membership? When the CBI took a similar stance before the 2014 Scottish independence referendum, in which it was down as one of the official supporters of the anti-independence side, several firms quit the CBI in protest. The BBC, with its impartiality requirements, was put in a tricky spot and had to suspend its CBI membership during the referendum campaign. Why on earth was the Beeb a member of the CBI in the first place?

These special-interest foot-stampers have wormed their way into the body politic and have acquired behind-the-scenes heft. Let us therefore consider some members of the CBI's executive team. Are they colossi of Western enterprise, or something less scintillating?

Director general Carolyn Fairbairn, who studied economics at Cambridge, went on to the European-Establishment hothouse INSEAD, started her working days as an economist at the World Bank and became a journalist at *The Economist* (which nowadays supports the Lib Dems). She worked at Downing Street in the John Major years as an adviser on health and social services before going into quangoland and the non-executive director belt. Among those to employ Ms Fairbairn was public-sector leech Capita – the firm which last year was caught using vicious little ruses and stratagems to collect TV licence money from the public. With such a CV, the sleek Fairbairn is naturally a devoted supporter of the EU.

Rhian Kelly, the CBI's director of infrastructure, worked previously for the EU Chamber of Commerce. Sarah Green, director of member relations, was a consultant with Arthur Andersen. Josh Hardie, deputy director general for policy and campaigns, was head of corporate responsibility for Tesco. The CBI's chief economist, Rain Newton-Smith, worked previously at the Bank of England as an economic forecaster (oh no!). She did time at the IMF and was once nominated as a 'young global leader' by the World Economic Forum in Davos.

This lot are more like civil servants than business moguls. They are no more likely to welcome 'disruption' than cats in sunshine.

No business conference is complete without a speech by a social-media bod who walks around the stage in casual manner, illustrating pro-tech parables with oh-so-zany images of a toothbrush, baby chimpanzee or such like. At the CBI conference two years ago the social-media slot was filled by Facebook executive Lady (Nicola) Mendelsohn, who strolled around like a catwalk model. Between bursts of jargon delivered in a transatlantic accent, she instructed the CBI audience members that they should have at least one 'hard conversation' a day with their staff. By this she did not mean the sort of conversation that goes, 'Blimey, Nicola, you made a dreadful speech yesterday.' The term 'hard conversation' or 'difficult conversation' has become managerial jargon for a disciplinary warning.

A whole branch of the human resources sector is now devoted to 'difficult conversations'. Arbitration service ACAS has leaflets, films and 'online toolkits' to help managers admonish staff in a touchy-feely way. Training is offered to help bosses open confrontations with gentle enquiries about an employee's family – before turning towards the meat of the encounter by saying, 'I need your help with what just happened – do you have a few minutes to talk?' Techniques on maintaining voice control and self-belief during a 'difficult conversation' are explained. The NHS has a 'London Leadership Academy', which teaches executives the Change Curve theory of a 1960s management guru, Elisabeth Kübler-Ross. This has a wiggly line going through a multicoloured graph marked with words such as 'denial', 'anger', 'depression' and 'acceptance'. 'Leadership toolkit modules' are provided to help 'leaders' prepare not only 'difficult conversations' but also 'influencing, collaboration and networking' and 'success strategies'.

If we cock up at work, do we want to be taken into a side office by our boss to answer simpering questions about our family before being disciplined in phrases rote-learned on an anger-management course? Is it not preferable for a telling-off to be genuine and brisk? A furious 'you cack-handed nincompoop – don't you ever do that again' is much less offensive than the Kübler-Ross Change Curve.

Ivan Off

An ambassador who spoke
for the diplomatic elite

———————•———————

When Sir Ivan Rogers quit in January 2017 as Britain's ambassador to the European Union there was an acrid tang not sniffed on England's breeze since Edward Wightman went to the stake in a Lichfield square, April 1612: the smell of burning martyr. Sir Ivan pouted and puffed. How he cast his 'I'm too good for 'em' gaze at the heavens. The BBC led its bulletins with the departure – the *suttee* – of this obscure diplomat.

Sir Ivan, fifty-seven, had been an exemplar of federalist orthodoxy, a back-room cardinal of the Eurocracy. For decades he had known everyone who mattered on Brussels's Avenue d'Auderghem, where the flagpoles outside the British embassy fly both the Union and the EU flags. And yet he had reached an impasse. Malvolio had lost his wicket. He'd be revenged on the lot of them.

Over the centuries diplomats have resigned without public histrionics. This was different. Sir Ivan took his punishment with a zealot's relish, greedy for indignation. He was right and 'they' (whoever they were – basically the

'Sir Ivan certainly brought a nervous energy
to his diplomacy'

electors of Britain, who voted to leave the EU) would learn their stupidity when they settled their broiling buttocks on hell's hot coals. He wrote a letter. He himself subscribed to 'nuanced' thinking – 'nuanced' being a favourite word of patronising bastards – but ministers were 'sloppy thinkers'.

In a trice Sir Ivan's letter was made public. Nothing sloppy about that! And so the outside world was able to savour his superior opinion. Without him and his technocrats in UKREP (the UK's mission to the EU), Britain was doomed. Europhile broadcasters were in heaven. Clear the schedules, team. We want vox pops, talking heads, interviews with anonymised ex-diplomats in darkened rooms. Create a sense of terror, of truth besieged. Eurosceptic newspapers quite enjoyed the story, too, for what Sir Ivan could not see was that he was a perfect example of the snoot who had been snotted.

For years he had devoted his career to Brussels matters. Careerism began with an EU, as far as he and his chums were concerned. Britain was but a province on the fringes of the empire, as it had been in the days of Asterix the Gaul. Devotees of Brussels pooh-pooh the nation state and patriotism, that they consider feebly romantic.

Rogers, schooled at a Bournemouth grammar, was a Balliol man – Roy Jenkins's old Oxford college – and did a year at the École Normale Supérieure, a Paris establishment that produces members of the French and European administrative cadre. It poses as an 'École Normale' but it has 'Supérieure' airs and graces. It is one of France's *Grandes écoles*, whose grip on that country's elite may be comparable to the Oxford and Cambridge old-boy network in Britain forty years ago. After entering the civil service as a fast-track graduate, Rogers arrived at the Treasury in 1992 and soon found himself private secretary to the Chancellor of the Exchequer, fervently pro-EU Kenneth Clarke. Rogers's next position was in Brussels where, aged thirty-five, he became chief of staff to European Commissioner Leon Brittan. When Brussels old-timers look back at Brittan's *cabinet* they pucker their lips with appreciation. In addition to Rogers it comprised Catherine Day, who would become the Commission's secretary general, Robert Madelin, who became its director general, Joost Korte, who became a deputy director general and Simon Fraser, who rose to the top of the British diplomatic service. Also in the team was a bum-fluffed twenty-seven-year-old, Nick Clegg.

From 1999 to 2003, Rogers worked at the Treasury, some of the time as 'director of EU policy and strategy'. Later he became principal private secretary to Prime

Minister Tony Blair. His predecessor in that job was Jeremy Heywood. Connections, connections. It was therefore no great surprise when, after a spell in corporate banking (Citigroup) during the less *gemütlich* Gordon Brown years, Rogers in 2012 became David Cameron's adviser on Europe. Heywood by now was Cameron's cabinet secretary and was delighted to have his old friend back. A year later Rogers was running UKREP.

Few ambassadorial roles offer such executive power. The EU has become such a Tower of Babel, its procedures so complex that ministers have neither time nor intellectual ability to monitor every tiny decision made in Brussels. The head of UKREP sponges up that work. It is like being a minister but (usually) with greater job security.

Sir Ivan was told to manage Cameron's renegotiation with Brussels. The deal would be presented to the British voters a few weeks before their June 2016 referendum on EU membership. The renegotiation was a non-event. Cameron was so laidback and confident he would win his referendum, the Europeans concluded they need not offer him any big concessions.

Cameron's resignation left Sir Ivan feeling the draught. Sir Ivan wrote a memo (soon leaked), which said the EU departure negotiations could take a decade. Downing Street was displeased. Sir Ivan quit.

The Establishment guard was swift to praise him. It was almost as if some of them had been given advance warning that he was going. Get your soundbites ready, old bean. Shall I give the BBC chaps your number in Wiltshire so they can get you just after the New Year? Tony Blair's former chief of staff, Jonathan Powell, castigated Downing Street for politicising the civil service. Magnificent! No regime did more to politicise the civil service than that of the wretched Blair and Powell. Lord Macpherson, former Treasury mandarin and another ex-colleague of Sir Ivan, took to Twitter, thumbs and fingers feverishly working his keyboard to type 'Ivan Rogers huge loss. Can't understand wilful&total destruction of EU expertise.' No time even to operate his space bar! The European Commission, unusually, passed comment on Sir Ivan's abilities, calling him 'very professional, very knowledgeable'. Professional? To write a foot-stamping letter slagging off your bosses as you resign?

Would it not have been more worrying if the EC had welcomed Sir Ivan's departure? Would that not have suggested that he was a genuine fighter for British interests?

Here is a shortened version of Sir Ivan's extremely long letter and (in italics) my no doubt grossly unfair interpretation of his words:

Dear All,

Happy New Year! I hope that you have all had/ are still having, a great break, and that you will come back refreshed and ready for an exciting year ahead.

Unhappy New Year!

I am writing to you all on the first day back to tell you that I am today resigning as Permanent Representative.

I'm buggering off. Can't bear it any more.

As most of you will know, I started here in November 2013. My four-year tour is therefore due to end in October – although in practice if we had been doing the Presidency my time here would have been extended by a few months. […] I have therefore decided to step down now, having done everything that I could in the last six months to contribute my experience, expertise and address book to get the new team at political and official level under way.

I was due to leave in October anyway – ya boo sucks! – but it's a slow news week and a BBC chum says I might be able to grab a few headlines if I commit hara kiri *now. I might have stayed if we'd been doing the Presidency, yum yum.*

This will permit a new appointee to be in place by the time Article 50 is invoked.

Importantly, it will also enable that person to play a role in the appointment of Shan's replacement as DPR. [Shan Morgan was Deputy Permanent Representative.]

I want to put on record how grateful I am to Shan for the great working relationship we have had.

She will be hugely missed in UKREP, and by many others here in Brussels, but she will be a tremendous asset to the Welsh government.

Wales! The poor woman must be desperate.

I know that this news will add, temporarily, to the uncertainty that I know, from our many discussions in the autumn, you are all feeling about the role of UKREP in the coming months and years of negotiations over "Brexit".

'Brexit' (I give it inverted commas because I regard this vile thing as a loathsome neologism!) is going to take forever to negotiate.

We do not yet know what the government will set as negotiating objectives for the UK's relationship with the EU after exit. Serious multilateral negotiating experience is in short supply in Whitehall, and that is not the case in the Commission or in the Council.

London hasn't a clue. Brussels is wonderful. Brussels is going to thrash us. Ha!

The government will only achieve the best for the country if it harnesses the best experience we have – a large proportion of which is concentrated in UKREP – and negotiates resolutely. Senior ministers, who will decide on our positions, issue by issue, also need from you detailed, unvarnished – even where this is uncomfortable – and nuanced understanding of the views, interests and incentives of the other 27.

David Davis, Boris Johnson and Liam Fox don't know their acquis communautaires from their EEAs. They will be easily baffled. Use our old friend 'nuance', comrades, and their eyeballs will soon be revolving in different directions!

The great strength of the UK system – at least as it has been perceived by all others in the EU – has always been its unique combination of policy depth, expertise and coherence, message co-ordination and discipline, and the ability to negotiate with skill and determination.

UKREP has always been key to all of that. [...] Meanwhile, I would urge you all to stick with it, to keep on working at intensifying your links with opposite numbers in DEXEU [Department for Exiting the EU] and line ministries and to keep on contributing your expertise to the policy-making process as negotiating objectives get drawn up. The famed UKREP combination of immense creativity with realism ground in negotiating experience, is needed more than ever right now.

British civil servants have long been brilliant at baffling ministers. Our own ministers, that is.

On a personal level, leaving UKREP will be a tremendous wrench. I have had the great good fortune, and the immense privilege, in my civil service career, to have held some really interesting and challenging roles: to have served four successive UK prime ministers very closely; to have been EU, G20 and G8 Sherpa; to have chaired a G8 Presidency and to have taken part in some of the most fraught, and fascinating, EU negotiations of the last 25 years – in areas from tax, to the MFF to the renegotiation.

God, I was good.

Of all of these posts, I have enjoyed being the Permanent Representative more than any other I have ever held. That is, overwhelmingly, because of all of you and what you all make UKREP: a supremely professional place, with a fantastic co-operative culture, which brings together talented people whether locally employed or UK-based and uniquely brings together people from the home civil service with those from the Foreign Office.

I hope you will continue to challenge ill-founded arguments and muddled thinking and that you will never be afraid to speak the truth to those in power.

David Davis really IS a moron.

I hope that you will support each other in those difficult moments where you have to deliver messages that are disagreeable to those who need to hear them.

I hope that you will continue to be interested in the views of others, even where you disagree with them, and in understanding why others act and think in the way that they do.

Ivan Off

I want to thank my agent, my fans, my beautiful family, all of Hollywood ... Boo hoo!

Ivan

The Tut-Tut Brigade

Regulators who think they
rule the ranch

———————•———————

Forces of the Crown once went to battle with lances and longbows. Their weaponry today? Clipboard and disappointed eyebrow. Meet the regulators. These superior quibblers supervise everything from tap water to roulette wheels, masseurs and pension yields. The tiniest shortcoming, the most minute departure from best-practice standards ordained by officialdom? Scribble scribble goes ballpoint pen. Another wretch has been snared.

Regulators are bureaucracy's traffic wardens. They are the crack troops of the Tut-Tut Brigade and they are, naturally, both well paid and royally honoured. OBEs are sprinkled on them like Dolly Mixture.

The inspectorate class has swollen since the 1990s, acquiring money and status. Where once we entrusted professional supervision to the chartered bodies and guilds and a few outfits such as the General Medical Council and Bar Council, now we have a welter of arm's-length bureaucracies: the Environment Agency, the Care Quality Commission, Ofcom, Ofgem, Ofwat, Ofqual,

Offwithyourknickers. There is the laidback British Board of Film Censors and the more picky Forensic Science Regulator. There is the politically driven Equality and Human Rights Commission, Citizens Advice, the Payment Systems Regulator, the Financial Conduct Authority, Financial Reporting Council, Pensions Regulator, Prudential Regulation Authority and the Regulator of Community Interest Companies. Medicine now has at least fifteen separate regulators, each with its own secretariat, strategic plan, statement on equality and diversity, governance procedures, mission and values statement and more. More functions. More statutory requirements. More office space. Empire building.

This cadre of licensed busybodies can jaw about outreach, risk-control and 'ongoing conversations with stakeholders' (yet miss looming disasters like Grenfell Tower) – and it is all paid for by the state. Top regulators draw salaries worthy of the private sector but face none of the attendant risks. The chief executive will often have a blog, written by a heavily staffed press office. The annual report will be published on glossy paper and launched at a press conference necessitating high-tech conference facilities and overnight stays in a smart hotel. Opportunities for all.

The regulatory sector has long outgrown the post-war functionalism of the Drinking Water Inspectorate and HM Inspector of Mines, the Fish Health Inspectorate and HM Chief Inspector of Prisons. Now there is a British Egg Industry Council, which presumably sits for days on end. There is a Utility Regulator, Legal Services Board, the Building Regulations Advisory Committee, the Reviewing Committee on the Export of Works of Art and Objects of Cultural Interest, countless Park authorities, the Aid Impact Commission, the Forestry Commission, Statistics Authority and more. Corporate logos. Executive obeisance. Career structures. All of these web-weaving spiders comply enthusiastically with their public sector equality duties, quizzing staff and suppliers about their ethnicity and sexuality and inside-leg measurements.

There is a quintessentially British expression 'Oh, go on then!' It is used by gluttons and tipplers when offered a second helping. More sherry trifle, Grandma? 'I really shouldn't, dear – oh, go on then!'

Professor Dame Sally Davies, Chief Medical Officer,

One of the fattest regulators is Ofsted, inspecting schools. Its reports are mired in jargon about frameworks and criteria, leadership teams and standardised assessment data. Ofsted frets more about record-keeping than about classroom flair. It sees schools not as nurseries of humanity but as bureaucratic engines in which every administrative cylinder must gleam. But even Ofsted robots can make fools of themselves. Its report on our children's primary school a few years ago complained that pupils did not have a big enough area in which to play with their bicycles. Our little ones needed 'more space for peddling'. What? Drugs?

---

would not approve. Dame Sally is that arid nanny forever telling us to eat better and to drink less. She reckons that as a nation we booze too much and that our young women in particular have been overdoing it. And so the sprightly sixty-eight-year-old gives us regular drubbings about intake levels. How prissily she does it. Would it not be more effective if done with an element of wit and by someone who herself went on occasional benders?

'Do as I do,' instructs the dry dame. 'When I reach for my glass of wine, think "do I want the glass of wine or do I want to raise my own risk of breast cancer?"' Crikey. What

---

Just beyond the regulator world sits the Association of Chief Executives of Voluntary Organisations (ACEVO), a lobby for big-salary charity bosses. It tries to defend the ripe emoluments paid to charity professionals. ACEVO's own past chief executive was until recently incorrigible braggart Sir Stephen Bubb (nickname 'Bubblet'), paid more than £100,000 and prone to speaking of himself in the third person. Acquaintances found it hard to believe that so egregious a self-publicist as Bubblet, so blatant a hustler, was taken seriously by the government. Bubblet published an online diary that gassed about his goodly acquaintance with top people in politics – his great friends Tony and Cherie, his man-to-man chats with David Cameron. Alongside his blog was a panel in which he told readers: 'Sir Stephen Bubb is globally recognised as a leading voice in philanthropy, charity governance and leadership and corporate social responsibility. He has provided strategic advice to governments and businesses, usually at Prime Minister, Mayor and Chairman level.' This peacock had his sixtieth-birthday party in a room at the House of Lords, complete with pink-iced Caribbean rum-soaked fruitcake. The knees-up was in part paid for with ACEVO funds.

---

is it to be, gringo: a second squirt of Tio Pepe or a double mastectomy? At a parliamentary inquiry Dame Sally said: 'I take a decision each time I have a glass.' Some of the MPs blanched. *I take a decision each time I have a glass.* We don't have many like that at the splashy Palace of Westminster. But is it remotely likely that many of us will *take a decision* (by which she means, conduct a serious health audit) every time we accept another splash of plonk? Would you like the elderflower cordial or the ductal carcinoma?

Dame Sally – an active Remainer – gave an interview to the *Sunday Times* 'A Life in the Day' column. It offered an account of such dietary virtue, we can only presume her gastric passages shine like tin whistles. Her personal routine involved a two and a half mile run two early mornings a week, followed by decaffeinated coffee, berries and yoghurt for breakfast. She prepared herself zip bags of raw, chopped vegetables for lunch (complete with fennel, in case they were not disgusting enough already), and maybe risked an Ottolenghi-style salad or fish dish or soup with more fresh vegetables for supper. She and her husband – a Cambridge professor of experimental haematology – 'enjoy good wine, but only on the weekends'. Meanwhile, she described how 'worrying' she found it when she saw the lumpen masses piling their supermarket trolleys with junk food.

Dame Sally must be a nightmare at a Christmas drinks party. Round comes the cheery host, bottle in hand, saying: 'Let me take the air out of your glass.' Dame Sally cogitates. She replies, 'I am running this data through my decision-making processes'. Eventually she reaches the decision. 'No. I have reached the conclusion that today I would rather not have cancer.'

That is her job, you say. The rise of ladette behaviour, with so many girls knocking back the booze, has left Britain's women blotchy-livered and lardy. Given the health-spending required to put right that damage, it is not unreasonable for our chief quack to read us the riot act. But there are other ways to persuade people to cut back on drink. You could tell them to spend their money on wiser things. You could tell them they will end up looking frightful slappers. You could tell them that they will spoil their career prospects, set a bad example to the young and develop stinky breath – and that the rest of us are anyway fed up with drunken Dorises screaming in the streets. But officialdom shies away from such an approach because it might sound judgemental. It couldn't suggest that there was something slatternly about drunkenness because for decades it has tried to banish that sort of morality.

Look what happened to a judge who suggested that women who drink too much left themselves vulnerable to attack. At the March 2017 sentencing of a rapist, Judge Lindsey Kushner said: 'Girls are perfectly entitled to drink themselves into the ground but should be aware that people who are potential defendants to rape gravitate towards girls who have been drinking. It shouldn't be like that but it does happen and we see it time and time again.' Judge Kushner was stating the obvious but she was swiftly pecked and mobbed for doing so. Campaign group End Violence Against Women declared that the judge was 'blaming victims' and 'removing responsibility' from male rapists. This was 'exactly the kind of thing that deters women from reporting rape'. Northumbria's police and crime commissioner, former Labour MP Dame Vera Baird, also fanned her face and deplored the judge's 'victim-blaming' comments.

Is it not 'victim-blaming' to suggest that if you drink more than half a glass of wine a day, you may end up with breast cancer?

Warning to public figures: You are perfectly entitled to think politically incorrect thoughts but if you voice them out loud you may be violated by lurking Left-wing clap-trappers. They often gravitate towards people who speak plain good sense.

Expectant mums have long been told to beware alcohol. Wise? Or (shock horror) inegalitarian? A displeased Ellie Lee, director of the University of Kent's Centre for Parenting Culture Studies (now there's a discipline vital to the future of Western civilisation), said: 'The exclusion of women from an ordinary activity on the basis of a precaution is sexist.' Quite right. Pregnant men should also avoid the booze.

Court at It

News update: Justice not blind after all

———————————————————●———————————————————

What would we think if, at the end of a criminal trial, the jury foreman said, 'M'lud, we find the accused not guilty because he's white'? We would be outraged. The judge would surely have to order a re-trial. To decide a legal matter on the basis of a person's skin colour would be rotten. But the legal class in Britain has got itself into a tangle. While much public-sector recruitment is done on a 'name-blind' basis to prevent favouritism, some of our most senior judges may be selected specifically on race grounds.

Is race discrimination a good or bad thing? If the judiciary is tinged by racial differentiation, where does that leave the rest of us?

Consider Lady Justice. She is the shimmering ideal, allegorical representation of impartiality, her statue found above many of the world's courthouses. Sometimes she is a glamour puss of enviable curves and scant wardrobe. You might almost think that she has been based on Miss Anthea Redfern, sometime *Generation Game* assistant to the late Sir Bruce Forsyth. I understand she is in fact based on Brenda 'Cop That, Carruthers' Hale, the terrifyingly beady-eyed Lady Hale of our Supreme Court.

Justice, in addition to her robes, tiara, scales and sword, often wears a blindfold. Being unable to see, she is not swayed by appearances. She does not know how able-bodied you are, if you have a skull and crossbones tattooed across your forehead or if you wear one of those Nigel Farage coats with a velvet collar and a bookie's docket sticking from the top pocket. Justice is above visual distractions. There she stands on the Supreme Court building in Washington, DC under the motto 'Equal Justice Under The Law'. Oscar Niemeyer's timeless 1961 statue of Justice in Brasilia also has her eyes covered. Yet the statue of Lady Justice above England's central criminal court, the Old Bailey in London, does not wear a blindfold. This is just as well. She needs to be able to see the colour of the judges' skin.

The selection process for judges contains something called the 'equal merit provision'. That is a fancy way of saying 'we can bend the reed to favour minorities'. A woman or someone from a racial minority may legally be chosen in preference to a rival candidate who is just as well qualified. Remember, we are not talking here about shoe-shop assistants. We are talking about judges, custodians of justice, people who can rise to become such arbiters of constitutional law that they can rule that Parliament is more important than the electorate. Is it right that such public dignitaries be chosen on a politicised, token-minority basis?

The equal merit provision was included in the Crime and Courts Act 2013, co-sponsored by the then Home Secretary, one Theresa May. It was designed to correct a lack of 'diversity' in the judiciary. By that they do not

London Fashion Week takes an unexpected turn

mean that there is a lack of diversity of political opinion, with too many of them being Centrist, Europhile, second-home-owning readers of *The Times* who went to public school and belong to the Garrick Club. Ah, lovely, Blairite Centrism. Our elite likes Centrism because it does not change the status quo. Centrism is no threat to subsidised sinecures.

The two categories of diversity specified by the 2013 Act are race and gender. Too many top judges, it was felt, were male (bad thing) and white (bad thing). At legal dinners in Middle Temple Hall, pasty-faced jurists would summon a pained expression to their faces and say, 'It's time we did something to get more women and blacks on the bench.' Politicians, driven by the politics of identity, agreed. Intellectuals, newspaper columnists and think-tanks also seized on it, not because it was a novel thing to say but because it helped them to parade their goodness. Conservatives would once have argued for appointments to be made solely on merit but the Cameroon modern-isers of the Tory party were eager to neutralise politically correct opinion. They calculated that if they supported touchy-feely causes such as this, they would receive a more favourable treatment from 'thought leaders' and damp down anti-Tory zealots on social media.

Under the Crime and Courts Act 2013 the Judicial Appointments Commission could discriminate if its Selection and Character committee put forward two equally qualified candidates for a judge vacancy. If one of those characters was a white male and the other was female or from a BAME (black, Asian and minority ethnic) background – or even better both, as that would tick two boxes – well, it was goodbye to the male whitey. And is it not desirable that judges look more like the rest of society? Maybe, if only because black judges might be less simperingly, idealistically indulgent of black defendants than some of their white colleagues. Your average Islamist thug will probably be far more frightened of a sharia law court than going up before some Crown court full of soft-hearted atheist ex-Christians.

How often are two candidates for a judicial vacancy truly equally qualified? Being a judge is not just about hav-ing legal qualifications. It includes less easily defined – yet easily discerned – things such as temperament, stamina, bearing, tact and imagination. Are we really to believe that the people who appoint our judges are unable to form a clear view as to which of two final candidates is the more able? Is it not more likely that the equal merit provision is an elaborate excuse for officialdom to promote second raters? But it allows those simpering sheep at Middle Temple Hall dinners to pat new female and BAME judges on the head and say, 'Very well done on your promotion,' while simultaneously congratulating themselves on being so enlightened.

The equal merit provision was keenly welcomed by legal boffins. In an article for the UK Constitutional Law Association, legal wonks Graham Gee and Kate Malleson dwelt at length on what they saw as an advance for the judiciary. They spoke of the 'key stakeholders' of the judicial appointments process – 'ministers, judges and practitioners' (practitioners being people who work in and around the courts). Gee and Malleson did not include the public in their definition of stakeholders.

The judicial oath, uttered by judges when they take office, states: 'I will do right to all people after the laws and usages of this realm, without fear or favour, affection or ill will.' How does the equal merit provision – which favours people on a racial and gender basis – sit with that oath?

But I should watch my step. Criticising the law is close to a thought crime, as was made clear in November 2016 when the *Daily Mail* took a pop at three High Court judges who found against the government in Gina Miller's anti-Brexit case. Miller wanted to force Theresa May to submit Brexit to Parliament for approval. The judges agreed. The keenly pro-Brexit *Mail*, in noisy campaign mode, ran a headline calling them 'Enemies of the People'.

One of the pleasures of writing for the *Mail* is that it makes Establishment bores so terribly cross. For journalists, it is much more fun to write for an iconoclastic paper than one which sucks up to the powerful. And, boy, the high and snooty certainly went nuts about that headline. Lofty Lord Hope (lawyer) declared that democracy was imperilled and that youngsters might be deterred from seeking a career in the law. Cue a chorus of the Bee Gees' 'Tragedy'. If democracy was being placed in danger it was possibly being done so by a political class outsourcing our law-making to unelected foreigners. All manner of accusations were thrown at the *Mail*: it opposed the rule of law, was an agent of tyranny, was fascist, etc., etc. No, it wasn't. It was pointing out, with the brio to be expected from a popular newspaper, that although the nation had voted for Brexit, lawyers were forcing that vote to be approved by a Parliament composed largely of Remain supporters. The paper also reported, quite legitimately, that these bewigged Cocklecarrots were being called 'activist judges' by some pro-Brexit politicians.

For a prize example of the activist barrister, let us consider Jolyon Maugham QC. He once advised Ed Miliband on tax policy. More recently this tweezered Tweeter has set himself up as a one-man opposition unit to Brexit, to the point where he proposed setting up a political party called 'Spring'. 'We will collect members. We will build a brand,' asserted Maugham. He would stand against Theresa May in her Maidenhead constituency. Referring to himself in the third person, he devised a plan: 'Step one – Jolyon announces to the *Maidenhead Advertiser* that he's standing. It filters out to the national press. The website goes up with a short biog, a teaser, a "register" button and a "donate" button.' None of this came to pass. Do you think he's any better as a barrister?

Must judges remain above any criticism? What of certain vicious beaks in the 1960s? Lord Justice Goddard, a notorious hanging judge, allegedly liked to masturbate while pronouncing the death penalty. Timothy Evans was sent to the gallows for the 10 Rillington Place murders after an appeal in which the judges included the prosecuting lawyer's father. What of the notoriously corkscrewed summing-up of Mr Justice Caulfield in the Jeffrey Archer libel trial in 1987? And then there was the conduct of Phil Shiner, a much-vaunted human-rights solicitor who in February 2017 was struck off after repeated dishonesty as he chased British soldiers for alleged war crimes in Iraq. The law and its acolytes had long defended Shiner. The *Law Society Gazette*, no less, ran a June 2014 editorial that praised him and said that the press had irresponsibly turned him into a hate-figure. 'We need more lawyers like Shiner,' cried the *Gazette*.

Earlier journalists such as Ludovic Kennedy and the great Richard Ingrams overcame deference to lawyers and revealed some judges to be grievous Establishment stoodges. Are we to accept that today's judges, miraculously, have quite, quite altered and are above such traits? You would certainly think so from the scorn that was thrown at journalists who questioned the ability of the Supreme Court's top judge, Lord Neuberger, to chair the Miller case's appeal. Charles Moore, a former *Daily Telegraph* editor, discovered that Neuberger's wife had publicly (on Twitter, repeatedly) raged against Brexit, calling it 'mad and bad'; yet here was her husband about to sit in judgement on a Brexit-related case. The Supreme Court's guidelines acknowledge that political activity by a close family member can imperil public trust in a judge.

Those guidelines were pushed aside like sprouts on a fussy child's plate. Lord Neuberger was permitted to continue on his way, a court spokesman saying that Neuberger would be able to separate political views from points of law. Oh really? The points of law were sufficiently debatable for the court's judges to be split in their verdicts.

I came across Neuberger once, at a dinner in Oxford. He sidled up to me and said we should get to know one another. Maybe he was just being friendly. Maybe it was more careerist than that. Far from coming across as a distant, dispassionate figure, he struck me as a networker, eager to 'make contact, put a face to the name, always been an admirer of your work' and all that. Not ideal in a judge, really.

While watching wagtails

While I was writing this book, my sister Penny died aged fifty-nine, weeks short of retiring from the school in Cheltenham where she was a housemistress. She left three fine children who must somehow cope with this pulverising loss. Over the years Penny looked after hundreds of teenage girls who will, I hope, remember 'Mrs R' for her crisp Christian kindness. There, perhaps, lies real duty.

The death of a sibling unsettles you. Much else – the power-jockeying, greed, the preening of politics – becomes unimportant. Dawn after dawn, as I worked in my Herefordshire study watching wagtails hop on the glistening grass, certain things fell into perspective. What value has political vainglory when the very breath in our bodies is so fleeting?

My brother-in-law Stuart, whom I mentioned at the start of the book, may have been a Leaver; dear Penny thought we should stay in the EU. She had no private gain to make from her vote. Nor did millions of others – 48 per cent of the electorate – who honourably cast their ballots for Remain in that great plebiscite. My beef is not with those people. Good grief, no. It is with the sticklers and swaggerers, the hectoring Snoots Who Know Best, the plotters and schemers who for years have bent the rules to their professional convenience. My target is the techno-crats who dehumanise our country's institutions, replacing common sense with rigid procedure. It has been the pros-elytising know-alls who, cork-bobbling on the swell, think they have some right to tell us how to lead what the Prayer Book calls our 'transitory' lives. Stuart and Penny would have agreed on that. So can the rest of us.

Much has been omitted: theatres' pre-show warnings to audiences that 'cigarettes are smoked during the per-formance'; phone-tree answering machines that treat us like idiots; children's commissioners; the National Trust, usurious high-street banks that advertise themselves as our friends; the 'Do you know who I am?' brigade who like that odd man David Mellor shout at cab drivers; supermarket check-outs that say 'unexpected item in the bagging area' when they mean 'stop shoplifting'; identity politics; the way Health and Safety saw off those lovely new Boris buses; think-tanks producing reams of political research that means nothing to the general public. But I have tried to describe at least some of the people and prac-tices that have infuriated and, until now, enslaved.

Britons voted for Brexit because they were fed up being taken for fools. A year later they declined to give Mrs May a parliamentary majority because she was a complacent glumbucket who looked too much like a continuation of the same. The patronising bastards for years thought 'the people are revolting' and eventually the people said 'yup, we most certainly are'. Good for them.

Top 100
Patronising Bastards

1. Sir Richard Branson
2. Nick Clegg
3. Sir Nicholas Serota
4. Emma Thompson
5. Lord Ashdown
6. David Beckham
7. James Purnell
8. Ian McEwan
9. Tony Blair
10. George Clooney and his woman
11. A.C. Grayling
12. Gina Miller
13. Gary Lineker
14. Michael Eavis
15. Lily Allen
16. Steve Coogan
17. Alan Yentob
18. Mark Carney
19. Bob Shennan
20. Sir Mark Lowcock
21. Alan Bennett
22. Emily Thornberry
23. Richard Dawkins
24. Bono
25. Lord Mandelson

26. Lord Neuberger

27. Harriet Harman

28. Julia Middleton

29. Jon Snow

30. Lord (Chris) Patten

31. George Osborne

32. Glynis Breakwell

33. David Tennant

34. Sir David King

35. Lady Hale

36. Hugh Grant

37. Lord Heseltine

38. The Kinnocks

39. Jonathan Powell

40. Phil Shiner

41. Blue Peter presenters

42. David Cameron

43. Ella Mills

44. The Hemsley sisters

45. Alan Milburn

46. Lord (Richard) Rogers

47. Theresa May

48. Sir Lynton Crosby

49. Sir David Attenborough

50. Peter Atkins

51. Polly Toynbee

52. Lord Stern

53. Stephen Fry

54. Viscount Hailsham

55. Lord (Roger) Liddle

56. Sally Davies

57. Lord Pannick

58. Bob Geldof

59. Lord (Rowan) Williams

60. Camila Batmanghelidjh

61. Sir Mike Rake

62. Warren East

63. Sadiq Khan

64. Dame Vivienne Westwood

65. Shami Chakrabarti

66. Benedict Cumberbatch

67. Dame Amelia Fawcett

68. Alice Rawsthorn

69. Sir John Major

70. Evan Davis

71. Rupert Soames

72. Carolyn Fairbairn

73. Paul Drechsler

74. Maurice Saatchi

75. Nicky Morgan

76. Angela Eagle

77. Lady Wheatcroft

78. Lord Harries

79. Sir Ivan Rogers

80. Sir Jeremy Heywood

81. Dan Snow

82. Ed Miliband

83. Stephanie Flanders

84. Michel Barnier

85. Dame Sandi Toksvig, Bt.

86. Philip Hammond

87. Sir Tom Stoppard

88. Jo Johnson

89. Zeinab Badawi

90. Wolff Olins & Co

91. Fiona Millar

92. Lord Hannay

93. Simon Schama

94. Lord (Quentin) Davies

95. Marcus Brigstocke

96. Nicholas Boyle

97. Sir Anish Kapoor

98. Jolyon Maugham

99. Alain de Botton

100. Gaz & Leccy